朗文
外研社

新概念英语

NEW CONCEPT ENGLISH

1

New Edition 新版

First Things First
英语初阶

亚历山大（L. G. ALEXANDER）何其莘　著

外语教学与研究出版社

PEARSON　LONGMAN

京权图字：01-2004-4972

图书在版编目(CIP)数据 *

朗文·外研社新概念英语(新版)(1) ／(英)亚历山大(Alexander, L. G.)，何其莘著.--
北京：外语教学与研究出版社，1997.10 (2016.5 重印)
ISBN 978-7-5600-1346-6

Ⅰ. 朗… Ⅱ. ①亚… ②何… Ⅲ. 英语—教材 Ⅳ. H31

中国版本图书馆 CIP 数据核字 (2006) 第 163559 号

地图审图号：GS(2012)1676 号

出 版 人：蔡剑峰
出版发行：外语教学与研究出版社
社　　　址：北京市西三环北路 19 号 (100089)
网　　　址：http://www.fltrp.com
印　　　刷：河北鹏盛贤印刷有限公司
开　　　本：787×1092　1/16
印　　　张：20.5
版　　　次：1997 年 10 月第 1 版　2019 年 3 月第 210 次印刷
印　　　数：12341000—12541000 册
书　　　号：ISBN 978-7-5600-1346-6
定　　　价：29.90 元

＊　　＊　　＊
购书咨询：(010)88819926　　电子邮箱：club@fltrp.com
外研书店：http://waiyants.tmall.com
凡印刷、装订质量问题，请联系我社印制部
联系电话：(010)61207896　　电子邮箱：zhijian@fltrp.com
凡侵权、盗版书籍线索，请联系我社法律事务部
举报电话：(010)88817519　　电子邮箱：banquan@fltrp.com
法律顾问：立方律师事务所　刘旭东律师
　　　　　　中咨律师事务所　殷　斌律师
物料号：113460003

朗文
外研社　　**新概念英语**（新版）

NEW CONCEPT ENGLISH (*New Edition*)
FIRST THINGS FIRST *Students' Book* 英语初阶　学生用书1

English edition © L. G. Alexander 1967
Original English material © Addison Wesley Longman Ltd. 1997
This revised edition of New Concept English with the addition of Chinese material is
published by arrangement with Addison Wesley Longman Limited, London and
Longman Asia Limited, Hong Kong.

Licensed for sale in the mainland territory of the People's Republic of China only

This simplified Chinese characters edition first published
in 1997 jointly by Foreign Language Teaching and Research Press
and Longman Asia Ltd.

双语版出版人：沈维贤
合作出版人：李朋义
合作编著者：亚历山大（L. G. Alexander），何其莘
策划编辑：赵嘉文，蔡女良
责任编辑：（朗文）王德厚，梅丹心；（外研社）孙蓓，任小玫
封面设计：梁若基

外语教学与研究出版社　联合出版
朗文出版亚洲有限公司

What's new in this edition?

This is the only new edition ever to be undertaken since *NCE* was originally published. The classic course continues to provide a complete and well-tried system for learning English, enabling students to reach their maximum potential in the four primary skills of understanding, speaking, reading and writing. The sound basic principles which made *NCE* a world-famous course have been retained. However, the following important features have been introduced in the new edition:

- All topical references in the texts and exercises have been brought up to date.
- All outdated texts have been completely replaced and accompanied by new exercises and new artwork.
- The original methodology has been modified to improve communication skills, with active training in listening comprehension right from the very first lesson.
- Drills and written exercises, previously published separately as supplementary materials, have been incorporated into the main coursebooks.
- The following features have been added to help Chinese learners of English: Bi-lingual vocabulary lists; notes in Chinese on texts and exercises and suggested translations of the texts.
- The pages have been enlarged and, where possible, are self-contained, so that lessons are easy to conduct.

本版本有什么新内容？

本版是《新概念英语》首次出版以来第一次推出的新版本。这套经典教材一如既往地向读者提供一个完整的、经过实践检验的英语学习体系，使学生有可能在英语的 4 项基本技能——理解、口语、阅读和写作——方面最大限度地发挥自己的潜能。新版本保留了《新概念英语》得以成为世界闻名英语教程的一整套基本原则，同时又包含了以下重要特色：

- 所有课文和练习中有关时事的内容都已更新。
- 所有过时的课文都已更换，由新课文和配套的新练习、新插图取代。
- 原有的教学法经过调整，以利于提高学生的交际能力。从第一课开始就安排了有效的听力训练。
- 教材更简洁精练，过去作为补充材料单独出版的句型训练和笔头练习均已取消，其精华纳入主干教程。
- 为了帮助中国的英语学习者，新版增加了英汉对照词汇表、课文注释、简短的练习讲解和课文的参考译文。
- 版面加大，在可能情况下，每课书相对独立，以方便课堂教学。

（注：本册双课正文内容请参见《教师用书1》及其盒带。）

CONTENTS 目录

To the teacher and student
Learning a foreign language in the classroom

General principles

Traditional methods of learning a foreign language die hard. As long ago as 1921, Dr. Harold Palmer pointed out the important difference between understanding how a language works and learning how to use it. Since that time, a great many effective techniques have been developed to enable students to learn a foreign language. In the light of intensive modern research, no one would seriously question the basic principles that have evolved since Palmer's day, though there is considerable disagreement about how these principles can best be implemented. Despite the great progress that has been made, teachers in many parts of the world still cling to old-fashioned methods and to some extent perpetuate the systems by which they themselves learnt a foreign language. It may, therefore, not be out of place to restate some basic principles and to discuss briefly how they can best be put into effect in the classroom.

Learning a language is not a matter of acquiring a set of rules and building up a large vocabulary. The teacher's efforts should not be directed at informing his students about a language, but at enabling them to use it. A student's mastery of a language is ultimately measured by how well he can use it, not by how much he knows about it. In this respect, learning a language has much in common with learning a musical instrument. The drills and exercises a student does have one end in sight: to enable him to become a skilled performer. A student who has learnt a lot of grammar but who cannot *use* a language is in the position of a pianist who has learnt a lot about harmony but cannot play the piano. The student's command of a language will therefore be judged not by how much he knows, but by how well he can perform in public.

In order to become a skilled performer, the student must become proficient at using the units of the language. And the unit of a language is not, as was once commonly supposed, the word, but the sentence. Learning words irrespective of their function can be a waste of time, for not all words are equal. We must draw a distinction between *structural* words and *lexical* items. Words like *I*, *you*, *he*, etc. are *structural*. Their use can be closely defined; they are part of a grammatical system. Words like *tree*, *plant*, *flower*, etc. are purely *lexical* items and in no way part of a grammatical system. From the learner's point of view, skill in handling structural words is the key to mastering a language, for the meaning that is conveyed in sentence-patterns depends largely on the function of the structural words that hold them together.

It is possible, though this has yet to be proved scientifically, that every student of a foreign language has what might be called a 'language ceiling', a point beyond which he cannot improve very much. If we accept this supposition, our aim must be to enable every student to learn as much as he is capable of learning in the most efficient way.

The old-fashioned translation and grammar-rule methods are extremely wasteful and inefficient, for the student is actually encouraged to make mistakes: he is asked to perform skills before he is adequately prepared. Teachers who use such methods unwittingly create the very problems they seek to avoid. At some point in the course their students inevitably become incapable of going *on*: they have to go *back*. They have become remedial students and the teacher is faced with the problem of remedying what has been incorrectly learnt. No approach could be more ineffective, wasteful and inefficient.

The student should be trained to learn by making as few mistakes as possible. He should never be required to do anything which is beyond his capacity. A well-designed course is one which takes into account what might be called the student's 'state of readiness': the point where he can proceed from easy to difficult. If the student is to make the most of his abilities, he must be trained to adopt correct learning habits right from the start.

What has to be learnt

The student must be trained adequately in all four basic language skills: *understanding*, *speaking*, *reading* and *writing*. In many classroom courses the emphasis is wholly on the written language. The student is trained to use his eyes instead of his ears and his inability to achieve anything like correct pronunciation, stress and intonation must be attributed largely to the tyranny of the printed word. If the teacher is to train his students in all four skills, he must make efficient use of the time at his disposal. Efficiency presupposes the adoption of classroom procedures which will yield the best results in the quickest possible time. The following order of presentation must be taken as axiomatic:
Nothing should be spoken before it has been heard.
Nothing should be read before it has been spoken.
Nothing should be written before it has been read.

Present-day techniques and the classroom

Any language course represents an attempt on the part of its designer to implement a number of basic principles. To do this, the designer will inevitably draw on techniques old and new which will best fulfil his purpose. A great many terms are used today to describe new methods and it may be of help to define and illustrate some of these terms in the light of this course.

Structural grading: grading sentence-patterns in order of increasing difficulty and complexity.

It is, or should be, an obvious requirement of any course that it should proceed from easy to difficult without sharp breaks or sudden 'jumps'. In a carefully graded course, the student learns to use a few patterns at a time. Ideally, these patterns should be interrelated and should be presented in a carefully ordered sequence. In traditional courses, grammatical items are often artificially grouped together. For instance, all the personal pronouns may be presented in a table which the student is expected to learn. The table is presented in isolation and is divorced from any context.

But learning facts about the language in this way is of no real help to the student, for he is in no position to apply what he has learnt. In a structurally graded course, the student acquires a little information at a time and learns to make meaningful statements. He therefore learns to use relatively simple structural words like personal pronouns over a long period, instead of being given a large, indigestible dose of information at any one time.

Contextualization: presenting grammatical items in a meaningful context.

When a student has practised a new pattern orally, he should encounter it, if possible, in an actual text so that he can see how it has been used. Obviously, such texts have to be specially written by the course designer. New items are introduced into a natural context: they are 'contextualized'. In well-written contextualized passages, the reiterated patterns should be unobtrusive: their use should strike the listener as being inevitable rather than artificially superimposed. This is a highly effective way of presenting the student with new information.

Situation teaching: teaching a language by presenting a series of everyday situations.

In this method, little structural grading is possible. The situation takes precedence over the structures. The patterns that are included arise naturally out of the situation itself: they have a thematic significance rather than a structural one. This system has serious drawbacks.

The dialogues which the student hears are refreshingly natural, but the teaching of basic patterns inevitably becomes much less controlled.

Structurally controlled situation teaching: teaching a language by means of a series of everyday situations, while at the same time grading the structures which are presented.

This method makes use of all the techniques outlined above: structural grading, contextualization, and situational teaching. In the early stages it is possible to use very few patterns indeed. This means that the 'situations' are often unconvincing and barely possible. Despite this disadvantage, it would seem to be one of the best methods for learning a language, for it is possible to exercise linguistic control and yet to present new information in an interesting way.

The teaching of grammar

Presenting new information is one thing; getting the student to apply the new information another. So far, we have been concerned with how to present the student with new material; but how is he to apply what he has learnt?

The basic aim in any language teaching is to train the student to use new patterns. In traditional textbooks, all information is presented in the form of 'rules' which the student applies in a series of disconnected sentences by filling in blank spaces, or by giving the correct form of words in parentheses. It has become abundantly clear that this approach to language-learning is highly ineffective. It encourages the teacher to talk *about* the language, instead of training his students to use it. The emphasis is on written exercises. The greatest weakness in this approach is that the student cannot transfer what he has learnt from abstract exercises of this kind to other language skills like understanding, speaking and creative writing.

In modern textbooks, the aim is exactly the same: the student must be trained to use patterns. Before considering how this can be done, it should be noted that the patterns in a language fall into two distinct categories: *progressive* and *static*. For instance, learning how to answer and to ask questions involves the use of *progressive* patterns. They are *progressive* because the student's skill in handling these complex forms must be developed over a long period, beginning with a simple response like 'Yes, it is' and culminating, towards the end of the course, in complex responses like 'Yes, I should, shouldn't I'. A *static* pattern, on the other hand, like the comparison of adjectives can be taught in a limited number of lessons, not over a long period. This distinction between *progressive* and *static* patterns is rarely recognized in traditional textbooks. The result is that even advanced students are often incapable of handling progressive patterns with any degree of skill.

Progressive patterns should be practised through comprehension exercises which require the student to answer and to ask questions which become increasingly complex as the course proceeds. The student should be trained to give tag answers; give answers to questions beginning with *Who*, *Which* or *What;* make negative and affirmative statements to answer double questions joined by *or*; answer general questions which begin with question-words like *When*, *Where*, *How*, etc.; and at each stage, the student should be trained to ask questions himself. It is obvious that these skills cannot be dealt with in one or two lessons: the student requires practice of this kind in *every* lesson.

At the same time, static patterns should be practised by means of taped drills. In each of these drills, the teacher seeks to elicit a particular kind of response. He provides the student with a stimulus to elicit the new pattern in a series of oral drills until the student is able to respond accurately and automatically. Each new pattern is not presented as the exemplification of some abstract grammar-rule, but as *a way of saying something* and no further explanation or elucidation is necessary. The student is trained to use correct forms automatically, rather than by applying 'grammar logic'. Where explanation is necessary, it can be done by relating a new pattern to one that has already been learnt. If, for instance, the student has learnt the use of 'must', he can be taught the use of 'have to' by being made to see a meaningful relationship between the two.

In certain taped drills, the stimulus the teacher provides may be given in the form of 'call words'. Let us suppose that the teacher wishes to elicit the response: 'I can't buy very much' and 'I can't buy very many'. The drill might be conducted in the following way:

TEACHER: What about pencils?
STUDENT: I can't buy very many.
TEACHER: What about coffee?
STUDENT: I can't buy very much.

In this particular exercise, the teacher would supply countable and uncountable nouns in the question 'What about ...?' as 'call words'.

Traditional filling-in-the-blank exercises still have a place in a modern course, but with one important difference: they should not be used as a means of teaching new patterns, but as a means of consolidating what has been learnt. They are an end, not a means to an end. In this respect, they are extremely useful in tests and can be employed for diagnostic purposes or to enable the teacher to assess students' level of achievement.

Audio visual aids and translation

In a monolingual course we are faced with the tremendous task of having to convey meaning without making use of the student's mother tongue. It follows that textbook illustrations become extremely important: at the beginner's level, they are far from being merely decorative. However, textbook illustrations have severe limitations, for many of the statements that are made in everyday speech are not visually presentable. Some linguists have experimented with artificial visual devices which require the student to interpret each illustration according to particular rules. They have evolved what might be called a 'visual language' which the student has to master before he can begin the course. The difficulty here is that if the student fails to interpret an illustration (and this can easily happen) he will fail to understand, or even worse, he will misinterpret what he hears.

At the beginner's level, this difficulty can be resolved in two ways. Where the meaning of a statement or a series of statements cannot be adequately conveyed by the illustration, the teacher should make use of gesture and mime. If the student still fails to understand, the teacher may translate, *providing that he translates lexical items and not patterns*. In this instance, translation is used not as a 'method', but as a means to an end. As such it can be extremely useful and time-saving.

Natural English

There is a great temptation in the early stages to encourage the student to make statements which he will never have to use. Statements like 'I have a nose', 'Have you a nose?', 'Is this my foot?' are ridiculous. This distortion of the language can never be justified. After all, the whole point of teaching a language is to train students to make useful statements which might normally be made in real-life situations. This criterion must be observed at the most elementary level. The peculiar type of 'textbook English' which is to be found in many traditional courses must be avoided at all costs.

The teacher's book and the students' book

In the past, no distinction was drawn between information intended for the teacher and information intended for the student. Everything was printed in one and the same volume. Early in the course, the student would find extremely complex information in his book like: 'With most nouns the plural is made by adding "s" to the singular' or: 'We form the negative of the verbs "to be" and "to have" by putting "not" after the verbs'. Now it is inconceivable that any beginner would be able to understand such instructions. What is more, from the learner's point of view, this information is totally irrelevant: it is really telling the teacher what to teach.

It should be recognized that the students' book is not a vehicle for conveying information, but an aid for practising the language. It should be pleasing to look at and attractively laid out. It should only contain material which the student will actually use.

At the beginner's level, a teacher's handbook is absolutely necessary. This should be in every way complementary to the students' book and should contain practical information and material which will be used in each lesson — not merely hints and suggestions. At the intermediate level, the teacher's handbook becomes less necessary, for the student is in a position to work from printed instructions.

Speed and intensity

Traditional courses are often divided into 'lessons', but these 'lessons' do not take into account what can be done in an average teaching period of forty-five minutes or an hour. They simply consist of 'an amount of information' and may run on for a great many pages. In the classroom, one of these 'lessons' might drag on for weeks because so much has to be done.

A lesson must be precisely what the word implies: an amount of material that can reasonably be covered in a teaching period, possibly with additional material which can be done as homework. In other words, a lesson must be considered as a unit of instruction and no more. Now it is extremely difficult for the course designer to decide what can be done in an average period. Obviously a class of bright students will cover more ground than a class of less able ones. This problem can be overcome if the lesson contains material which can be omitted at the discretion of the teacher, providing that these omissions do not hamper the students' progress.

Levels

Finally, it might be worth noting that a full-scale course would resolve itself into three parts, each of which would consist of two stages:

Stage 1: Pre-elementary level.
Elementary level.
Stage 2: Pre-intermediate level.
Intermediate level.
Stage 3: Pre-advanced level.
Advanced level.

About this course

From theory to practice: basic aims

This course attempts to put into practice all the theories about language learning outlined above. Briefly, the aims may be stated as follows:

1 To provide a course for the secondary school or adult beginner. No previous knowledge is assumed. There is sufficient material for one year's work which will completely meet the requirements of the pre-elementary and elementary levels. It is assumed that the student will be able to work at the course for a complete academic year of about thirty-six weeks. It is also assumed that the student will receive about four hours' instruction each week: i.e. four one-hour lessons on four separate occasions, or two 'double periods' each consisting of two hours or ninety minutes. The student will receive most of his training in the classroom and will be required to do a little extra work in his own time.

2 To train the student in all four skills: *understanding, speaking, reading* and *writing* — in that order. The exercises in this course are largely aural/oral. Full-scale training in the written language should only be undertaken when this course has been completed. It must be clearly understood that this course has been designed entirely to meet the needs of the teacher working in the classroom, not of the student working on his own.

3 To provide the student with a book which will enable him, with the aid of a teacher, to *use* the language.

4 To provide the teacher with well co-ordinated and graded material which will enable him to conduct each lesson with a minimum of preparation. Taken together, the students' book and the teacher's book form a complete course: it is not possible to use one without the other.

5 To provide the teacher and student with recorded material which can be used in the classroom and at home. It must be emphasized, however, that this is in no way a full-scale self-study course. It is essentially a classroom course, with taped material that can also be used at home. The recorded drills supplement drills done in the classroom.

The components of the course

The course consists of the following:
- The Students' Book.
- The Teacher's Book.
- A set of cassettes, on which the multi-purpose texts have been recorded.
- Another set of cassettes, on which 'Repetition drill' in the Teacher's Book has been recorded.

A description of the course

In this course, two lessons, each of about an hour's duration, are considered as one teaching unit. The student will spend about an hour on each lesson and will complete two teaching units each week. There are seventy-two teaching units in all, that is, sufficient material for thirty-six weeks' work.

The Students' Book

The first part of each teaching unit consists of a structurally controlled situational dialogue or narrative piece in which the new linguistic features introduced in the lesson are contextualized. The passage will be used for training in understanding and speaking, reading, and practising progressive patterns.

The second part of each teaching unit usually consists of sets of numbered illustrations which will be used for understanding and speaking practice. Where possible, new vocabulary items are not presented in print until the student has mastered them orally. The new linguistic features introduced in the contextualized passage are isolated and drilled intensively. This oral work is followed by a very short written exercise which seeks to consolidate skills which have already been acquired.

The Teacher's Book

In the first part of each teaching unit, the teacher is provided with the following information:

Content and basic aims: A list of patterns, structural words and content words which the student will actually use.

General remarks: A summary of the main grammatical items that are introduced in the unit.

Listening comprehension: The nine steps for presenting the text, so students will be trained to understand spoken English.

Comprehension: Constant practice in answering and asking questions based on the text.

Pattern drill: A brief drill on a particular difficulty is given occasionally, or the ground is prepared for the exercises which are to follow in the second part of the teaching unit.

Activities: Material is provided occasionally for particular activities, such as telling the story, games or some kind of classroom activity.

In the second part of the teaching unit, the teacher is provided with material to practise the new patterns. These exercises generally take two forms: Repetition drill and Pattern drill. Pieces for dictation are recommended from Teaching Unit 17 onwards.

The tapes

Two sets of tapes accompany the course for use in the classroom and for home study.

1 A set of cassettes, on which the situational dialogue or narrative piece in the first part of each teaching unit is recorded at less than normal speed (100 words per minute). These cassettes are intended for use in the classroom when the teacher is working through the nine steps when presenting each text. However, students studying at home may also make use of these cassettes to improve their listening comprehension.

2 Another set of cassettes, on which the 'Repetition drill' in the second part of each teaching unit is recorded for use in the classroom or at home. There are 72 drills in all. These cassettes are intended for teachers to use in the classroom and for students who decide to do the drills on their own with the aid of a cassette-player at home.

The drills consist of three phrases: stimulus/*student response*/correct response. The drills are based entirely on the main grammatical item introduced in each lesson. The tapescript of the drills is included in the second part of each teaching unit in the Teacher's Book.

How to use this course

The teacher's notes

The notes which accompany each teaching unit should be treated as suggestions. The teacher may depart from the scheme that is laid down if he wishes to, or he may omit any exercise which does not seem to suit his purpose. However, the intention behind the notes is to enable the teacher to drill the patterns that are introduced. The exercises within each lesson are, where possible, graded in order of increasing difficulty. This means that if there is insufficient time, the final exercises may be omitted without seriously hampering the students' progress. Each teaching unit provides enough material for two hours' work. If the teacher can only devote forty-five minutes to each part of the unit, he may edit the drills to suit the time at his disposal.

All instructions and comments like *Listen*, *Sit down*, *Say it again*, *All together*, etc. which any teacher might use while conducting a lesson should be given in English. In the early stages, the meaning of these expressions may be conveyed through gesture and mime. Such patterns must be regarded as extraneous to the course, unless they are formally introduced. For the purpose of this course, it is not assumed that a student is familiar with a pattern until he is actually made to use it. That is why many of the instructions commonly used in the classroom are not given in the pattern and vocabulary lists which precede each lesson in the Teacher's Book.

All the information in the notes is given under headings and each item will now be considered.

Content and basic aims — general remarks

The information given under these two headings summarizes briefly what will be taught in terms of patterns and content words. This summary is purely for the teacher's information.

Listening comprehension

Detailed instructions are given at the beginning of the course, which are gradually reduced as teachers get used to the procedure. There are nine recommended steps for presenting each text which will train students to understand spoken English. The steps are as follows:
1 Introduce the story
2 Understand the situation
3 Listening objective
4 Play the tape or read the text
5 Answer the question
6 Intensive reading

7 Play the tape or read the text again
8 Repetition
9 Reading aloud

Every one of these steps must be very brief. Let's see how this works in practice:

1 Introduce the story

The teacher introduces the text with a few words, so the student clearly understands what's going on and is not obliged to guess. At the very beginning, some Chinese may be used, but the teacher should use English as early as possible. For example:

Today we'll listen to a story about a handbag.

2 Understanding the situation

The students are asked to look at the pictures to see if they can understand what is going on in the text. At the very beginning, a few prompts can be given in Chinese, but the teacher should use English as early as possible. For example:

Look at the pictures and tell me what is happening here. (You may add one or two questions as prompts.)

3 Listening objective

The teacher sets the students 'a listening objective', by setting them a question they will try to find the answer to. This means, the students will listen to the text *actively* rather than *passively*. For example: *Listen to the story, then tell me: Whose handbag is it?*

4 Play the tape or read the text

The teacher plays the tape or reads the text just once while the students simply listen without interruption.

5 Answer the question

Now the teacher asks the question (3 above) again and the students try to answer it: *Now you've heard the story, whose handbag is it?* Don't let students shout out the answer. Train them to raise their hands if they think they know the answer. Get one student to answer, then ask the others, *How many of you agree with him/her? Put up your hands if you agree with him/her. You don't agree* (to another student) *so what do you think the answer is? How many of you agree with him/her? Put up your hands.* This keeps the students guessing and involves *the whole class*. Students should be trained to listen right from the start without 'preparation' or 'translation'. They will soon get used to the sound of English and to understanding the meaning of what they hear.

6 Intensive reading

Now the teacher plays the tape or reads the text again, pausing after every line to check the students understand. This is an extremely important part of the lesson as the students must make every effort to understand the text through the pictures. If the students fail to understand the meaning of parts of the text through the pictures (and this will inevitably occur at times), the teacher should explain by gesture and mime. If the teacher still fails to communicate the meaning, he should ask the best students in the class for a 'confirmatory translation' of a particular word or phrase for the benefit of other students who haven't grasped the meaning. Translation, however, must be regarded as a last resort. This difficulty of conveying meaning is acute in the early stages, but becomes less of a problem as the course progresses.

7 Play the tape or read the text again
Play the tape or read the text again right through without interruption. This time, the students will understand it without difficulty because of the careful explanation you provided in 6 above.

8 Repetition
Play the tape or read the text again, pausing after every line. Ask the students to repeat (a) in chorus, (b) in small groups (say, row by row in the class) and (c) individually. When conducting chorus and group repetition, make sure the students repeat all together after you give them a clear signal. You can give such a signal simply by nodding or with a pencil in your hand. Imagine you're conducting an orchestra! The broken lines in the text represent 'reading units', which match the students' eye-span.

9 Reading aloud
Ask one or two students to take parts and to read the text aloud. You will be able to tell from this how well particular students can pronounce correctly the English they have already heard.

This presentation should not take more than about twenty-five minutes. As the students make progress, the teacher may simplify the procedure if necessary, so that more time can be devoted to the exercises that follow.

Students working at home on their own should listen to the recording of each text as often as is necessary for them to become completely familiar with it, and should even learn the texts by heart if they wish to.

Comprehension

This stage consists of two exercises:
1 Students answer questions
2 Students ask questions

1 Students answer questions
After presenting the text (the nine steps above), the teacher asks individual students questions round the class. If a student fails to answer, move quickly on to another student, so that this part of the lesson has *pace*. All the questions you will ask and the appropriate answers are printed for you in the Teacher's Book. Of course, you can ask additional questions of your own if you want to. The questions fall into two categories:

a **Yes/No questions**
It is generally considered rude to answer a question with just 'Yes' or 'No'. The student is trained to listen to the first word in the yes/no question and to use the same word in the answer:
TEACHER: *Is* Anna's dress new? (The first word in the question is *Is*.)
STUDENT: Yes, it *is*. (*is* forms part of the answer.)
TEACHER: *Is* Anna's dress blue?
STUDENT: No, it *isn't*.

b   Wh-questions and questions with How

The student is trained to answer questions beginning with When, Where, Which, How, etc. (Of course, these take time to develop during the course.) The student may provide complete answers, or short natural ones.

TEACHER: Whose dress is new?

STUDENT: Anna's dress is new. Or simply: Anna's.

In this way, the student is trained over a period to associate When? with time, Where? with place, Why? with reason, Who? with identity, Whose? with possession, Which? with choice, What? with choice, identity or activity, How? with manner, etc.

2 Students ask questions

In order to prevent incorrect forms like *Where he went?*, students are trained to ask two questions at a time. The first of these is a yes/no question and the second a Wh-question. For example:

TEACHER: Ask me if Sally is in the garden.

STUDENT: Is Sally in the garden?

TEACHER: Where …?

STUDENT: Where is Sally? (Not *Where Sally is?* or *Where Sally?*)

Of course, these questions take time to develop during the course.

All the asking questions exercises are printed for you in the Teacher's Book. You can add some of your own if you want to.

Activities

Suggestions for activities are usually given at the end of the first part of each teaching unit. If there is insufficient time, they may be omitted altogether. Every effort should be made to introduce activities occasionally as they liven up the class and make language learning an enjoyable task. Two forms of activity are suggested.

Games

There are a number of ideas for games which enable the students to practise particular patterns.

Tell the story

The students may be asked to reconstruct the dialogue by referring only to the pictures. Adult students are usually too self-conscious to 'act' the dialogues in class and this is a good compromise. It is an extremely valuable exercise in recall and helps to lay the foundations of speech.

Extension exercises

In the students' book, the second part of each teaching unit (all even-numbered lessons) consists of numbered pictures and sometimes printed words and statements. As was pointed out earlier, where possible, a new word is printed *after* it has been learnt orally. That is why this page often consists only of pictures. With the aid of these illustrations, the student will practise particular patterns (both *progressive* and *static*, depending on the lesson).

The Extension exercises usually begin with a short drill which deals with a special problem: e.g. the use of numbers, dates, telling the time, the use of the alphabet and spelling difficulties, etc. Difficulties of this sort are practised over a very long period and are not dealt with in single lessons. The student then continues with Repetition drill and Pattern drill.

Repetition drill

The students practise the taped drill. They may do this with the aid of a cassette player in the classroom, or at home if they are working on their own. Alternatively, the teacher may conduct the drill 'live' from the tapescript printed in the lesson.

Pattern drill

These make up the main part of the lesson. In these drills, the teacher seeks to elicit a number of different patterns from the class. The students may respond in chorus, small groups or individually: this is left for the teacher to decide.

Each time a new pattern drill is introduced, the teacher should illustrate the type of response he requires. He may do this orally, or by writing the response on the blackboard. It should not be necessary to give grammatical explanations. Each new pattern should simply be presented as *a way of saying something*. However, the way new patterns are to be presented is left to the teacher's discretion.

When conducting a drill, the teacher provides a stimulus and the student responds to it by referring to his book:

To elicit statements involving the use of the present perfect.

TEACHER: Look at the first picture.
         What has she just done?
STUDENT *(consulting illustration):* She has just aired the room.
TEACHER: Look at the second picture.
         What have they just done?
STUDENT *(consulting illustration):* They have just cleaned their shoes.

In a number of drills, the student is not required to refer to illustrations but to make use of "call words" which are supplied by the teacher. The call words to be used are always provided in the teacher's notes and are drawn only from vocabulary the student knows well. Here is an example of this type of exercise:

To elicit statements involving the use of *very much* and *very many*:
I can't buy very much/many.
TEACHER: What about pencils?
STUDENT: I can't buy very many.
TEACHER: What about coffee?
STUDENT: I can't buy very much.

The following call words will be substituted in the question 'What about ...?': bread, cheese, soap, steak, biscuits, eggs, vegetables, fruit, flowers, cakes, paper, ink, glue, clothes, aspirins, medicine, jam, honey, envelopes, magazines, wine, milk.

The Pattern drill is followed by written exercises.

Writing	Written exercises take two forms: structural exercises and dictation.

Structural exercises

In the first few teaching units, the student begins with copying before proceeding to actual exercises. Examples of the script used and the type of answer to be given are always printed in the students' book. It should be noted that in the early stages the instructions for the written exercises, though simple, will be outside the students' vocabulary range and will have to be explained. The aim of these exercises is not to teach the new patterns, but to reinforce and consolidate what has been learnt orally. They should always be done *after* the oral exercises have been completed and may be set as homework. The student must not merely fill in blank spaces but copy out the whole exercise.

Dictation

Dictation exercises are not introduced till Teaching Unit 17. No 'unseen' dictations are given. The teacher always dictates the answer to the written exercise given in the preceding teaching unit.

There is sufficient material in the Extension exercises for about one hour's work. As the exercises are arranged in order of increasing difficulty, it is always possible to omit the last few if there is insufficient time.

Testing	A test is included in the middle of the course to enable the teacher to assess the students' progress.

Homework	**The tapes**

Apart from being given written exercises, students who possess the tapes should be encouraged to play the recording of the new dialogue several times at home and if possible to memorise it. They should also be advised to practise the recorded drills. Taken together, the seventy-two passages form a carefully graded and structurally controlled survey of elementary English. All the passages are short and easy to memorise and will enable the complete beginner to use the language with increasing confidence and skill.

Future work	This course is completely self-contained and covers one year's work. At the end of it, the student should have a reasonable command of spoken English. If he wishes to proceed further, the student may go on to the following books which 'overlap' each other so that he can continue his studies without difficulty:

Practice and Progress:
An integrated course for pre-intermediate students
Developing Skills:
An integrated course for intermediate students
Fluency in English:
An integrated course for advanced students
In these books, the student continues with the oral work begun in this course and is also taught to write English in a systematic way.

致教师和学生

外语的课堂教学

基本原理

学习外语的传统方法根深蒂固。早在 1921 年, 哈罗德·帕尔默博士就指出, 理解一种语言是如何运作的与学会如何使用这种语言之间存在着重大的差别。从那时以来, 人们已经找到了许多卓有成效的方法教授学生外语。根据当代所作的深入细微的研究, 没有人会对自帕尔默以来发展而成的学习外语的基本原理提出重大质疑, 尽管在如何才能最好地贯彻这些原理方面仍有相当大的分歧。虽然在外语教学上取得了重大的进步, 但是世界上许多地方的教师依然眷恋着过时的教学方法, 在一定程度上, 他们是用当年自己学外语的方法使旧的教学体系永久化。因此, 重述一遍其中一些基本原理, 简要探讨如何在课堂上有效地实施这些原理, 大概不算不合时宜吧。

学习一门语言, 不仅仅是掌握一套规则, 积累大量词汇。教师工作的重点不应是告诉学生关于一门语言的知识, 而应是使学生能够使用这门语言。衡量学生是否掌握一门语言, 最终是要看他运用如何, 而不是懂了多少。在这方面, 学习语言与学习乐器十分相似。学生所做的操练与练习都是为了达到一个明确的目标: 使他成为一个熟练的操作者。一个学生学了许多语法知识却不会**运用**语言, 就像一个弹钢琴的学了许多有关和声的知识却不会弹钢琴一样。因此, 衡量学生是否掌握语言并不看他懂了多少, 而要看他在众人面前语言运用得如何。

学生要想成为熟练的语言运用者, 就必须能够熟练地使用语言单位, 而语言单位并不是人们曾经普遍认为的单词, 而是句子。学习单词而不考虑它们的作用可能会白白浪费时间, 因为单词并不都是同样重要的。我们必须把**结构词**和**词项**加以区别。像 I, you, he 等词便是结构词, 它们的作用可以准确地加以界定, 它们是语法体系的一部分; 而像 tree, plant, flower 等词则是单纯的词项, 与语法体系毫无关系。就学生而言, 运用结构词的技巧是掌握一门语言的关键, 因为由句型表达的含义主要依靠把句子联结起来的结构词所起的作用。

虽然以下一点仍有待于科学地论证, 但每个学习外语的学生可能都有一个也许可以称为"语言极点"的地方, 即过了这点他的水平不可能有很大的提高。如果我们接受这一假设, 那么, 我们的目标就必须是用最有效的方法使学生在其能力范围内尽量多学到一点东西。过时的翻译－语法教学法极端浪费时间而且效率很低, 因为这种方法实际上是鼓励学生犯错误: 让学生在没有充分准备的情况下运用语言技能。使用这种方法的教师无意中制造了他们企图避免的问题。他们的学生在学到一定程度后会不可避免地无法继续往下学: 他们不得不**回过头来重新开始**。他们成了需要补课的学生, 教师面临的问题是为学生补课, 纠正他们所学到的错误的内容。同别的教学方法相比, 这是一种最无益、最浪费时间和效率最低的方法。

应该训练学生学会尽量少犯错误。决不应该要求学生去做力所不及的事情。一本精心设计的教材应考虑到学生所谓的"准备状况"即可以使他从易到难循序渐进的那个交接点。要使学生最充分地发挥自己的能力, 必须训练他从一开始就采用正确的学习方法。

学什么

学生必须在语言的 4 项基本技能方面得到充分的训练。这些技能是: **理解**、**口语**、**阅读和写作**。在课堂教学中, 许多教师把重点完全放在书面文字上。学生接受的训练是如何用眼而不是如何用耳来学习。学生不能掌握正确的发音、重音和语调, 不得不主要归罪于书面文字的束缚。教师若想培养学生全面的 4 项基本技能, 就必须有效地使用自己的时间。要做到有效, 首先就要采用能在最短时间内产生最佳效果的课堂教学法。下列讲课顺序务必作为格言来遵循:

听到的再说；

说过的再读；

读过的再写。

现代手段和教室

任何语言教程都包含着设计者的一种意图，即在教学中贯彻一系列基本原则。为了做到这一点，设计者不可避免地会从新老教学手段中选择最有助于达到他的目标的方法。如今大量术语被用来描述新的教学方法，按照这本教程来解释和说明其中的一些术语是有帮助的。

按结构分级：按句型的难度和复杂程度来分级。

循序渐进、没有明显的断层或突然的"跳跃"是——或应该是——对任何教程的一个显而易见的要求。在一个仔细分级的教程中，学生每次学会使用几个句型。理想的做法是这些句型相互关联，并按照一种精心排列的顺序介绍给学生。在传统教程中，语法项目常常被人为地组合到一起。例如，所有人称代词都被列在一个表中，让学生去学习。这个表是孤立的，不与任何上下文有关系。按照这种方法来学习语言的细节对学生并没有真正的帮助，因为他不可能运用他所学到的知识。在一个按结构分级的教程中，学生每次得到一点信息，然后学会在有意义的表述中运用这些知识。这样，他就能在很长一段时间里，学习运用诸如人称代词这类相对简单的结构词，而不是在某一时刻得到一大堆无法消化的信息。

语境化教学：在有意义的上下文中来解释语法项目。

学生口头练习了一个新句型时，如有可能，他应该在实际的课文中接触这个句型，看一看这个句型是如何使用的。很明显，这些课文必须由教程设计者专门撰写。新句型在一个自然的语境中介绍给学生：它们被"融入上下文中"。在精心编写的有语境的课文中，反复重复的句型必须不十分注目：要使听者觉得使用这些句型是不可避免的，而不是人工堆砌在一起的。这是向学生介绍新信息的一种有效方式。

情景教学：通过介绍一系列日常的情景来讲授语言。

使用这种方法几乎不可能按结构分级。情景领先于结构，课文中所含有的句型自然而然地从情景中产生：它们具有一个主题含义，而不是一个结构含义。这种方式有着严重的缺陷。

学生听到的对话与众不同地自然，但是，基本句型的教学不可避免地变得更难控制。

限定结构的情景教学：通过一系列日常情景来讲授语言，同时，将介绍的句型按结构分级。

这种方法利用了以上简略介绍的所有手段：按结构分级、语境化教学、情景教学。在开始阶段确实可以仅仅使用少数几个句型。这就意味着"情景"常常令人难以置信，几乎不可能实现。尽管有不利的一面，这种方法仍被认为是学习语言的最好的方法之一，因为它可以从语言学角度来控制，并能用一种有趣的方法来介绍新的信息。

讲授语法

介绍新的信息是一回事儿，让学生使用这些新的信息是另一回事儿。至此，我们关心的是如何向学生介绍新的材料，但是学生如何运用他所学的知识呢？

语言教学的首要目标是训练学生使用新句型。在传统教材中，所有信息都是以"规则"的形式来介绍的，学生将这些规则用于相互没有关联的句子的填空练习或填上括号中所列词的正确词形的练习之中，这种讲授语言的方法收效甚微，这点现在已经变得非常清楚。这种方法鼓励教师**谈论语言**，却不是训练学生去使用语言。侧重点是在书面练习上。这种方法的最大弱点是，学生不能将他从这种抽象的练习中所学到的知识转化成其他语言技能，如理解，口语和创作性写作。

在现代教材中，目标也是同样的：训练学生运用句型。在考虑如何实现这一目标之前，应该注意到语言中的句型可以分成两种截然不同的类型："渐进型的"和"静态型的"。例如，学习提出问题和回答问题就涉及了渐进型的句型。它们属于渐进型，是因为学生运用这些复杂形式的技能要在很长的一段时间里才能培养起来。从一开始的简单回答 "Yes, it is" 发展到这本教材结尾部分的复杂回答方式 "Yes, I should, shouldn't I"。而静态型的句型，如形容词的比较级，可以在有限的几课课文中讲授，不必占用很长时间。在传统教材中，渐进型的和静态型的句型之间的差别几乎没有作任何区分，其结果是，即使是学习好的学生也常常不能比较熟练地运用渐进型句型。

渐进型句型必须在检查学生理解能力的练习中进行训练。这种练习要求学生回答问题并提出问题，而问题的难度则随着教程的进展而不断加深。必须训练学生用简略形式回答一般疑问句；为以 Who, Which, What 开头的疑问句提供答案；用肯定形式和否定形式来回答用 or 联结的选择疑问句；回答用 When, Where, How 等疑问词开头的问句。而在每一个阶段，必须训练学生自己提问题。很明显，这些技能不可能在一两课书中学会：在每课书中都必须有这种练习。

与此同时，静态型的句型必须在录音练习中得到训练。在每一个录音练习中，教师试图引出某一特定的回答。他在一系列口头练习中给学生某种诱导以引出新句型，直到学生可以准确地、下意识地作出反应。每个新句型不是作为某一种抽象的语法规则的范例来介绍，而是作为**表达某种思想的方法**，也不需要进一步的说明和解释。学生在训练中学会下意识地运用正确的句型，而不是用"语法逻辑"去进行推理。如果需要解释，可以把新句型与已经学会的旧句型联系起来。举例来说，如果学生已经学会了 must 的用法，那么在讲授 have to 的用法时，可以让学生领会这两个句型之间有机的联系。

在部分录音练习中，教师提供的诱导可以采用"提示词"的形式。假设教师想引出 "I can't buy very much"（我不能买许多）和 "I can't buy very many"（我不能买很多个）的回答，这个练习可以用以下形式来进行：

教师：What about pencils?（那么铅笔呢?）
学生：I can't buy very many.（我不能买很多支。）
教师：What about coffee?（那么咖啡呢?）
学生：I can't buy very much.（我不能买许多。）

在这一特定的练习中，教师可以为 What about ... ? 这个句型提供可数名词和不可数名词来作为"提示词"。

在现代教程中，传统的填空练习仍有它的一席之地，但有一个重大的区别，即填空练习不应作为讲授新句型的一种手段，而应作为巩固已学知识的途径。它们是目的，而不是达到目的的一种手段。从这个意义上讲，填空练习在测试中尤其有用，可以用来分析学生的错误，或让教师评估学生所取得的成绩。

视听教具和翻译

在单语教程中，我们面临着不借助学生的母语来传授知识的艰巨任务。其结果是课文中的插图变得格外重要：在初级阶段，它们绝对不仅仅是起装饰作用。然而，课文插图有很大的局限性，因为日常生活中所讲的许多话根本不可能用图来表示。有些语言学家尝试过使用人造的视觉教具，这些教具要求学生根据某种规则来解释每一幅插图。他们已经逐渐形成了一种所谓的"视觉语言"，并要求学生在开始教程前就先掌握。但问题在于，如果学生无法解释一幅插图——这种情况很容易发生——他就会无法理解，更严重的情况是，他会误解他所听到的内容。

在初级阶段，这个难题可以用两种不同的方式来解决：当一句话或几句话的意思无法用插图准确地表达时，教师必须用手势和模仿动作。如果学生仍无法理解，教师可译成母语，**条件是教师翻译的仅**

是词组而不是整个句型。在这里，翻译不是作为一种教学法，而是达到目的的手段。这样做是非常有用的，而且节省时间。

真实英语

在课程的初级阶段，我们极可能鼓励学生去说一些他永远也不会说的话，诸如"我有一个鼻子"，"你有鼻子吗?"，"这是我的脚吗?"这类句子非常荒唐。这种对语言的歪曲是根本没有道理的。毕竟讲授一种语言的全部目的在于训练学生去说那些在真实的生活环境中通常使用的有意义的话。在初级阶段必须遵循这个标准。必须不惜任何代价避免使用那种在传统教科书中可以找到的特殊的"教科书英语"。

教师用书和学生用书

在过去，我们没有区分开哪些信息是给教师的，哪些是给学生的。所有的内容都印在一本书中。在教程的初级阶段，学生会在他的书中发现特别复杂的内容，如"对大多数名词来说，其复数形式是在单数名词后面加 -s 而成"，或"'是'和'有'动词的否定形式是在动词后面加 not 构成的"。不能想像初学者可能懂得这些指令。更重要的是，从学习者的角度来说，这种信息是与他们不相干的：实际上它是告诉教师应教什么。

应该认识到，学生用书并不是用来传达信息，而是训练语言的一种工具。它必须很漂亮，版面很吸引人，而且包含对学生有用的内容。

在初级阶段，教师用书是非常必要的。教师用书必须在各个方面与学生用书相互补充，而且必须包含每课书中会用到的、有实用价值的信息和材料，而不仅仅是提示和建议。在中级阶段，教师用书就变得不那么需要，因为到那时学生可以跟随书上的指令自己进行学习了。

速度和深度

传统的教程往往分为"课"，而这些"课"却没有考虑一般长度为 45 分钟或 1 小时的课中可以做些什么。它们只是简单地包含"一定量的信息"，而且常常是洋洋洒洒好几页。在课堂教学中，这些"课"可能讲上好几周，因为要做的事情太多了。

"课"应该名符其实：教学内容一般可以在一个课时内完成，可能再加上一些补充的内容在课下作为作业。换句话说，一课书应被视作一个教学单位，仅此而已。现在，让教程设计者决定一个课时内可以做些什么是极其困难的。显然，由聪明学生组成的一个班所完成的内容要多于由不太聪明的学生组成的另一个班。如果课文中含有可以由教师决定取舍的内容，这个问题就可以迎刃而解，当然这种删节不应妨碍学生水平的提高。

程度

最后，值得注意的是，一个完整的教程一般分为 3 个阶段，而每个阶段又分成两个级别：

第 1 阶段：初级以下
　　　　　　初级
第 2 阶段：中级以下
　　　　　　中级
第 3 阶段：高级以下
　　　　　　高级

关于本教材的说明

从理论到实践: 基本目的

这本教材试图将上面简述的关于语言学习的理论付诸实践。现将目的简述如下:

1 为中学生和成年初学者提供一本教材。假定学生没有学过英语。这本教材的内容足够 1 年使用, 可以使学生达到初级以下和初级的水平。假定学生 1学年上课 36 周, 可在 1 学年内结束这本教材。这就是说, 学生每周上课约 4 个课时, 即互不相连的 4 个课时, 每课时为 1 小时, 或两个"双课时", 每个双课时为 2 小时或 90 分钟。学生主要在课上接受训练, 在课下仅做一点额外的作业。

2 全面训练学生的 4 项技能: 理解、口语、阅读、写作——按此顺序进行训练。本书的练习大多数是听说方面的, 笔语方面的全面训练要到本书学完后才开始。应该明确, 这本书是为满足教师课堂教学的需要而设计的, 而不是为自学的学生设计的。

3 为学生提供一本令他能够在教师的帮助下自己使用语言的教材。

4 为教师提供配合得当、循序渐进的教材, 使他们在上课前只需做极少的准备。教师用书和学生用书组成一个完整的教程, 两者不可缺一。

5 为教师和学生提供可在课堂和家里使用的录音材料。然而, 必须强调的是, 这不是一本全面供自学者使用的教程。从根本上来说, 这是一本供课堂使用的教材, 但它的录音材料也可以在家里使用。录音练习对课堂练习是一个补充。

教材内容

这本教材由以下各部分组成:
- 学生用书
- 教师用书
- 一组录有多功能课文的盒式磁带
- 一组录有教师用书中的"重复训练"的盒式磁带

教材介绍

在这本教材中, 每两课课文——每课大约为 1 课时——被看成 1 个教学单元。学生学每课书大概用 1 小时, 每周学完两个教学单元。全书共有 72 个教学单元, 因此足够 36 周使用。

学生用书

每个教学单元的前半部分有一篇按句型结构编排的情景对话或描述性文字, 其中每课书介绍的新的语言内容被融进了上下文之中。课文用于训练学生的理解能力, 以及学生说、读和运用渐进型句型的能力。

每个教学单元的后半部分通常有几组有编号的插图, 用于理解和口语练习。在可能的情况下, 新词汇在学生口头掌握之后才见之于文字。在具有语境的课文中介绍的新的语言现象被单列出来，并进行反复练习。在这种口头练习之后有一小段笔头练习，用来巩固已经学到的技能。

教师用书

在每个教学单元的前半部分，教师可以找到如下几部分内容：

<u>内容和基本目标</u>：列出学生将要使用的句型、结构词和词项。

<u>总体评论</u>：介绍本教学单元的主要语法项目。

<u>听力理解</u>：介绍课文的 9 个步骤，用以训练学生听懂英语口语的能力。

<u>理解</u>：训练学生根据课文回答问题和提出问题。

<u>句型训练</u>：有时会有某个语言难点的简单训练，或为本教学单元后半部分的练习铺平道路。

<u>活动</u>：有时为某些活动提供素材，例如：讲故事，玩游戏或其他课堂活动。

在每个教学单元的后半部分，教师可为新句型的训练找到素材。这些练习往往采用两种形式：重复训练和句型训练。从第 17 教学单元起，书中列出了建议听写的段落。

录音带

与教程相配套的两组录音磁带，可用于课堂教学，也可供自学使用。

1　　第 1 组录音磁带含有每个教学单元前半部分的情景对话或描述性文字的录音，录音速度比正常语速慢一些（每分钟 100 个单词）。这些磁带是为教师在课堂上使用而设计的，以便按照 9 个步骤来介绍课文。然而，自学的学生也可以用这些录音带来提高他们听的能力。

2　　第 2 组录音磁带含有每个教学单元后半部分的"重复训练"，可用于课堂教学和课外自学。一共有 72 个练习。这些磁带是为教师在课堂上使用而设计的，决心借助于录音机在家里完成这些练习的学生也可使用这些磁带。

练习分成 3 个步骤：引导——**学生回答**——正确答案。这些练习是根据每课介绍的重点语法项目编写的。练习的书面材料刊印在教师用书中每个教学单元的后半部分。

本教材使用说明

教师按语

伴随每个教学单元的按语应该被视为建议。如果愿意，教师可以偏离所规定的教学计划，或是省略他认为不符合他教学目标的练习。然而，写上按语的目的是帮助教师组织训练所介绍的句型。在可能的情况下，每课书的练习均按难易程度分级。这就意味着，如果时间不够，最后的练习可以删去，而不至于严重影响学生的学习进程。每个教学单元包含两小时的内容。如果教师仅有 45 分钟用于每个单元的前半部分或后半部分，那么他就要根据他所能使用的时间来重新编排这些练习。

每个教师上课时都会使用的那些指令和评语——如"请听"、"坐下"、"再说一遍"、"一起来"等等——应该用英语来说。在初级阶段，这些短语的含义可用手势和模仿动作来表述。这些短语必须被看成与课文无关，除非它们正式在课文中出现。按照本教材的目的，只有当学生学会使用某个句型他才算是熟悉了这一句型。这就是为什么课堂教学中常用的指令并没有列入教师用书课文之前的句型和词汇表内。

按语分列在不同的标题之下。现在我们来介绍其中的每一项。

内容和基本目标——总体评论

这两个标题下的内容简要地归纳了课文所教的句型和语项。归纳完全是为教师准备的。

听力理解

详尽的指令在课程之初便作了交代，但随着教师慢慢适应这一程序，指令便逐渐简化。我们推荐介绍课文的 9 个步骤，用以训练学生听懂英语口语的能力。这 9 个步骤如下：

1　介绍故事
2　了解情景
3　听力训练目标
4　播放录音或朗读课文
5　回答问题
6　精读
7　再次播放录音或朗读课文
8　重复
9　大声朗读

每一个步骤都必须简洁。让我们来看一下如何在实践中运用这 9 个步骤：

1　介绍故事

教师用几句话介绍课文，使学生能清楚了解所发生的事情，而不需要去猜测。开始可以用少量的中文，但教师必须尽早开始用英语。例如：Today we'll listen to a story about a handbag.（今天，我们要听一个有关手提包的故事。）

2　了解情景

要求学生看插图，以便检查学生是否了解课文中所发生的事情。在最初阶段可以给少量的中文作为提示，但教师必须尽早开始使用英语。例如：Look at the pictures and tell me what is happening here.（看图，然后告诉我这里发生了什么事情。）（你可以再加上 1 至 2 个问题作为提示。）

3 听力训练目标

通过给学生提个问题, 让他们寻找答案的方式, 教师为学生确立一个"听力训练目标"。这就意味着学生会积极地而不是消极地去听课文录音。例如: Listen to the story, then tell me: Whose handbag is it? (听故事, 然后告诉我: 这是谁的手提包?)

4 播放录音或朗读课文

教师播放录音或朗读课文, 在不停顿的情况下让学生静听一遍课文。

5 回答问题

现在教师再一次问第 3 步骤中的问题, 让学生试着回答 Now you've heard the story, whose hand-bag is it? (你现在听了这个故事, 这是谁的手提包?) 训练学生不要集体回答, 如果他们认为自己知道答案, 就让他们举手。问一个学生, 然后再问其他的人: "你们中有多少人同意他/她的回答?""如果你们同意请举起手来。""[对另一个学生]如果你不同意, 那么你认为答案是什么?""你们中有多少人同意他/她的回答?""同意的请举起手来。"这样就能让学生不断地猜测, 而且把全班学生都调动起来。从一开始就要训练学生不做"任何准备"地去听, 也不通过"翻译"。很快, 他们就会适应英语的语音, 并理解他们所听到的内容。

6 精读

现在教师重放录音或重读课文, 每行后稍稍停顿, 检查学生是否理解。这是课堂教学中非常重要的一个环节, 因为学生必须全力通过图片去理解课文。如果学生不能通过图片来理解部分课文的内容——这种情况总会发生的——教师必须用手势和模拟动作来进行解释。如果仍不能表述那一含义, 教师就应该请班上学得最好的学生给出一个单词或词组的译文, 以照顾尚未理解词义的学生。把翻译看成最后一种手段。在开始阶段, 传达意思是很难的一个环节, 但随着课程的进展, 困难就会越来越小。

7 再次播放录音或朗读课文

不停顿地再次从头播放录音或课文。经过以上 6 个步骤的精心讲解, 这次学生应毫无困难便可听懂。

8 重复

再次播放录音或朗读课文, 每行后停顿一下, 让学生全体、小组 (如教室里每一行) 和单个地重复。当全体和小组重复时, 要求学生在看到你的明确信号后一起开始。你可用点头或以手中的铅笔来做信号, 想像你自己在指挥一个交响乐团。课文中的断句标志着不同的"阅读单元", 它们的长度与学生视线的宽度是一致的。

9 大声朗读

让一两个学生扮演对话中的角色, 大声朗读。从中你可以了解到不同学生是否能够准确地读出他们听到的英语。

这个介绍课文的过程不应超过 25 分钟。随着学生能力的提高, 教师可以根据需要简化其中的步骤, 这样就可以有更多的时间用于其后的练习。

在家中自学的学生应尽可能多听课文录音, 使自己完全熟悉课文。如果愿意, 甚至可以把课文背出来。

理解

这个阶段包含两个练习: 1 学生回答问题; 2 学生提问题。

1   学生回答问题

按照以上 9 个步骤介绍课文后,教师在班上向学生单独提问题。如果一个学生没能回答出来,很快转向另一个学生,因此,这部分练习要很注意节奏。教师提的问题和相应的答案都包括在教师用书中。当然,如果你愿意,可以提一些额外的问题。问题分成两类:

a   一般疑问句

一般来说,仅用 Yes(是)或 No(不)来回答一个问题是不礼貌的。要训练学生注意听一般疑问句的第一个单词,在回答时用同样的词。

教师:*Is* Anna's dress new?(安娜的连衣裙是新的吗?) (问题中的第一个词是 *Is*)

学生:Yes, it *is*.(是,它是新的。) (*is* 是答案的一部分)

教师:*Is* Anna's dress blue?(安娜的连衣裙是蓝色的吗?)

学生:No, it *isn't*.(不,它不是。)

b   特殊疑问句 (以 Wh- 开头和以 How 开头的疑问句)

训练学生回答以 When, Where, Which, How 等词开头的疑问句(当然,在这本教材中要花一些时间才能逐渐达到这个目标)。学生可以用完整的句子回答,也可以用简短的、较自然的回答方式。

教师:Whose dress is new?(谁的连衣裙是新的?)

学生:Anna's dress is new. 或 Anna's.(安娜的连衣裙是新的。或简短回答:安娜的。)

就这样,经过一段时间的训练,学生会把 When 和时间、Where 和地点、Why 和原因、Who 和身份、Whose 和所有权、Which 和选择、What 和选择、身份或活动、How 和方式联系起来。

2   学生提问题

为了防止类似 Where he went 的错误问题,需要训练学生同时问两个问题。第 1 个是一般疑问句第 2 个是特殊疑问句。例如:

教师:Ask me if Sally is in the garden.(问我萨莉是否在花园里。)

学生:Is Sally in the garden?(萨莉是不是在花园?)

教师:Where ... ?(……在哪里?)

学生:Where is Sally?(萨莉在哪里?) (而不是 Where Sally is? 或 Where Sally?)

当然,在这本教材中要经过一段时间问题才能发展到这个形式。所有的这类问题都包括在教师用书中。如果教师愿意,可以增加一些问题。

活动

在每个教学单元第 1 部分的结尾处,有一些关于课堂活动的建议。如果没有足够的时间,它们可以全部省略。应该尽一切可能不时地介绍一些课堂活动,因为它们会活跃课堂气氛,为语言教学增添乐趣。所建议的课堂活动有两种形式。

游戏

一系列关于游戏的建议可以帮助学生操练某些句型。

讲故事

可以要求学生仅仅依靠插图来重新组合对话。成年学生在课堂上"表演"对话通常会感到不自然,讲故事活动是一个很好的折衷办法。这也是非常有用的锻炼记忆力的方式,同时为讲话打下基础。

附加练习

在学生用书中,每个教学单元的后半部分(所有双数课文)都有一些标了数字的插图,有些还有单词和句子。正如前面所指出的,在可能的情况下,一个单词要在口语中出现后才正式在文字中出现。

这就是为什么这些双数课文常常仅有插图。在这些插图的帮助下，学生可以练习某些句型（句型既有**渐进型的**又有**静态型的**，取决于课文）。

附加练习往往从一个简短的练习开始，这个练习仅仅针对一个特殊的问题，如数字的用法、日期、时间、字母的使用、拼写难点等等。这类难点要在很长的一段时间里反复练习，不可能在一两课中解决。在此练习之后，学生继续进行重复训练和句型训练。

重复训练

学生进行重复训练。他们可以利用录音机和录音磁带在课堂上进行这种训练，如果是自学，也可以在家里进行。但也可采用另一种方式，即由教师"现场"口头指导，利用书中的录音材料进行训练。

句型训练

这种句型训练是双数课文的主体。在这些训练中，教师试着引导班上的学生练习一系列不同的句型。学生可以全班、小组或个人进行回答，形式可以由教师来决定。

每次给学生介绍一个新的句型练习时，教师应该说明所需要的回答形式，可以用口头说明或将回答写到黑板上。不需要从语法上进行解释。每一个新句型都应该作为**口头表述的形式**来介绍。但介绍新句型的方法则由教师自己决定。

在进行句型操练时，教师提供诱导，学生看着自己的书作出回答。例如引导有关现在完成时用法的句子可以这样进行：

教师：Look at the first picture. What has she just done?（请看第 1 幅画。她刚刚做完了什么?）

学生：She has just aired the room.（[看插图]她刚刚给房间通了通风。）

教师：Look at the second picture. What have they just done?（请看第 2 幅画。他们刚刚做完了什么?）

学生：They have just cleaned their shoes.（[看插图]他们刚刚擦了鞋。）

在部分练习中，没有要求学生去查看插图，只让学生使用"提示词"。所用的提示词都列在教师用书中，而且是从学生所熟悉的词汇中选出来的。下面是这种练习的一个例子。

引导使用 *very much* 和 *very many* 的句子 I can't buy very much/many.（我不能买很多。）

教师：What about pencils?（那么铅笔呢?）

学生：I can't buy very many.（我不能买很多枝。）

教师：What about coffee?（那么咖啡呢?）

学生：I can't buy very much.（我不能买许多。）

以下是可用在问题 What about ...? 中的提示词：面包、奶酪、肥皂、牛排、饼干、鸡蛋、蔬菜、水果、鲜花、蛋糕、纸张、墨水、胶水、衣服、阿斯匹林、药品、果酱、蜂蜜、信封、杂志、葡萄酒、牛奶。

句型训练之后是书面练习。

书面练习

书面练习有两种形式：结构练习和听写。

结构练习

在最初的几个教学单元，学生在开始正式的书面练习前应先抄书。在学生用书中印有要求使用的手写体格式和所要求的回答形式。应该注意到，在开始阶段，虽然书面练习的指令很简单，但所用的语汇是学生所不熟悉的，需要解释。这些练习的目的不是学习新的句型，而是去重复和巩固已经口头学会的内容。它们必须置于口头训练**之后**，而且可以作为家庭作业。学生不应仅填几个空，而应抄写整个练习。

听写

听写练习在第 17 教学单元之后才开始，听写的内容均是课文中见过的语言。教师用来听写的总是前一个教学单元笔头练习的答案。

附加练习部分有将近 1 小时的素材。由于练习是按难易程度编排的，因此，如果时间不够，可以省略最后几项。

测试

在全书的中部有一个测验，教师可以用这套试题来评估学生的学习成果。

课外作业

录音磁带

除了布置书面作业外，必须鼓励有配套录音磁带的学生在家里多次播放新学对话的录音。如有可能，应要求他们背诵对话。同时也应建议学生跟随录音带上的练习进行训练。全书的 72 篇课文组成了一个循序渐进、按语言结构难度分级的基础英语概论。课文短小精悍，便于记忆，可以使零起点的学生在使用语言过程中逐渐增强信心，提高能力。

继续深造

这本教材是完全独立的，足够 1 年使用。在课程结束后，学生应能较好地掌握英语口语。凡打算继续深造的学生，可以接着学习以下各册。教材各册之间的内容相互"重叠"，学生继续学习不会感到困难。

Practice and Progress《实践与进步》：中级以下水平综合教材

Developing Skills《培养技能》：中级水平综合教材

Fluency in English《流利英语》：高级水平综合教材

在这几本书中，学生将继续他们在这本教材中开始的口语训练，并系统地接受英语写作的训练。

Lesson 1　Excuse me! 对不起!

Listen to the tape then answer this question. Whose handbag is it?
听录音, 然后回答问题 。这是谁的手袋?

Excuse me!	1
Yes?	2
Is this your handbag?	3
Pardon?	4
Is this your handbag?	5
Yes, it is.	6
Thank you very much.	7

1

New words and expressions 生词和短语

excuse /ɪksˈkjuːz/ v. 原谅
me /mɪ/ pron. 我（宾格）
yes /jes/ adv. 是的
is /ɪz/ v. be 动词现在时第三人称单数
this /ðɪs/ pron. 这
your /jɔː/ possessive adjective 你的, 你们的

handbag /ˈhændbæg/ n. （女用）手提包
pardon /ˈpɑːdn/ int. 原谅, 请再说一遍
it /ɪt/ pron. 它
thank you /ˈθæŋk-juː/ 感谢你（们）
very much /ˈveri-mʌtʃ/ 非常地

Notes on the text 课文注释

1 Excuse me.
   这个短语常用于与陌生人搭话, 打断别人的说话或从别人身边挤过。在课文中, 男士为了吸引女士的注意力而用了这个表示客套的短语。
2 Pardon?
   全句为 I beg your pardon. 意思是请求对方把刚才讲过的话重复一遍。

参考译文

对不起!

什么事?

这是您的手提包吗?

对不起, 请再说一遍。

这是您的手提包吗?

是的, 是我的。

非常感谢!

Lesson 2   Is this your . . . ?   这是你的……吗？

 Listen to the tape and do the exercises.
听录音并回答问题 。

1

2

3

4

5

6

7

8

9

10

New words and expressions 生词和短语

pen /pen/ *n.* 钢笔

pencil /'pensəl/ *n.* 铅笔

book /bʊk/ *n.* 书

watch /wɒtʃ/ *n.* 手表

coat /kəʊt/ *n.* 上衣, 外衣

dress /dres/ *n.* 连衣裙

skirt /skɜːt/ *n.* 裙子

shirt /ʃɜːt/ *n.* 衬衣

car /kɑː/ *n.* 小汽车

house /haʊs/ *n.* 房子

Written exercise 书面练习

Copy these sentences.

抄写以下句子。

Excuse me!

Yes?

Is this your handbag?

Pardon?

Is this your handbag?

Yes, it is.

Thank you very much.

Lesson 3   Sorry, sir. 对不起, 先生。

Listen to the tape then answer this question. Does the man get his umbrella back?

听录音, 然后回答问题。这位男士有没有要回他的雨伞?

My coat and my umbrella please.

1

Here is my ticket.

2

Thank you, sir.
Number five.

3

Here's your umbrella
and your coat.

4

This is not my umbrella.
Sorry, sir.

5

Is this your umbrella?
No, it isn't.

6

Is this it?
Yes, it is.
Thank you very much.

7

New words and expressions 生词和短语

umbrella /ʌmˈbrelə/ n. 伞

please /pliːz/ int. 请

here /hɪə/ adv. 这里

my /maɪ/ possessive adjective 我的

ticket /ˈtɪkɪt/ n. 票

number /ˈnʌmbə/ n.号码

five /faɪv/ num. 五

sorry /ˈsɒri/ adj. 对不起的

sir /sɜː/ n. 先生

cloakroom /ˈkləʊkrʊm/ n. 衣帽存放处

Notes on the text 课文注释

1 Here's 是 Here is 的缩写形式, 类似的例子有 He's (He is), It's (It is) 等 。缩写形式和非缩写形式在英语的书面用语和口语中均有, 但非缩写形式常用于比较正式的场合 。

2 Sorry = I'm sorry. 这是口语中的缩略形式, 用于社交场合, 向他人表示歉意 。

3 sir, 先生, 这是英美人对不相识的男子, 年长者或上级的尊称 。

4 Is this it?
本句中 it 是指 your umbrella 。由于前面提到了, 后面就用代词 it 来代替, 以免重复 。

参考译文

请把我的大衣和伞拿给我 。

这是我（寄存东西）的牌子 。

谢谢, 先生 。
是5号 。

这是您的伞和大衣 。

这不是我的伞 。
对不起, 先生 。

这把伞是您的吗?
不, 不是！

这把是吗?
是, 是这把 。
非常感谢 。

Lesson 4　Is this your . . . ?　这是你的……吗?

🎙 Listen to the tape and answer the questions.
听录音并回答问题。

1

Is this your pen?

2

Is this your pencil?

3

Is this your book?

4

Is this your watch?

5

Is this your coat?

6

Is this your dress?

7

Is this your skirt?

8

Is this your shirt?

9

Is this your car?

10

Is this your house?

11

Is this your suit?

12

Is this your school?

13

Is this your teacher?

14

Is this your son?

15

Is this your daughter?

7

New words and expressions 生词和短语

suit /suːt/ *n.* 一套衣服

school /skuːl/ *n.* 学校

teacher /'tiːtʃə/ *n.* 老师

son /sʌn/ *n.* 儿子

daughter /'dɔːtə/ *n.* 女儿

Written exercises 书面练习

A Copy these sentences.
    抄写以下句子。

This is not my umbrella.
Sorry, sir.
Is this your umbrella?
No, it isn't!

B Answer these questions.
    模仿例句回答以下问题。

Example:

Is this your umbrella?

No. It isn't my umbrella. It's your umbrella.

1 Is this your pen?

2 Is this your pencil?

3 Is this your book?

4 Is this your watch?

5 Is this your coat?

6 Is this your dress?

7 Is this your skirt?

8 Is this your shirt?

9 Is this your car?

10 Is this your house?

Lesson 5　Nice to meet you.　很高兴见到你。

 Listen to the tape then answer this question. Is Chang-woo Chinese?
听录音，然后回答问题。昌宇是中国人吗？

MR. BLAKE :	Good morning.
STUDENTS :	Good morning, Mr. Blake.

MR. BLAKE :	This is Miss Sophie Dupont.
	Sophie is a new student.
	She is French.

MR. BLAKE :	Sophie, this is Hans.
	He is German.
HANS :	Nice to meet you.

MR. BLAKE :	And this is Naoko.
	She's Japanese.
NAOKO :	Nice to meet you.

MR. BLAKE :	And this is Chang-woo.
	He's Korean.
CHANG-WOO :	Nice to meet you.

MR. BLAKE :	And this is Luming.
	He's Chinese.
LUMING :	Nice to meet you.

MR. BLAKE :	And this is Xiaohui.
	She's Chinese, too.
XIAOHUI :	Nice to meet you.

New words and expressions 生词和短语

Mr. /'mɪstə/ 先生
good /gʊd/ *adj.* 好
morning /'mɔːnɪŋ/ *n.* 早晨
Miss /mɪs/ 小姐
new /njuː/ *adj.* 新的
student /'stjuːdənt/ *n.* 学生
French /frentʃ/ *adj. & n.* 法国的; 法国人

German /'dʒɜːmən/ *adj. & n.* 德国的; 德国人
nice /naɪs/ *adj.* 美好的
meet /miːt/ *v.* 遇见
Japanese /dʒæp'niːz/ *adj. & n.* 日本的; 日本人
Korean /kə'rɪən/ *adj. & n.* 韩国的; 韩国人
Chinese /ˌtʃaɪ'niːz/ *adj. & n.* 中国的; 中国人
too /tuː/ *adv.* 也

Notes on the text 课文注释

1 Good morning.
  早上好。英语中常见的问候用语。
2 This is Miss Sophie Dupont.
  一般用于将某人介绍给他人的句式。一般指未婚女子。
3 Nice to meet you.
  用于初次与同学、朋友见面等非正式场合。正式的场合常用 How do you do?

参考译文

布莱克先生： 早上好。
学　　　生： 早上好, 布莱克先生。

布莱克先生： 这位是索菲娅·杜邦小姐。索菲娅是新来的学生。她是法国人。

布莱克先生： 索菲娅, 这位是汉斯。他是德国人。
汉　　　斯： 很高兴见到你。

布莱克先生： 这位是直子。她是日本人。
直　　　子： 很高兴见到你。

布莱克先生： 这位是昌宇。他是韩国人。
昌　　　宇： 很高兴见到你。

布莱克先生： 这位是鲁明。他是中国人。
鲁　　　明： 很高兴见到你。

布莱克先生： 这位是晓惠。她也是中国人。
晓　　　惠： 很高兴见到你。

Lesson 6 What make is it? 它是什么牌子的？

Listen to the tape and answer the questions.
听录音并回答问题。

8

It's a Volvo. (Swedish)

9

It's a Peugeot. (French)

10

It's a Mercedes. (German)

11

It's a Toyota. (Japanese)

12

It's a Daewoo. (Korean)

13

It's a Mini. (English)

14

It's a Ford. (American)

15

It's a Fiat. (Italian)

New words and expressions 生词和短语

make /meɪk/ *n.* （产品的）牌号

Swedish /'swiːdɪʃ/ *adj.* 瑞典的

English /'ɪŋglɪʃ/ *adj.* 英国的

American /ə'merɪkən/ *adj.* 美国的

Italian /ɪ'tæliən/ *adj.* 意大利的

Volvo /'vɒlvəʊ/ *n.* 沃尔沃

Peugeot /'pɜːʒəʊ/ *n.* 标致

Mercedes /mə'seɪdiːz/ *n.* 梅赛德斯

Toyota /'təʊjəʊtə/ *n.* 丰田

Daewoo /'dɑːwuː/ *n.* 大宇

Mini /'mɪnɪ/ *n.* 迷你

Ford /fɔːd/ *n.* 福特

Fiat /'fiːæt/ *n.* 菲亚特

Written exercises 书面练习

A Complete these sentences using *He, She* or *It*.
完成以下句子，用 *He, She* 或 *It* 填空。

Examples:

Stella is a student. _____ isn't German. _____ is Spanish.

Stella is a student. She isn't German. She is Spanish.

Alice is a student. _____ isn't German. _____ is French.
This is her car. _____ is a French car.
Hans is a student. _____ isn't French. _____ is German.
This is his car. _____ is a German car.

B Write questions and answers using *He, She, It, a* or *an*.
模仿例句写出相应的疑问句，并回答。选用 *He, She, It, a* 或 *an* 等词。

Examples:

This is Miss Sophie Dupont. French/(Swedish)

Is she a French student or a Swedish student?
She isn't a Swedish student. She's a French student.

This is a Volvo. Swedish/(French)

Is it a Swedish car or a French car?
It isn't a French car. It's a Swedish car.

1 This is Naoko. Japanese/(German)
2 This is a Peugeot. French/(German)
3 This is Hans. German/(Italian)
4 This is Xiaohui. Chinese/(Italian)
5 This is a Mini. English/(American)
6 This is Chang-woo. Korean/(Japanese)

7 This is a Fiat. Italian/(English)
8 This is Luming. Chinese/(English)
9 This is a Mercedes. German/(French)
10 This is a Toyota. Japanese/(Chinese)
11 This is a Ford. American/(English)
12 This is a Daewoo. Korean/(Japanese)

Lesson 7   Are you a teacher? 你是教师吗?

Listen to the tape then answer this question. What is Robert's job?
听录音,然后回答问题 。罗伯特是做什么工作的?

ROBERT : I am a new student.
             My name's Robert.
SOPHIE : Nice to meet you.
             My name's Sophie.

ROBERT : Are you French?
SOPHIE : Yes, I am.

SOPHIE : Are you French, too?
ROBERT : No, I am not.

SOPHIE : What nationality are you?
ROBERT : I'm Italian.

ROBERT : Are you a teacher?
SOPHIE : No, I'm not.

ROBERT : What's your job?
SOPHIE : I'm a keyboard operator.

SOPHIE : What's your job?
ROBERT : I'm an engineer.

New words and expressions 生词和短语

I /aɪ/ *pron.* 我

am /æm/ *v.* be 动词现在时第一人称单数

are /ɑ:/ *v.* be 动词现在时复数

name /neɪm/ *n.* 名字

what /wɒt/ *adj. & pron.* 什么

nationality /ˌnæʃəˈnælɪti/ *n.* 国籍

job /dʒɒb/ *n.* 工作

keyboard /ˈkiːbɔːd/ *n.* 电脑键盘

operator /ˈɒpəreɪtə/ *n.* 操作人员

engineer /endʒɪˈnɪə/ *n.* 工程师

Notes on the text 课文注释

1 My name's = My name is.

2 I'm /aɪm/ = I am.
   口语中经常使用这种缩略形式 。

3 What's your job? 你是做什么工作的?
   What's = What is.

4 What nationality are you?
   用来询问对方国籍 。也可以问 Where are you from?

参考译文

罗伯特 ： 我是新来的学生, 我的名字叫罗伯特 。
索菲娅 ： 很高兴见到你 。我的名字叫索菲娅 。

罗伯特 ： 你是法国人吗?
索菲娅 ： 是的, 我是法国人 。

索菲娅 ： 你也是法国人吗?
罗伯特 ： 不, 我不是 。

索菲娅 ： 你是哪国人?
罗伯特 ： 我是意大利人 。

罗伯特 ： 你是教师吗?
索菲娅 ： 不, 我不是 。

罗伯特 ： 你是做什么工作的?
索菲娅 ： 我是电脑录入员 。

索菲娅 ： 你是做什么工作的?
罗伯特 ： 我是工程师 。

Lesson 8　What's your job?　你是做什么工作的？

 Listen to the tape then answer the questions.
听录音并回答问题。

11

I'm a policeman.

12

I'm a policewoman.

13

I'm a taxi driver.

14

I'm an air hostess.

15

I'm a postman.

16

I'm a nurse.

17

I'm a mechanic.

18

I'm a hairdresser.

19

I'm a housewife.

20

I'm a milkman.

New words and expressions 生词和短语

policeman /pə'liːsmən/ *n.* 警察

policewoman /pə'liːswʊmən/ *n.* 女警察

taxi driver /'tæksɪ-'draɪvə/ 出租汽车司机

air hostess /'eə-'həʊstəs/ 空中小姐

postman /'pəʊstmən/ *n.* 邮递员

nurse /nɜːs/ *n.* 护士

mechanic /mɪ'kænɪk/ *n.* 机械师

hairdresser /'heə͵dresə/ *n.* 理发师

housewife /'haʊswaɪf/ *n.* 家庭妇女

milkman /'mɪlkmən/ *n.* 送牛奶的人

Written exercises 书面练习

A Complete these sentences using *am* or *is*.
   完成以下句子, 用 *am* 或 *is* 填空 。

Example:

My name _____ Xiaohui. I _____ Chinese.

My name is Xiaohui. I am Chinese.

1 My name _____ Robert. I _____ a student. I _____ Italian.
2 Sophie _____ not Italian. She _____ French.
3 Mr. Blake _____ my teacher. He _____ not French.

B Write questions and answers using *his, her, he, she, a* or *an*.
   模仿例句写出相应的疑问句, 并回答 。选用 *his, her, he, she, a* 或 *an* 等词 。

Examples:

keyboard operator

What's her job? Is she a keyboard operator? Yes, she is.

engineer

What's his job? Is he an engineer? Yes, he is.

1 policeman

2 policewoman

3 taxi driver

4 air hostess

5 postman

6 nurse

7 mechanic

8 hairdresser

9 housewife

10 milkman

Lesson 9   How are you today? 你今天好吗？

Listen to the tape then answer this question. How is Emma?
听录音，然后回答问题。埃玛身体好吗？

STEVEN : Hello, Helen.

HELEN :   Hi, Steven.

1

STEVEN : How are you today?

HELEN :   I'm very well, thank you.
          And you?

2

STEVEN : I'm fine, thanks.

3

STEVEN : How is Tony?

HELEN :   He's fine, thanks.
          How's Emma?

STEVEN : She's very well, too, Helen.

4

STEVEN : Goodbye, Helen.
          Nice to see you.

HELEN :   Nice to see you, too, Steven.
          Goodbye.

5

New words and expressions 生词和短语

hello /hə'ləʊ/ *int.* 喂（表示问候）

hi /haɪ/ *int.* 喂，嗨

how /haʊ/ *adv.* 怎样

today /tə'deɪ/ *adv.* 今天

well /wel/ *adj.* 身体好

fine /faɪn/ *adj.* 美好的

thanks /θæŋks/ *int.* 谢谢

goodbye /'gʊd'baɪ/ *int.* 再见

see /siː/ *v.* 见

Notes on the text 课文注释

1 How are you?
   这是朋友或相识的人之间见面时问对方身体情况的寒暄话，一般回答是：Fine, thank you.
2 And you? 即And how are you? 的简略说法。
3 Nice to see you. 是 It's nice to see you.的简略说法。
   这一句也是见面时的客气话，一般回答是：Nice to see you, too. 见到你, 我也很高兴。也可说：Nice to meet you. 很高兴遇到你。

参考译文

史蒂文：你好, 海伦。

海　伦：你好, 史蒂文。

史蒂文：你今天好吗?

海　伦：很好, 谢谢你。你好吗?

史蒂文：很好, 谢谢。

史蒂文：托尼好吗?

海　伦：他很好, 谢谢。埃玛好吗?

史蒂文：她也很好, 海伦。

史蒂文：再见, 海伦。见到你真高兴。

海　伦：我见到你也很高兴, 史蒂文。再见。

Lesson 10   Look at . . . 看……

 Listen to the tape and answer the questions.
听录音并回答问题。

11

that man!
(fat)

12

that woman!
(thin)

13

that policeman!
(tall)

14

that policewoman!
(short)

15

that mechanic!
(dirty)

16

that nurse!
(clean)

17

Steven!
(hot)

18

Emma!
(cold)

19

that milkman!
(old)

20

that air hostess!
(young)

21

that hairdresser!
(busy)

22

that housewife!
(lazy)

New words and expressions 生词和短语

fat /fæt/ adj. 胖的
woman /ˈwʊmən/ n. 女人
thin /θɪn/ adj. 瘦的
tall /tɔːl/ adj. 高的
short /ʃɔːt/ adj. 矮的
dirty /ˈdɜːti/ adj. 脏的
clean /kliːn/ adj. 干净的

hot /hɒt/ adj. 热的
cold /kəʊld/ adj. 冷的
old /əʊld/ adj. 老的
young /jʌŋ/ adj. 年轻的
busy /ˈbɪzi/ adj. 忙的
lazy /ˈleɪzi/ adj. 懒的

Written exercises 书面练习

A Complete these sentences using *He's, She's* or *It's*.
完成以下句子, 用 *He's, She's* 或 *It's* 填空 。

Example:

Robert isn't a teacher. _____ an engineer.
Robert isn't a teacher. He's an engineer.

1 Mr. Blake isn't a student. _____ a teacher.
2 This isn't my umbrella. _____ your umbrella.
3 Sophie isn't a teacher. _____ a keyboard operator.
4 Steven isn't cold. _____ hot.
5 Naoko isn't Chinese. _____ Japanese.
6 This isn't a German car. _____ a Swedish car.

B Write sentences using *He* or *She*.
模仿例句写出相应的句子 。

Example:

Helen/well
Look at Helen. She's very well.

1 man/fat
2 woman/thin
3 policeman/tall
4 policewoman/short
5 mechanic/dirty
6 nurse/clean

7 Steven/hot
8 Emma/cold
9 milkman/old
10 air hostess/young
11 hairdresser/busy
12 housewife/lazy

Lesson 11 Is this your shirt ? 这是你的衬衫吗?

Listen to the tape then answer this question. Whose shirt is white?

听录音,然后回答问题 。谁的衬衣是白色的?

TEACHER : Whose shirt is that?

TEACHER : Is this your shirt, Dave?

DAVE :　　No, sir.

　　　　　It's not my shirt.

DAVE :　　This is my shirt.

　　　　　My shirt's blue.

TEACHER : Is this shirt Tim's?

DAVE :　　Perhaps it is, sir.

　　　　　Tim's shirt's white.

TEACHER : Tim!

TIM :　　 Yes, sir?

TEACHER : Is this your shirt?

TIM :　　 Yes, sir.

TEACHER : Here you are.

　　　　　Catch!

TIM :　　 Thank you, sir.

21

New words and expressions 生词和短语

whose /huːz/ *pron.* 谁的　　　　　　　white /waɪt/ *adj.* 白色的
blue /bluː/ *adj.* 蓝色的　　　　　　　catch /kætʃ/ *v.* 抓住
perhaps /pəˈhæps/ *adv.* 大概

Notes on the text 课文注释

1　Whose shirt is that?
　　疑问代词 Whose 在本句中作定语, 修饰 shirt 。
2　Is this shirt Tim's?
　　Tim's 是 Tim 的所有格形式, 为避免重复, Tim's 后面可以省去 shirt 。
　　例: It isn't my pen, it's Frank's. 这不是我的钢笔, 是弗兰克的 。
3　Here you are.或Here it is.
　　是给对方东西时的用语, 句中的 are 和 is 应重读 。

参考译文

老师：那是谁的衬衫?

老师：戴夫, 这是你的衬衫吗?
戴夫：不, 先生 。这不是我的衬衫 。

戴夫：这是我的衬衫 。我的衬衫是蓝色的 。

老师：这件衬衫是蒂姆的吗?
戴夫：也许是, 先生 。蒂姆的衬衫是白色的 。

老师：蒂姆!
蒂姆：什么事, 先生?

老师：这是你的衬衫吗?
蒂姆：是的, 先生 。

老师：给你 。接着!
蒂姆：谢谢您, 先生 。

Lesson 12 Whose is this . . . ? This is my/your/his/her . . .
这……是谁的？这是我的／你的／他的／她的……
Whose is that . . . ? That is my/your/his/her . . .
那……是谁的？那是我的／你的／他的／她的……

Listen to the tape and answer the questions.
听录音并回答问题。

22

handbag
It's Stella's.

23

car
It's Paul's.

24

coat
It's Sophie's.

25

umbrella
It's Steven's.

26

pen
It's my son's.

27

dress
It's my daughter's.

28

suit
It's my father's.

29

skirt
It's my mother's.

30

blouse
It's my sister's.

31

tie
It's my brother's.

New words and expressions 生词和短语

father /ˈfɑːðə/ n. 父亲

mother /ˈmʌðə/ n. 母亲

blouse /blaʊz/ n. 女衬衫

sister /ˈsɪstə/ n. 姐, 妹

tie /taɪ/ n. 领带

brother /ˈbrʌðə/ n. 兄, 弟

his /hɪz/ possessive adjective 他的

her /hɜː/ possessive adjective 她的

Written exercises 书面练习

A Complete these sentences using *my, your, his* or *her.*
完成以下句子, 用 *my, your, his* 或 *her* 填空 。

Example:

Hans is here. That is _____ car.

Hans is here. That is his car.

1 Stella is here. That is _____ car.

2 Excuse me, Steven. Is this _____ umbrella?

3 I am an air hostess. _____ name is Britt.

4 Paul is here, too. That is _____ coat.

B Write questions and answers using *'s, his* and *hers.*
模仿例句提问并回答, 选用名词所有格形式 *'s* 或代词所有格形式 *his* 或 *hers* 。

Example:

shirt/Tim

Whose is this shirt? It's Tim's. It's his shirt.

1 handbag/Stella

2 car/Paul

3 coat/Sophie

4 umbrella/Steven

5 pen/my daughter

6 dress/my son

7 suit/my father

8 skirt/my mother

9 blouse/my sister

10 tie/my brother

11 pen/Sophie

12 pencil/Hans

Lesson 13　A new dress　一件新连衣裙

Listen to the tape then answer this question. What colour is Anna's hat?
听录音, 然后回答问题 。安娜的帽子是什么颜色的?

LOUISE :　What colour's your new dress?

ANNA :.　It's green.

1

ANNA :　Come upstairs and see it.

LOUISE :　Thank you.

2

ANNA :　Look!

　　　　Here it is!

LOUISE :　That's a nice dress.

　　　　It's very smart.

3

ANNA :　My hat's new, too.

LOUISE :　What colour is it?

4

ANNA :　It's the same colour.

　　　　It's green, too.

5

LOUISE :　That *is* a lovely hat!

6

25

New words and expressions 生词和短语

colour /'kʌlə/ *n.* 颜色
green /griːn/ *adj.* 绿色
come /kʌm/ *v.* 来
upstairs /ʌp'steəz/ *adv.* 楼上

smart /smɑːt/ *adj.* 漂亮的, 时髦的
hat /hæt/ *n.* 帽子
same /seɪm/ *adj.* 相同的
lovely /'lʌvli/ *adj.* 可爱的, 秀美动人的

Notes on the text 课文注释

1 What colour's = What colour is
2 Come upstairs and see it.
句中 and 不当"和"讲, 而是表示目的, 例: Come and see me. 来见我。在英文中不能用 Come upstairs to see it.

参考译文

路易丝：你的新连衣裙是什么颜色的?
安　娜：是绿色的。

安　娜：到楼上来看看吧。
路易丝：谢谢。

安　娜：瞧, 就是这件。
路易丝：这件连衣裙真好, 真漂亮。

安　娜：我的帽子也是新的。
路易丝：是什么颜色的?

安　娜：一样的颜色, 也是绿的。
路易丝：真是一顶可爱的帽子!

Lesson 14   What colour's your . . .? 你的……是什么颜色的？

🎞 Listen to the tape and answer the questions.
听录音并回答问题。

20

umbrella   black

30

car   blue

40

shirt   white

50

coat   grey

60

case   brown

70

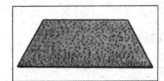

carpet   red

80

blouse   yellow

90

tie   orange

100

hat   grey and black

101

dog   brown and white

New words and expressions 生词和短语

case /keɪs/ *n.* 箱子

carpet /ˈkɑːpɪt/ *n.* 地毯

dog /dɒg/ *n.* 狗

Written exercises 书面练习

A   Rewrite these sentences.

模仿例句将下列各组句子合二为一 。

Example:

This is Stella. This is her handbag.

This is Stella's handbag.

1   This is Paul. This is his car.
2   This is Sophie. This is her coat.
3   This is Helen. This is her dog.
4   This is my father. This is his suit.
5   This is my daughter. This is her dress.

B   Write sentences using *'s, his* or *her.*

模仿例句提问并回答, 选用名词所有格形式 's或代词所有格形式 *his* 或 *her* 。

Example:

Steven/umbrella/black

What colour's Steven's umbrella? His umbrella's black.

1   Steven/car/blue
2   Tim/shirt/white
3   Sophie/coat/grey
4   Mrs. White/carpet/red
5   Dave/tie/orange
6   Steven/hat/grey and black

7   Helen/dog/brown and white
8   Hans/pen/green
9   Luming/suit/grey
10   Stella/pencil/blue
11   Xiaohui/handbag/brown
12   Sophie/skirt/yellow

Lesson 15　Your passports, please. 请出示你们的护照 。

Listen to the tape then answer this question.
Is there a problem with the Customs officer?
听录音, 然后回答问题 。海关官员有什么疑问吗?

CUSTOMS OFFICER :　Are you Swedish?

GIRLS :　　　　　　No, we are not.

We are Danish.

CUSTOMS OFFICER :　Are your friends Danish, too?

GIRLS :　　　　　　No, they aren't.

They are Norwegian.

CUSTOMS OFFICER :　Your passports, please.

GIRLS :　　　　　　Here they are.

CUSTOMS OFFICER :　Are these your cases?

GIRLS :　　　　　　No, they aren't.

GIRLS :　　　　　　Our cases are brown.

Here they are.

CUSTOMS OFFICER :　Are you tourists?

GIRLS :　　　　　　Yes, we are.

CUSTOMS OFFICER :　Are your friends tourists too?

GIRLS :　　　　　　Yes, they are.

CUSTOMS OFFICER :　That's fine.

GIRLS :　　　　　　Thank you very much.

New words and expressions 生词和短语

customs /'kʌstəmz/ *n.* 海关
officer /'ɒfɪsə/ *n.* 官员
girl /gɜːl/ *n.* 女孩, 姑娘
Danish /'deɪnɪʃ/ *adj. & n.* 丹麦的；丹麦人
friend /frend/ *n.* 朋友

Norwegian /nɔːˈwiːdʒən/ *adj. & n.* 挪威的；挪威人
passport /'pɑːspɔːt/ *n.* 护照
brown /braʊn/ *adj.* 棕色的
tourist /'tʊərɪst/ *n.* 旅游者

Note on the text 课文注释

可数名词的复数形式一般是在单数名词后面加上-s, 如课文中的 friend — friends /frendz/; tourist — tourists /'tʊərɪsts/; case — cases /'keɪsɪz/。请注意 -s 的不同发音。

参考译文

海关官员：你们是瑞典人吗?
姑 娘 们：不, 我们不是瑞典人。我们是丹麦人。

海关官员：你们的朋友也是丹麦人吗?
姑 娘 们：不, 他们不是丹麦人。他们是挪威人。

海关官员：请出示你们的护照。
姑 娘 们：给您。

海关官员：这些是你们的箱子吗?
姑 娘 们：不, 不是。

姑 娘 们：我们的箱子是棕色的。在这儿呢。

海关官员：你们是来旅游的吗?
姑 娘 们：是的, 我们是来旅游的。

海关官员：你们的朋友也是来旅游的吗?
姑 娘 们：是的, 他们也是。

海关官员：好了。
姑 娘 们：非常感谢。

Lesson 16 Are you . . . ? 你们是……吗？

 Listen to the tape and answer the questions.
听录音并回答问题。

20	30	40	50

Russian?	English?	American?	Dutch?

Are these your . . . ? What colour are your . . . ? 这些是你的……吗？你的……是什么颜色？

60	70	80
red books	white shirts	grey coats

90	100	101
yellow tickets	blue suits	black and grey hats

102	103	104
green passports	black umbrellas	white handbags

105	106	107
orange ties	brown and white dogs	blue pens

108	109	110
red cars	green dresses	yellow blouses

New words and expressions 生词和短语

Russian /'rʌʃən/ *adj. & n.* 俄罗斯的；俄罗斯人　　grey /greɪ/ *adj.* 灰色的

Dutch /dʌtʃ/ *adj. & n.* 荷兰的；荷兰人　　yellow /'yeləʊ/ *adj.* 黄色的

these /ðiːz/ *pron.* 这些（this 的复数）　　black /blæk/ *adj.* 黑色的

red /red/ *adj.* 红色的　　orange /'ɒrɪndʒ/ *adj.* 橘黄色的

Notes on the text 课文注释

1　如果名词是以-s 结尾的，变成复数时要加-es，如 dress — dresses 。

2　表示复数的-s 或-es 一般遵循以下发音规则：

(1)　如果名词词尾的发音是一个清辅音（/s/, /ʃ/, /tʃ/ 除外），-s发/s/的音，如

books /bʊks/,

suits /suːts/;

(2)　如果名词词尾的发音是一个浊辅音（/z/, /ʒ/, /dʒ/ 除外）或元音，-s发/z/的音，如

ties /taɪz/,

dogs /dɒgz/;

(3)　如果名词词尾的发音是/s/, /z/, /ʃ/, /ʒ/, /tʃ/ 或/dʒ/，-s发/ɪz/的音，如

dresses /'dresɪz/,

blouses /'blaʊzɪz/ 。

Written exercises 书面练习

A　Complete these sentences using *a* or *an*.

完成以下句子，用冠词 *a* 或 *an* 填空 。

Examples:

It is _____ Swedish car. *It is a Swedish car.*

She is _____ air hostess. *She is an air hostess.*

1　It is _____ English car.　　3　It is _____ Italian car.　　5　It is _____ American car.

2　It is _____ Japanese car.　　4.　It is _____ French car.　　6　Robert is not _____ teacher.

B　Write questions and answers using *our*.

模仿例句提问并用 *our* 来回答 。

Example:

books/red

What colour are your books? Our books are red.

1　shirts/white　　4　suits/blue　　7　umbrellas/black　　10　dogs/brown and white

2　coats/grey　　5　hats/black and grey　　8　handbags/white　　11　pens/blue

3　tickets/yellow　　6　passports/green　　9　ties/orange　　12　cars/red

Lesson 17　How do you do?　你好!

Listen to the tape then answer this question.
What are Michael Baker and Jeremy Short's jobs?
听录音,然后回答问题。迈克尔·贝克和杰里米·肖特是做什么工作的?

MR. JACKSON : Come and meet our employees,
　　　　　　　Mr. Richards.

MR. RICHARDS : Thank you, Mr. Jackson.

1

MR. JACKSON : This is Nicola Grey,
　　　　　　　and this is Claire Taylor.

MR. RICHARDS : How do you do?

2

MR. RICHARDS : Those women are very hard-working.
　　　　　　　What are their jobs?

MR. JACKSON : They're keyboard operators.

3

MR. JACKSON : This is Michael Baker,
　　　　　　　and this is Jeremy Short.

MR. RICHARDS : How do you do?

4

MR. RICHARDS : They aren't very busy!
　　　　　　　What are their jobs?

MR. JACKSON : They're sales reps.
　　　　　　　They're very lazy.

5

MR. RICHARDS : Who is this young man?

MR. JACKSON : This is Jim.
　　　　　　　He's our office assistant.

6

33

New words and expressions 生词和短语

employee /ˌɪmplɔɪˈiː/ *n.* 雇员

hard-working /ˌhɑːdˈwɜːkɪŋ/ *adj.* 勤奋的

sales rep /ˈseɪlz-ˈrep/ 推销员

man /mæn/ *n.* 男人

office /ˈɒfɪs/ *n.* 办公室

assistant /əˈsɪstənt/ *n.* 助手

Notes on the text 课文注释

1 How do you do? 您好（用于第一次见面时）。一般用同样的话来回答。见第 5 课课文注释 3。

2 sales reps 是 sales representatives 的缩写形式, 常用于口语。

3 office assistant 是指办公室干杂务的工作人员。

参考译文

杰克逊先生： 来见见我们的雇员, 理查兹先生。

理查兹先生： 谢谢, 杰克逊先生。

杰克逊先生： 这位是尼古拉·格雷, 这位是克莱尔·泰勒。

理查兹先生： 你们好!

理查兹先生： 那些姑娘很勤快。她们是做什么工作的?

杰克逊先生： 她们是电脑录入员。

杰克逊先生： 这位是迈克尔·贝克, 这位是杰里米·肖特。

理查兹先生： 你们好!

理查兹先生： 他们不很忙吧! 他们是做什么工作的?

杰克逊先生： 他们是推销员, 他们非常懒。

理查兹先生： 这个年轻人是谁?

杰克逊先生： 他是吉姆, 是我们的办公室助理。

Lesson 18   What are their jobs? 他们是做什么工作的？

 Listen to the tape and answer the questions.
听录音并回答问题 。

100

sales reps

200

keyboard operators

300

mechanics

400

engineers

500

hairdressers

600

teachers

700

Customs officers

800

taxi drivers

900

nurses

1,000

air hostesses

1,001

housewives

1,002

milkmen

1,003

postmen

1,004

policemen

1,005

policewomen

Notes on the text 课文注释

1　如果名词是以 -f 或 -fe 结尾的, 变成复数时, 一般要把 -f 或 -fe 变成 -v, 再加 -es, 如 housewife — housewives 。

2　英语中有一些名词的复数形式是不规则的, 如 man, woman, 以及由这两个词组成的复合名词:

man — men; woman — women;

milkman — milkmen;

policewoman — policewomen.

Written exercises 书面练习

A　Complete these sentences using *He, She, We* or *They.*
　　完成以下句子, 用 *He, She, We* 或 *They* 填空 。

Example:

Those men are lazy. _____ are sales reps.

Those men are lazy. They are sales reps.

1　That man is tall. _____ is a policeman.

2　Those girls are busy. _____ are keyboard operators.

3　Our names are Britt and Inge. _____ are Swedish.

4　Look at our office assistant. _____ is very hard-working.

5　Look at Nicola. _____ is very pretty.

6　Michael Baker and Jeremy Short are employees. _____ are sales reps.

B　Write questions and answers.
　　模仿例句提问并回答 。

Example:

(mechanics)/sales reps

What are their jobs?

Are they mechanics or sales reps?

They aren't mechanics. They're sales reps.

1　(keyboard operators)/air hostesses

2　(postmen)/policemen

3　(policewomen)/nurses

4　(customs officers)/hairdressers

5　(hairdressers)/teachers

6　(engineers)/taxi drivers

7　(policewomen)/keyboard operators

8　(milkmen)/engineers

9　(policemen)/milkmen

10　(nurses)/housewives

Lesson 19　Tired and thirsty　又累又渴

Listen to the tape then answer this question.
Why do the children thank their mother?
听录音,然后回答问题。为什么孩子们向母亲致谢?

MOTHER :	What's the matter, children?	1
GIRL :	We're tired . . .	
BOY :	. . . and thirsty, Mum.	
MOTHER :	Sit down here.	2
MOTHER :	Are you all right now?	3
BOY :	No, we aren't.	
MOTHER :	Look!	4
	There's an ice cream man.	
MOTHER :	Two ice creams please.	5
MOTHER :	Here you are, children.	6
CHILDREN :	Thanks, Mum.	
GIRL :	These ice creams are nice.	7
MOTHER :	Are you all right now?	8
CHILDREN :	Yes, we are, thank you!	

New words and expressions 生词和短语

matter /'mætə/ *n.* 事情
children /'tʃɪldrən/ *n.* 孩子们（child 的复数）
tired /taɪəd/ *adj.* 累, 疲乏
boy /bɔɪ/ *n.* 男孩
thirsty /'θɜːsti/ *adj.* 渴

Mum /mʌm/ *n.* 妈妈（儿语）
sit down /'sɪt-daʊn/ 坐下
right /raɪt/ *adj.* 好, 可以
ice cream /'aɪs-'kriːm/ 冰淇淋

Notes on the text 课文注释

1 What's the matter? = Tell me what's wrong. 怎么啦?
2 There's = There is.

参考译文

母　亲：怎么啦, 孩子们?
女　孩：我们累了……
男　孩：……口也渴, 妈妈 。

母　亲：坐在这儿吧 。

母　亲：你们现在好些了吗?
男　孩：不, 还没有 。

母　亲：瞧! 有个卖冰淇淋的 。

母　亲：请拿两份冰淇淋 。

母　亲：拿着, 孩子们 。
孩子们：谢谢, 妈妈 。

女　孩：这些冰淇淋真好吃 。

母　亲：你们现在好了吗?
孩子们：是的, 现在好了, 谢谢您!

Lesson 20　Look at them!　看看他们／它们！

 Listen to the tape and answer the questions.
听录音并回答问题。

105

They're clean.

106

They're dirty.

217

They're hot.

218

They're cold.

321

They're fat.

322

They're thin.

433

They're big.

434

They're small.

545

They're open.

546

They're shut.

657

They're light.

658

They're heavy.

769

They're old.

770

They're young.

881

They're old.

882

They're new.

998

They're short.

999

They're tall.

1,000

They're short.

1,001

They're long.

New words and expressions 生词和短语

big /bɪg/ *adj.* 大的
small /smɔːl/ *adj.* 小的
open /ˈəʊpən/ *adj.* 开着的
shut /ʃʌt/ *adj.* 关着的
light /laɪt/ *adj.* 轻的

heavy /ˈhevi/ *adj.* 重的
long /lɒŋ/ *adj.* 长的
shoe /ʃuː/ *n.* 鞋子
grandfather /ˈɡrændˌfɑːðə/ *n.* 祖父, 外祖父
grandmother /ˈɡrænˌmʌðə/ *n.* 祖母, 外祖母

Written exercises 书面练习

A Complete these sentences using *am, is* or *are*.
  抄写以下句子, 用 *am, is* 或 *are* 填空 。

Example:

Those children _____ thirsty.
Those children are thirsty.

1 Those children _____ tired.
2 Their mother _____ tired, too.
3 That ice cream man _____ very busy.
4 His ice creams _____ very nice.
5 What's the matter, children? We _____ thirsty.
6 What's the matter, Tim? I _____ tired.

B Write questions and answers.
  模仿例句提问并回答 。

Example:

his shoes/(dirty)/clean
Are his shoes dirty or clean?
They're not dirty. They're clean.

1 the children/(tired)/thirsty
2 the postmen/(cold)/hot
3 the hairdressers/(thin)/fat
4 the shoes/(small)/big
5 the shops/(shut)/open

6 his cases/(heavy)/light
7 grandmother and grandfather/(young)/old
8 their hats/(old)/new
9 the policemen/(short)/tall
10 his trousers/(short)/long

Lesson 21　　Which book?　哪一本书?

 Listen to the tape then answer this question.
Which book does the man want?
听录音, 然后回答问题 。 这位男士要哪本书?

MAN :　　　Give me a book please, Jane.

1

WOMAN : Which book?

2

WOMAN : This one?

3

MAN :　　　No, not that one. The red one.

4

WOMAN : This one?
MAN :　　　Yes, please.

5

WOMAN : Here you are.
MAN :　　　Thank you.

6

New words and expressions 生词和短语

give /gɪv/ v. 给
one /wʌn/ pron. 一个

which /wɪtʃ/ *question word* 哪一个

Notes on the text 课文注释

1　Give me a book, please.
　　这是祈使句, 省略了主语 you 。
2　Which book? 哪一本? 这是一种省略形式 。
3　This one? 句中的 one 是不定代词, 表示 book 。复数形式是 ones 。

参考译文

男人：请拿本书给我, 简 。

女人：哪一本?

女人：是这本吗?

男人：不, 不是那本 。是那本红皮的 。

女人：这本吗?
男人：是的, 请给我 。

女人：给你 。
男人：谢谢 。

Lesson 22   Give me/him/her/us/them a . . .
给我／他／她／我们／他们一……
Which one?
哪一……？

 Listen to the tape and answer the questions.
听录音并回答问题。

1,001 (dirty)

1,002 (clean)

1,003 (empty)

1,004 (full)

1,005 (large)

1,006 (small)

1,007 (big)

1,008 (little)

1,009 (new)

1,010 (old)

1,011 (sharp)

1,012 (blunt)

1,013 (new)

1,014 (old)

1,015 (large)

1,016 (small)

New words and expressions 生词和短语

empty /'empti/ *adj.* 空的

full /ful/ *adj.* 满的

large /lɑːdʒ/ *adj.* 大的

little /'lɪtl/ *adj.* 小的

sharp /ʃɑːp/ *adj.* 尖的, 锋利的

small /smɔːl/ *adj.* 小的

big /bɪg/ *adj.* 大的

blunt /blʌnt/ *adj.* 钝的

box /bɒks/ *n.* 盒子, 箱子

glass /glɑːs/ *n.* 杯子

cup /kʌp/ *n.* 茶杯

bottle /'bɒtl/ *n.* 瓶子

tin /tɪn/ *n.* 罐头

knife /naɪf/ *n.* 刀子

fork /fɔːk/ *n.* 叉子

spoon /spuːn/ *n.* 勺子

Written exercises 书面练习

A Complete these sentences using *His, Her, Our* or *Their*.
   完成以下句子, 用 *His, Her, Our* 或 *Their* 填空。

Example:

Is this Tim's shirt? No, it's not. _____ shirt is white.

Is this Tim's shirt? No, it's not. His shirt is white.

1 Is this Nicola's coat? No, it's not. _____ coat is grey.

2 Are these your pens? No, they're not. _____ pens are blue.

3 Is this Mr. Jackson's hat? No, it's not. _____ hat is black.

4 Are these the children's books? No, they're not. _____ books are red.

5 Is this Helen's dog? No, it's not. _____ dog is brown and white.

6 Is this your father's tie? No, it's not. _____ tie is orange.

B Write questions and answers.
   模仿例句写出相应的对话。

Example:

book/(this blue)/that red

Give me a book please.

Which one? This blue one?

No, not this blue one. That red one.

Here you are.

Thank you.

1 cup/(this dirty)/that clean

2 glass/(this empty)/that full

3 bottle/(this large)/that small

4 box/(this big)/that little

5 tin/(this new)/that old

6 knife/(this sharp)/that blunt

7 spoon/(this new)/that old

8 fork/(this large)/that small

Lesson 23   Which glasses? 哪几只杯子？

Listen to the tape then answer this question.
Which glasses does the man want?
听录音，然后回答问题。这位男士要哪些杯子？

MAN :   Give me some glasses please, Jane.

1

WOMAN : Which glasses?

2

WOMAN : These glasses?

3

MAN :   No, not those.
           The ones on the shelf.

4

WOMAN : These?
MAN :   Yes, please.

5

WOMAN : Here you are.
MAN :   Thanks.

6

New words and expressions 生词和短语

on /ɒn/ *prep.* 在……之上   shelf /ʃelf/ *n.* 架子, 搁板

Notes on the text 课文注释

1   在 Give me some glasses 中, 动词 give 后面有两个宾语, 即直接宾语 some glasses 和间接宾语 me 。
    人称代词作宾语时要用人称代词的宾格, 如 me (I 的宾格), us (we 的宾格), you (you 的宾格), him (he
    的宾格), her (she 的宾格), them (they 的宾格) 和 it (it 的宾格) 。

2   No, not those.
    句中 those 是指 those glasses 。

3   The ones on the shelf.
    本句是省略句 。句中的 ones 代表 glasses 。

参考译文

男人： 请拿给我几只玻璃杯, 简 。

女人： 哪几只?

女人： 是这几只吗?

男人： 不, 不是那几只 。是架子上的那几只 。

女人： 这几只?
男人： 是的, 请拿给我 。

女人： 给你 。
男人： 谢谢 。

Lesson 24   Give me/him/her/us/them some . . .
给我/他/她/我们/他们一些……
Which ones?
哪些?

 Listen to the tape and answer the questions.
听录音并回答问题。

1,117

pens/on the desk

1,218

ties/on the chair

1,319

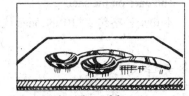

spoons/on the table

1,420

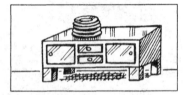

plates on the cupboard

1,521

cigarettes/on the television

1,622

boxes/on the floor

1,723

bottles/on the dressing table

1,824

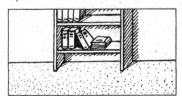

books/on the shelf

1,925

magazines/on the bed

2,000

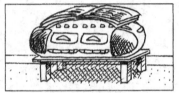

newspapers/on the stereo

New words and expressions 生词和短语

desk /desk/ n. 课桌
table /'teɪbl/ n. 桌子
plate /pleɪt/ n. 盘子
cupboard /'kʌbəd/ n. 食橱
cigarette /ˌsɪgə'ret/ n. 香烟
television /'telɪˌvɪʒən/ n. 电视机

floor /flɔː/ n. 地板
dressing table /'dresɪŋ-'teɪbl/ 梳妆台
magazine /mægə'ziːn/ n. 杂志
bed /bed/ n. 床
newspaper /'njuːspeɪpə/ n. 报纸
stereo /'steriəʊ/ n. 立体声音响

Written exercises 书面练习

A Complete these sentences using *me, him, her, us* or *them*.
　　完成以下句子,用 *me, him, her, us* 或 *them* 填空 。

Example:

Give Tim this shirt. Give _____ this one, too.
Give Tim this shirt. Give him this one, too.

1 Give Jane this watch. Give _____ this one, too.
2 Give the children these ice creams. Give _____ these, too.
3 Give Tom this book. Give _____ this one, too.
4 That is my passport. Give _____ my passport please.
5 That is my coat. Give _____ my coat please.
6 Those are our umbrellas. Give _____ our umbrellas please.

B Write questions and answers.
　　模仿例句写出相应的对话 。

Example:

glasses/on the shelf
Give me some glasses please.
Which ones? These?
No, not those. The ones on the shelf.

1 pens/on the desk
2 ties/on the chair
3 spoons/on the table
4 plates/on the cupboard
5 cigarettes/on the television

6 boxes/on the floor
7 bottles/on the dressing table
8 books/on the shelf
9 magazines/on the bed
10 newspapers/on the stereo

Lesson 25　Mrs. Smith's kitchen 史密斯太太的厨房

 Listen to the tape then answer this question.
What colour is the electric cooker?
听录音，然后回答问题。电灶是什么颜色的?

Mrs. Smith's kitchen is small.

There is a refrigerator in the kitchen.

The refrigerator is white.

It is on the right.

There is an electric cooker in the kitchen.

The cooker is blue.

It is on the left.

There is a table in the middle of the room.

There is a bottle on the table.

The bottle is empty.

There is a cup on the table, too.

The cup is clean.

New words and expressions 生词和短语

Mrs. /ˈmɪsɪz/ 夫人

kitchen /ˈkɪtʃən/ *n.* 厨房

refrigerator /rɪˈfrɪdʒəreɪtə/ *n.* 电冰箱

right /raɪt/ *n.* 右边

electric /ɪˈlektrɪk/ *adj.* 带电的, 可通电的

left /left/ *n.* 左边

cooker /ˈkʊkə/ *n.* 炉子, 炊具

middle /ˈmɪdl/ *n.* 中间

of /əv/ *prep.* （属于）……的

room /ruːm/ *n.* 房间

cup /kʌp/ *n.* 杯子

Notes on the text 课文注释

1 There is 的结构用来说明人或物的存在，在汉语中可以译为"有"。这个结构要跟单数名词，句中往往要有一个介词短语来表示位置或地点。

2 on the right (left), 在右边（左边），是介词短语, 在本句中作表语。

3 注意不要把 cooker 和 cook 混淆，cooker 是炉子、锅等炊具，不是"厨师"。厨师在英语中是 cook。

4 in the middle of, 在……中间。

5 在课文的第 2 行和第 3 行的名词 refrigerator 前面用了两种不同的冠词：a（不定冠词）和 the（定冠词）。在第 2 行，"冰箱"是第一次提到，是指冰箱这类电器中的一个，因此要用不定冠词 a。当第 2 次提到冰箱时，就不是泛指任何一个冰箱，而是特指第 2 行中的那个冰箱了，因此要用定冠词 the。

参考译文

史密斯太太的厨房很小。

厨房里有个电冰箱。

冰箱是白色的。

它位于房间右侧。

厨房里有个电灶。

电灶是蓝色的。

它位于房间左侧。

房间的中央有张桌子。

桌子上有个瓶子。

瓶子是空的。

桌子上还有一只杯子。

杯子很干净。

Lesson 26   Where is it? 它在哪里？

 Listen to the tape and answer the questions.
听录音并回答问题 。

3,000

There is a cup on the table.
The cup is clean.

4,000

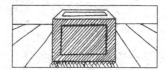

There is a box on the floor.
The box is large.

5,000

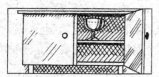

There is a glass in the cupboard.
The glass is empty.

6,000

There is a knife on the plate.
The knife is sharp.

7,000

There is a fork on the tin.
The fork is dirty.

8,000

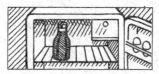

There is a bottle in the refrigerator.
The bottle is full.

9,000

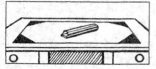

There is a pencil on the desk.
The pencil is blunt.

10,000

There is a spoon in the cup.
The spoon is small.

New words and expressions 生词和短语

where /weə/ *adv.* 在哪里   in /ɪn/ *prep.* 在······里

Written exercises 书面练习

A Complete these sentences using *a* or *the*.
   完成以下句子，用 *a* 或 *the* 填空。

Example:

Give me _____ book. Which book? _____ book on the table.
Give me a book. Which book? The book on the table.

1 Give me _____ glass. Which glass? _____ empty one.
2 Give me some cups. Which cups? _____ cups on the table.
3 Is there _____ book on _____ table? Yes, there is. Is _____ book red?
4 Is there _____ knife in that box? Yes, there is. Is _____ knife sharp?

B Write sentences using these words.
   模仿例句写出相应的句子。

Example:

refrigerator in the kitchen/white
There's a refrigerator in the kitchen.
The refrigerator is white.

1 cup on the table/clean   5 fork on the tin/dirty
2 box on the floor/large   6 bottle in the refrigerator/full
3 glass in the cupboard/empty   7 pencil on the desk/blunt
4 knife on the plate/sharp

Lesson 27 Mrs. Smith's living room 史密斯太太的客厅

 Listen to the tape then answer this question. Where are the books?
听录音, 然后回答问题 。书在哪里?

Mrs. Smith's living room is large.

There is a television in the room.

The television is near the window.

There are some magazines on the television.

There is a table in the room.

There are some newspapers on the table.

There are some armchairs in the room.

The armchairs are near the table.

There is a stereo in the room.

The stereo is near the door.

There are some books on the stereo.

There are some pictures in the room.

The pictures are on the wall.

New words and expressions 生词和短语

living room /'lɪvɪŋ-rʊm/ 客厅
near /nɪə/ prep. 靠近
window /'wɪndəʊ/ n. 窗户
armchair /'ɑːmtʃeə/ n. 扶手椅

door /dɔː/ n. 门
picture /'pɪktʃə/ n. 图画
wall /wɔːl/ n. 墙

Notes on the text 课文注释

1   There are 的结构中要用复数名词。
2   near the window (door), 靠近窗（门），为介词短语。在本句中作表语。
3   on the wall, 在墙上。介词短语作表语。

参考译文

史密斯太太的客厅很大。
客厅里有台电视机。
电视机靠近窗子。
电视机上放着几本杂志。
客厅里有张桌子。
桌上放着几份报纸。
客厅里有几把扶手椅。
这些扶手椅靠近桌子。
客厅里有台立体声音响。
音响靠近门。
音响上面有几本书。
客厅里有几幅画。
画挂在墙上。

Lesson 28　Where are they?　它们在哪里？

 Listen to the tape and answer the questions.
听录音并回答问题 。

1,120

There are some cigarettes
on the dressing table.
They are near that box.

2,230

There are some plates on the cooker.
They are clean.

3,340

There are some trousers on the bed.
They are near that shirt.

4,450

There are some bottles in the refrigerator.
They are empty.

5,560

There are some shoes on the floor.
They're near the bed.

6,670

There are some knives on the table.
They're in that box.

7,780

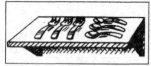

There are some forks on the shelf.
They're near those spoons.

8,890

There are some bottles on the cupboard.
They're near those tins.

9,999

There are some tickets on the shelf.
They're in that handbag.

10,001

There are some glasses on the television.
They're near those bottles.

55

New words and expressions 生词和短语

trousers /ˈtraʊzəz/ n. 〔复数〕长裤

Written exercises 书面练习

A Look at these words.
注意单数名词和复数名词的区别。

Examples:

a book — some books; a man — some men; a housewife — some housewives

Rewrite these sentences using *There are*.
模仿例句改用*There are*的结构。

Example:

There *is a book* on the desk.
There are some books on the desk.

1 There *is a pencil* on the desk.
2 There *is a knife* near that tin.
3 There *is a policeman* in the kitchen.
4 There *is a newspaper* in the living room.
5 There *is a keyboard operator* in the office.

B Write sentences using these words.
模仿例句写出相应的对话。

Example:

(books)/on the dressing table/cigarettes/near that box
Are there any books on the dressing table?
No, there aren't any books on the dressing table.
There are some cigarettes.
Where are they?
They're near that box.

1 (books)/in the room/magazines/on the television
2 (ties)/on the floor/shoes/near the bed
3 (glasses)/on the cupboard/bottles/near those tins
4 (newspapers)/on the shelf/tickets/in that handbag
5 (forks)/on the table/knives/in that box
6 (cups)/on the stereo/glasses/near those bottles
7 (cups)/in the kitchen/plates/on the cooker
8 (glasses)/in the kitchen/bottles/in the refrigerator
9 (books)/in the room/pictures/on the wall
10 (chairs)/in the room/armchairs/near the table

Lesson 29   Come in, Amy. 进来，艾米。

Listen to the tape then answer this question. How must Amy clean the floor?
听录音，然后回答问题。艾米需要如何来清扫地面？

MRS. JONES :   Come in, Amy.

1

MRS. JONES :   Shut the door, please.

2

MRS. JONES :   This bedroom's very untidy.

AMY :   What must I do, Mrs. Jones?

3

MRS. JONES :   Open the window and air the room.

4

MRS. JONES :   Then put these clothes in the wardrobe.

5

MRS. JONES :   Then make the bed.

6

MRS. JONES :   Dust the dressing table.

7

MRS. JONES :   Then sweep the floor.

8

New words and expressions 生词和短语

shut /ʃʌt/ v. 关门
bedroom /'bedrʊm/ n. 卧室
untidy /ʌn'taɪdi/ adj. 乱, 不整齐
must /mʌst/ modal verb 必须, 应该
open /'əʊpən/ v. 打开
air /eə/ v. 使……通风, 换换空气

put /pʊt/ v. 放置
clothes /kləʊðz/ n. 衣服
wardrobe /'wɔːdrəʊb/ n. 衣柜
dust /dʌst/ v. 掸掉灰尘
sweep /swiːp/ v. 扫

Notes on the text 课文注释

1 英文中需用祈使语气来表示直接的命令、建议、告诫、邀请等多种意图。祈使句一般省略主语you, 动词采用动词的原形。如本课对话中的 Come in, shut the door, open the window ... 等均为祈使句。

2 What must I do? 我应该做些什么呢? 其中的 must 是情态动词, 表示不可逃避的义务或不可推卸的责任。

3 make the bed, 铺床。

参考译文

琼斯夫人: 进来, 艾米。

琼斯夫人: 请把门关上。

琼斯夫人: 这卧室太不整洁了。

艾   米: 我应该做些什么呢, 琼斯夫人?

琼斯夫人: 打开窗子, 给房间通通风。

琼斯夫人: 然后把这些衣服放进衣橱里去。

琼斯夫人: 再把床整理一下。

琼斯夫人: 掸掉梳妆台上的灰尘。

琼斯夫人: 然后扫扫地。

Lesson 30　What must I do?　我应该做什么？

Listen to the tape and answer the questions.
听录音并回答问题。

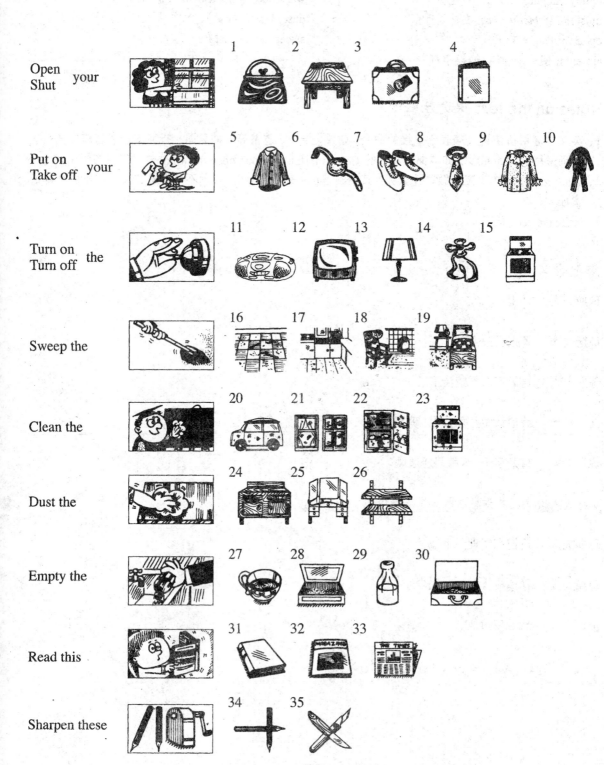

Open
Shut　your

Put on
Take off　your

Turn on
Turn off　the

Sweep the

Clean the

Dust the

Empty the

Read this

Sharpen these

New words and expressions 生词和短语

empty /'empti/ v. 倒空, 使……变空

read /ri:d/ v. 读

sharpen /'ʃɑːpən/ v. 削尖, 使锋利

put on /'pʊt-ɒn/ 穿上

take off /'teɪk-ɒf/ 脱掉

turn on /'tɜːn-ɒn/ 开（电灯）

turn off /'tɜːn-ɒf/ 关（电灯）

Written exercises 书面练习

A Rewrite these sentences.
   模仿例句写出相应的祈使句。

Example:

The cup isn't empty. *Empty it!*

1   The window isn't clean.
2   The door isn't shut.
3   The wardrobe isn't open.

B Look at this table:
   注意下表：

Shut the	stereo
Open the	tap
Put on your	blackboard
Take off your	cup
Turn on the	window
Turn off the	cupboard
Sweep the	magazine
Clean the	knives
Dust the	shirt
Empty the	door
Read this	floor
Sharpen these	shoes

Now write eleven sentences.
模仿下面的例句写出 11 句表示命令的句子。

Example:

Shut the door!

Lesson 31　Where's Sally?　萨莉在哪里?

Listen to the tape then answer this question. Is the cat climbing the tree?
听录音, 然后回答问题。猫正在爬树吗?

JEAN : Where's Sally, Jack?

JACK : She's in the garden, Jean.

JEAN : What's she doing?

JACK : She's sitting under the tree.

JEAN : Is Tim in the garden, too?

JACK : Yes, he is.

He's climbing the tree.

JEAN : I beg your pardon?

Who's climbing the tree?

JACK : Tim is.

JEAN : What about the dog?

JACK : The dog's in the garden, too.

It's running across the grass.

It's running after a cat.

New words and expressions 生词和短语

garden /'gɑːdn/ *n.* 花园

under /'ʌndə/ *prep.* 在……之下

tree /triː/ *n.* 树

climb /klaɪm/ *v.* 爬, 攀登

who /huː/ *pron.* 谁

run /rʌn/ *v.* 跑

grass /grɑːs/ *n.* 草, 草地

after /'ɑːftə/ *prep.* 在……之后

across /ə'krɒs/ *prep.* 横过, 穿过

cat /kæt/ *n.* 猫

Notes on the text 课文注释

1 在英文中表示说话时正在进行的动作或事件, 要用动词的现在进行时。现在进行时由 be 的现在时加上现在分词组成, 如课文中的 "She's sitting under the tree." 和 "He's climbing the tree." 等句子均为现在进行时。对大多数动词来说, 在动词后面直接加 -ing 即可组成现在分词, 如 doing, climbing。对以 -e 结尾的动词, 要去掉 -e, 再加 -ing, 如 making。如果动词只有一个元音字母, 而其后跟了一个辅音字母时, 则需将辅音字母双写, 再加 -ing, 如 running, sitting。

2 What about the dog? 那么狗呢? 这句话的意思是 What is the dog doing in the garden? 为了避免重复原句中的主语和谓语动词, 可以用 What about 这个结构, 用来询问情况。

3 run after, 追逐。

例: Look, Sally is running after her Mum. 瞧, 萨莉正在追赶她的母亲。

参考译文

琼　：杰克, 萨莉在哪儿?

杰克：她在花园, 琼。

琼　：她在干什么?

杰克：她正在树下坐着。

琼　：蒂姆也在花园里吗?

杰克：是的, 他也在花园里。他正在爬树。

琼　：你说什么? 谁在爬树?

杰克：蒂姆在爬树。

琼　：那么狗呢?

杰克：狗也在花园里。它正在草地上跑, 在追一只猫。

Lesson 32　What's he/she/it doing? 他／她／它正在做什么？

 Listen to the tape and answer the questions.
听录音并回答问题。

20,000

Nicola is typing
a letter.

30,000

She is emptying
a basket.

40,000

Mr. Richards is opening
the window.

50,000

My mother is making
the bed.

60,000

Sally is shutting
the door.

70,000

It is eating
a bone.

80,000

My sister is looking
at a picture.

90,000

Jack is reading
a magazine.

100,000

He is cleaning
his teeth.

200,000

She is dusting
the dressing table.

300,000

Emma is cooking
a meal.

400,000

The cat is drinking
its milk.

500,000

Amy is sweeping the floor.

600,000

Tim is sharpening a pencil.

700,000

He is turning on the light.

800,000

The girl is turning
off the tap.

900,000

The boy is putting
on his shirt.

1,000,000

Mrs. Jones is taking
off her coat.

New words and expressions 生词和短语

type /taɪp/ v. 打字
letter /'letə/ n. 信
basket /'bɑːskɪt/ n. 篮子
eat /iːt/ v. 吃
bone /bəʊn/ n. 骨头
clean /kliːn/ v. 清洗

tooth /tuːθ/ （复数teeth /tiːθ/） n. 牙齿
cook /kʊk/ v. 做（饭菜）
milk /mɪlk/ n. 牛奶
meal /miːl/ n. 饭，一顿饭
drink /drɪŋk/ v. 喝
tap /tæp/ n. （水）龙头

Written exercises 书面练习

A Complete these sentences.
   模仿例句把祈使句改写成现在进行时。

Example:

Sweep the floor! She *is sweeping it.*

1 Open the window! He _____ .
2 Sharpen this pencil! She _____ .
3 Dust the cupboard! She _____ .
4 Empty the basket! She _____ .
5 Look at the picture! He _____ .

B Write questions and answers.
   模仿例句提问并回答。

Example:

Nicola/emptying the basket/typing a letter
What is Nicola doing?
Is she emptying the basket?
No, she isn't emptying the basket.
She's typing a letter.

1 Mr. Richards/cleaning his teeth/opening the window
2 My mother/shutting the door/making the bed
3 The dog/drinking its milk/eating a bone
4 My sister/reading a magazine/looking at a picture
5 Emma/dusting the dressing table/cooking a meal
6 Amy/making the bed/sweeping the floor
7 Tim/reading a magazine/sharpening a pencil
8 The girl/turning on the light/turning off the tap
9 The boy/cleaning his teeth/putting on his shirt
10 Miss Jones/putting on her coat/taking off her coat

Lesson 33   A fine day 晴天

Listen to the tape then answer this question. Where is the Jones family?
听录音, 然后回答问题。琼斯一家人在哪里?

It is a fine day today.

There are some clouds in the sky,

but the sun is shining.

Mr. Jones is with his family.

They are walking over the bridge.

There are some boats on the river.

Mr. Jones and his wife are looking at them.

Sally is looking at a big ship.

The ship is going under the bridge.

Tim is looking at an aeroplane.

The aeroplane is flying over the river.

New words and expressions 生词和短语

day /deɪ/ *n.* 日子
cloud /klaʊd/ *n.* 云
sky /skaɪ/ *n.* 天空
sun /sʌn/ *n.* 太阳
shine /ʃaɪn/ *v.* 照耀
with /wɪð/ *prep.* 和……在一起
family /'fæmɪli/ *n.* 家庭（成员）
walk /wɔːk/ *v.* 走路, 步行

over /'əʊvə/ *prep.* 跨越, 在……之上
bridge /brɪdʒ/ *n.* 桥
boat /bəʊt/ *n.* 船
river /'rɪvə/ *n.* 河
ship /ʃɪp/ *n.* 轮船
aeroplane /'eərəpleɪn/ *n.* 飞机
fly /flaɪ/ *v.* 飞

Notes on the text 课文注释

1 It is a fine day today.
   句中的 it 是指天气。
2 some clouds, 几朵云。
   some 可以修饰可数名词, 也能修饰不可数名词。

参考译文

今天天气好。
天空中飘着几朵云, 但阳光灿烂。
琼斯先生同他的家人在一起。
他们正在过桥。
河上有几艘船。
琼斯先生和他的妻子正在看这些船。
莎莉正在看一艘大船。
那船正从桥下驶过。
蒂姆正望着一架飞机。
飞机正从河上飞过。

Lesson 34　What are they doing?　他们在做什么？

Listen to the tape and answer the questions.
听录音并回答问题。

220,231

cooking

331,342

sleeping

442,453

shaving

553,564

crying

664,675

eating

775,786

typing

886,897

doing

997,998

washing

1,000,001

flying

1,100,000

walking

1,500,000

waiting

2,000,000

jumping

New words and expressions 生词和短语

sleep /sliːp/ v. 睡觉
shave /ʃeɪv/ v. 刮脸
cry /kraɪ/ v. 哭, 喊

wash /wɒʃ/ v. 洗
wait /weɪt/ v. 等
jump /dʒʌmp/ v. 跳

Written exercises 书面练习

A Complete these sentences.
模仿例句用现在进行时完成以下句子。

Example:

take — taking
Take . . . He is *taking* his book.

注意以下例句:
如果动词是以 -e 结尾, 变成现在分词时要去掉-e, 然后再加-ing 。

1 Type . . .   She is _____ a letter.
2 Make . . .   She is _____ the bed.
3 Come . . .   He is _____ .
4 Shine . . .   The sun is _____ .
5 Give . . .   He is _____ me some magazines.

B Write questions and answers.
模仿例句提问并回答。

Example:

the children/looking at the boats on the river
What are the children doing?
They're looking at the boats on the river.

1 the men/cooking a meal
2 they/sleeping
3 the men/shaving
4 the children/crying
5 the dogs/eating bones
6 the women/typing letters

7 the children/doing their homework
8 the women/washing dishes
9 the birds/flying over the river
10 they/walking over the bridge
11 the man and the woman/waiting for a bus
12 the children/jumping off the wall

Lesson 35   Our village 我们的村庄

 Listen to the tape then answer this question.
Are the children coming out of the park or going into it?
听录音,然后回答问题。孩子们是正从公园里出来还是正在往里走?

This is a photograph of our village.

Our village is in a valley.

It is between two hills.

The village is on a river.

1

Here is another photograph of the village.

My wife and I are walking

along the banks of the river.

We are on the left.

There is a boy in the water.

He is swimming across the river.

2

Here is another photograph.

This is the school building.

It is beside a park.

The park is on the right.

Some children are coming out of the building.

Some of them are going into the park.

3

New words and expressions 生词和短语

photograph /ˈfəʊtəɡrɑːf/ n. 照片
village /ˈvɪlɪdʒ/ n. 村庄
valley /ˈvæli/ n. 山谷
between /bɪˈtwiːn/ prep. 在……之间
hill /hɪl/ n. 小山
another /əˈnʌðə/ det. 另一个
wife /waɪf/ n. 妻子
along /əˈlɒŋ/ prep. 沿

bank /bæŋk/ n. 河岸
water /ˈwɔːtə/ n. 水
swim /swɪm/ v. 游泳
building /ˈbɪldɪŋ/ n. 大楼, 建筑物
park /pɑːk/ n. 公园
into /ˈɪntə/ prep. 进入

Notes on the text 课文注释

1　The village is on a river.
　　这句话中的介词 on 不表示"在……上", 而是"邻近", "靠近"的意思。
2　My wife and I . . .
　　我和妻子……在英语中表达"我和……"时, 要把 I 放在别人的后面。
3　Some children are coming out of the building.
　　out of 表示"从里向外"的动作。

参考译文

这是我们村庄的一张照片。
我们的村庄坐落在一个山谷之中。
它位于两座小山之间。
它靠近一条小河。

这是我们村庄的另一张照片。
我和妻子正沿河岸走着。
我们在河的左侧。
河里面有个男孩。
他正横渡小河。

这是另一张照片。
这是学校大楼。
它位于公园的旁边。
公园在右面。
一些孩子正从楼里出来。
他们中有几个正走进公园。

Lesson 36 Where...? ……在哪里?

Listen to the tape and answer the questions.
听录音并回答问题。

1   one

going into

2   two

going out of

3   three

sitting beside

4   four

walking across

5   five

running along

6   six

jumping off

7   seven

walking between

8   eight

sitting near

9   nine

flying under

10   ten

flying over

11   eleven

sitting on

12   twelve

reading in

New words and expressions 生词和短语

beside /bɪˈsaɪd/ *prep.* 在……旁   off /ɒf/ *prep.* 离开

Written exercises 书面练习

A Complete these sentences.
  模仿例句用现在进行时完成以下句子。

注意：如果单音节动词仅有一个元音字母而其后跟一个辅音字母时，变成现在分词时要将此辅音字母双写。

Example:

put — putting

put . . . He is *putting* on his coat.

1 swim . . . He is _____ across the river.
2 sit . . . She is _____ on the grass.
3 run . . . The cat is _____ along the wall.

B Write sentences using these words.
  模仿例句提问并回答。

Examples:

boy swimming/across the river
Where is the boy swimming? He's swimming across the river.
children going/into the park
Where are the children going? They're going into the park.

1 man going/into the shop
2 woman going/out of the shop
3 he sitting/beside his mother
4 they walking/across the street
5 the cats running/along the wall
6 the children jumping/off the branch

7 man standing/between two policemen
8 she sitting/near the tree
9 it flying/under the bridge
10 the aeroplane flying/over the bridge
11 they sitting/on the grass
12 the man and the woman reading/in the living room

Lesson 37 Making a bookcase 做书架

Listen to the tape then answer this question. What is Susan's favourite colour?
听录音，然后回答问题 。苏珊最喜欢哪种颜色?

DAN :   You're working hard, George.

           What are you doing?

GEORGE : I'm making a bookcase.

GEORGE : Give me that hammer please, Dan.

DAN :   Which hammer?

           This one?

GEORGE : No, not that one.

           The big one.

DAN :   Here you are.

GEORGE : Thanks, Dan.

DAN :   What are you going to do now, George?

GEORGE : I'm going to paint it.

DAN :   What colour are you going to paint it?

GEORGE : I'm going to paint it pink.

DAN :   Pink!

GEORGE : This bookcase isn't for me.

           It's for my daughter, Susan.

           Pink's her favourite colour.

New words and expressions 生词和短语

work /wɜːk/ v. 工作
hard /hɑːd/ adv. 努力地
make /meɪk/ v. 做
bookcase /'bʊk-keɪs/ n. 书橱, 书架

hammer /'hæmə/ n. 锤子
paint /peɪnt/ v. 上漆, 涂
pink /pɪŋk/ n. & adj. 粉红色; 粉红色的
favourite /'feɪvərɪt/ adj. 最喜欢的

Notes on the text 课文注释

1 You're working hard, George. 在这句话中 hard 是一个副词, 修饰动词 work, 有"努力地"、"费劲地"的意思。hard 还常常与表示动作、举止的动词连用, 如 work, listen, play, try 等, 用来加强动作的强度, 常译成"拼命地"。

2 What are you going to do now, George?
你现在准备做什么, 乔治?
be going to, 是"打算"、"准备"、"按计划"在最近做某事, 表示将来。

3 paint it pink,
it 指 bookcase, 是宾语, pink是宾语补足语。

参考译文

丹　　：你干得真辛苦, 乔治。你在干什么呢?
乔治　：我正在做书架。

乔治　：请把那把锤子拿给我, 丹。
丹　　：哪一把? 是这把吗?

乔治　：不, 不是那把。是那把大的。

丹　　：给你。
乔治　：谢谢, 丹。

丹　　：你现在打算干什么, 乔治?
乔治　：我打算把它漆一下。

丹　　：你打算把它漆成什么颜色?
乔治　：我想漆成粉红色。
丹　　：粉红色!

乔治　：这个书架不是为我做的, 是为我的女儿苏珊做的。粉红色是她最喜欢的颜色。

Lesson 38   What are you going to do? 你准备做什么?
What are you doing now? 你现在正在做什么?

 Listen to the tape and answer the questions.
听录音并回答问题。

one

I am going to shave.

two

Now I am shaving.

three

I'm going to wait for a bus.

four

Now I'm waiting for a bus.

five

We're going to do our homework.

six

Now we're doing our homework.

seven

I'm going to paint this bookcase.

eight

Now I'm painting this bookcase.

nine

We're going to listen to the stereo.

ten

Now we're listening to the stereo.

eleven

I'm going to wash the dishes.

twelve

Now I'm washing the dishes.

New words and expressions 生词和短语

homework /'həʊmwɜːk/ n. 作业   dish /dɪʃ/ n. 盘子, 碟子
listen /'lɪsən/ v. 听

Written exercises 书面练习

A Complete these sentences using *am, is* or *are*.
   完成以下句子, 用 *am, is* 或 *are* 填空 。

Examples:

What _____ you doing?
What are you doing?
We _____ reading.
We are reading.

1 What _____ you doing? We _____ reading.
2 What _____ they doing? They _____ doing their homework.
3 What _____ he doing? He _____ working hard.
4 What _____ you doing? I _____ washing the dishes.

B Write questions and answers.
   模仿例句写出相应的对话 。

Example:

paint this bookcase
What are you going to do?
I'm going to paint this bookcase.
What are you doing now?
I'm painting this bookcase.

1 shave
2 wait for a bus
3 do my homework
4 listen to the stereo
5 wash the dishes

Lesson 39 Don't drop it! 别摔了!

 Listen to the tape then answer this question.
Where does Sam put the vase in the end?
听录音,然后回答问题。萨姆把花瓶放在什么地方?

SAM :   What are you going to do
         with that vase, Penny?

PENNY : I'm going to put it
         on this table, Sam.

SAM :   Don't do that.
         Give it to me.

PENNY : What are you going to do with it?
SAM :   I'm going to put it here,
         in front of the window.

PENNY : Be careful!
         Don't drop it!

PENNY : Don't put it there, Sam.
         Put it here,
         on this shelf.

SAM :   There we are!
         It's a lovely vase.
PENNY : Those flowers are lovely, too.

New words and expressions 生词和短语

front /frʌnt/ *n.* 前面

in front of 在……之前

careful /'keəfəl/ *adj.* 小心的, 仔细的

vase /vɑːz/ *n.* 花瓶

drop /drɒp/ *v.* 掉下

flower /'flaʊə/ *n.* 花

Notes on the text 课文注释

1 do with 指对某件事物或人的处理 。

2 在第 29 课中, 我们讲到在英文中需用祈使语气来表示直接的命令、建议等多种意图 。而祈使句的否定形式则由 don't 加上动词原形组成, 如课文中的 "Don't do that"; "Don't drop it" 等句子 。

3 在第 21 课有这样的句型 "give me a book", 在本课文中又出现了 "give it to me" 的句型 。在动词 give 后面可以有两个宾语: 直接宾语 (指物, 如 a book, it) 和间接宾语 (指人, 如 me) 。如果直接宾语置于动词 give 之后, 间接宾语则变成有 to 的介词短语 。

4 Be careful! 小心点! 这个固定结构常用来提醒他人可能发生的事故或困难 。

5 There we are! 放好了! 参见第 11 课课文注释 3 。

参考译文

萨姆: 你打算如何处理那花瓶?

彭妮: 我打算把它放在这张桌子上, 萨姆 。

萨姆: 不要放在那儿, 把它给我 。

彭妮: 你打算怎么办?

萨姆: 我准备把它放在这儿, 放在窗前 。

彭妮: 小心点! 别摔了!

彭妮: 别放在那儿, 萨姆 。放在这儿, 这个架子上 。

萨姆: 放好了! 这是只漂亮的花瓶 。

彭妮: 那些花也很漂亮啊 。

Lesson 40   What are you going to do? 你准备做什么？
I'm going to . . .   我准备……

Listen to the tape and answer the questions.
听录音并回答问题 。

| 13 thirteen | 14 fourteen | 15 fifteen | 16 sixteen |

put it . . . !   take it . . . !   turn it . . . !   turn it . . . !

What are you going to do with that/those . . .? 你准备把那个／
那些……？
I'm going to give/show/send/take . . . 我准备给／展示／送／拿……

| 17 seventeen | 18 eighteen | 19 nineteen | 20 twenty |

to my daughter   to my grandmother   to my father   to my mother

| 30 thirty | 40 forty | 50 fifty | 60 sixty |

to the children   to my wife   to my grandfather   to my sister

79

New words and expressions 生词和短语

show /ʃəʊ/ *v.* 给……看   take /teɪk/ *v.* 带给
send /send/ *v.* 送给

Written exercises 书面练习

A Rewrite these sentences.
   模仿例句改写以下句子。

Example:

Give me that vase.
Give that vase to me.

1 Send George that letter.
2 Take her those flowers.
3 Show me that picture.
4 Give Mrs. Jones these books.
5 Give the children these ice creams.

B Rewrite these sentences.
   模仿例句改写以下句子。

Examples:

Put on your coat!
I'm going to put it on.
Put on your shoes!
I'm going to put them on.

1 Put on your hat!   6 Take off your hat!
2 Take off your shoes!   7 Turn on the lights!
3 Turn on the taps!   8 Turn off the television!
4 Turn off the light!   9 Turn off the lights!
5 Put on your suit!   10 Turn on the stereo!

Lesson 41　Penny's bag　彭妮的提包

Listen to the tape then answer this question. Who is the tin of tobacco for?
听录音，然后回答问题。那盒烟丝是给谁买的？

SAM :　　Is that bag heavy, Penny?　　　　　　　　　1

PENNY :　Not very.

SAM :　　Here!

Put it on this chair.

What's in it?

PENNY :　A piece of cheese.　　　　　　　　　　　　2

A loaf of bread.　　　　　　　　　　　　3

A bar of soap.　　　　　　　　　　　　4

A bar of chocolate.　　　　　　　　　　5

A bottle of milk.　　　　　　　　　　　6

A pound of sugar.　　　　　　　　　　　7

Half a pound of coffee.　　　　　　　　8

A quarter of a pound of tea.　　　　　　9

And a tin of tobacco.　　　　　　　　　10

SAM :　　Is that tin of tobacco for me?

PENNY :　Well, it's certainly not for me!

81

New words and expressions 生词和短语

cheese /tʃiːz/ *n.* 乳酪, 干酪

bread /bred/ *n.* 面包

soap /səʊp/ *n.* 肥皂

chocolate /'tʃɒklɪt/ *n.* 巧克力

sugar /'ʃʊgə/ *n.* 糖

coffee /'kɒfɪ/ *n.* 咖啡

tea /tiː/ *n.* 茶

tobacco /tə'bækəʊ/ *n.* 烟草, 烟丝

Notes on the text 课文注释

1 Not very. 是 "It is not very heavy." 的省略形式, 常用于口语中。

2 a piece of, 一块, 一张, 一片, 用在不可数名词前, 表示数量, 又如: a piece of bread, 一片面包。

本课表示数量的短语还有:

a loaf of, 一条;

a bar of, 一块;

a bottle of, 一瓶;

a pound of, 一磅;

half a pound of, 半磅;

a quarter of, 四分之一 (1/4);

a tin of, 一罐, 一盒。

参考译文

萨姆: 那个提包重吗? 彭妮?

彭妮: 不太重。

萨姆: 放这儿。把它放在这把椅子上。里面是什么东西?

彭妮: 一块乳酪、一条面包、一块肥皂、一块巧克力、一瓶牛奶、一磅糖、半磅咖啡、1/4磅茶叶和一盒烟丝。

萨姆: 那盒烟丝是给我的吗?

彭妮: 噢, 当然不会是给我的!

Lesson 42   Is there a . . . in/on that . . . ?
在那个……中/上有一个……吗？
Is there any . . . in/on that . . . ?
在那个……中/上有……吗？

 Listen to the tape and answer the questions.
听录音并回答问题。

thirteen	fourteen	fifteen	sixteen
passport	milk	spoon	tie

seventeen	eighteen	nineteen	twenty
bread	hammer	tea	vase

thirty	forty	fifty	sixty
suit	tobacco	chocolate	cheese

70 seventy	80 eighty	90 ninety	100 a hundred
newspaper	car	soap	bird

New words and expressions 生词和短语

bird /bɜːd/ *n.* 鸟

any /'eni/ *det.* 一些

some /sʌm/ *det.* 一些

Note on the text 课文注释

some 和 any 是英文中表示数量的限定词, 它们一般不能精确地说明数量究竟有多大, 在汉语中往往译为 "一些"。some 一般用于肯定句中, any 一般用于不能确定答案是肯定还是否定的疑问句和含有 not 或 -n't 的否定句中。

Written exercises 书面练习

A Complete these sentences using *a, any* or *some*.
　完成以下句子, 用 *a, any* 或 *some* 填空。

Examples:

There's *a* photograph on the desk.

Is there *any* milk in the bottle?

There isn't *any* milk in the bottle.

There's *some* milk in that cup.

1 Is there _____ bread in the kitchen?

2 There's _____ loaf on the table.

3 There's _____ coffee on the table, too.

4 There isn't _____ chocolate on the table.

5 There's _____ spoon on that dish.

6 Is there _____ soap on the dressing table?

B Write questions and answers using these words.
　模仿例句提问并回答。

Examples:

passport/on the table

Is there a passport here?

Yes, there is. There's one on the table.

bread/on the table

Is there any bread here?

Yes, there is. There's some on the table.

1 spoon/on the plate

2 tie/on the chair

3 milk/on the table

4 hammer/on the bookcase

5 tea/on the table

6 vase/on the radio

7 suit/in the wardrobe

8 tobacco/in the tin

9 chocolate/on the desk

10 cheese/on the plate

Lesson 43   Hurry up! 快点!

Listen to the tape then answer this question.
How do you know Sam doesn't make the tea very often?
听录音, 然后回答问题 。你怎么知道萨姆不常沏茶?

PENNY : Can you make the tea, Sam?
SAM :   Yes, of course I can, Penny.

1

SAM :   Is there any water in this kettle?
PENNY : Yes, there is.

2

SAM :   Where's the tea?
PENNY : It's over there,
           behind the teapot.

3

PENNY : Can you see it?
SAM :   I can see the teapot,
           but I can't see the tea.

4

PENNY : There it is!
           It's in front of you!
SAM :   Ah yes, I can see it now.

5

SAM :   Where are the cups?
PENNY : There are some in the cupboard.

6

PENNY : Can you find them?
SAM :   Yes. Here they are.

7

PENNY : Hurry up, Sam!
           The kettle's boiling!

8

85

New words and expressions 生词和短语

of course /əv-'kɔːs/ 当然

kettle /'ketl/ *n.* 水壶

behind /bɪ'haɪnd/ *prep.* 在……后面

teapot /'tiːpɒt/ *n.* 茶壶

now /naʊ/ *adv.* 现在, 此刻

find /faɪnd/ *v.* 找到

boil /'bɔɪl/ *v.* 沸腾, 开

Notes on the text 课文注释

1   make the tea, 沏茶 。

2   over there 是指 "在那边", 指比较远的地方 。

3   在 There are some in the cupboard 中, some 是代词, 指 some cups 。

4   hurry up, 赶快, 在祈使语气中用来催促他人 。

参考译文

彭妮： 你会沏茶吗, 萨姆?
萨姆： 会的, 我当然会, 彭妮 。

萨姆： 这水壶里有水吗?
彭妮： 有水 。

萨姆： 茶叶在哪儿?
彭妮： 就在那儿, 茶壶后面 。

彭妮： 你看见了吗?
萨姆： 茶壶我看见了, 但茶叶没看到 。

彭妮： 那不是吗! 就在你眼前 。
萨姆： 噢, 是啊, 我现在看到了 。

萨姆： 茶杯在哪儿呢?
彭妮： 碗橱里有几只 。

彭妮： 你找得到吗?
萨姆： 找得到 。就在这儿呢 。

彭妮： 快, 萨姆! 水开了!

Lesson 44 Are there any . . . ? 有……吗?
Is there any . . . ? 有……吗?

 Listen to the tape and answer the questions.
听录音并回答问题。

seventy

bread on the table

eighty

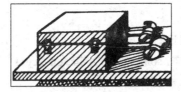

hammers behind that box

ninety

milk in front of the door

a hundred

soap on the cupboard

two hundred

newspapers behind that vase

three hundred

water in those glasses

four hundred

tea in those cups

five hundred

cups in front of that kettle

six hundred

chocolate behind that book

seven hundred

teapots in the cupboard

eight hundred

cars in front of that building

nine hundred

coffee on the table

Written exercises 书面练习

A Look at these:

注意名词的单数和复数形式：

glass — glasses; book — books; housewife — housewives.

Rewrite these sentences.

改写以下句子,用名词的复数形式填空 。

Example:

I can see some cups. But I can't see any _____ (glass).

I can see some cups, but I can't see any glasses.

1 I can see some spoons, but I can't see any _____ (knife).
2 I can see some hammers, but I can't see any _____ (box).
3 I can see some coffee, but I can't see any _____ (loaf) of bread.
4 I can see some cupboards, but I can't see any _____ (shelf).
5 I can see Mr. Jones and Mr. Brown, but I can't see their _____ (wife).
6 I can see some cups, but I can't see any _____ (dish).
7 I can see some cars, but I can't see any _____ (bus).

B Write questions and answers using these words.

模仿例句提问并回答 。

Examples:

bread/on the table
Is there any bread here?
Yes, there is. There's some on the table.

hammers/behind that box
Are there any hammers here?
Yes, there are. There are some on the table.

1 milk/in front of the door
2 soap/on the cupboard
3 newspapers/behind that vase
4 water/in those glasses
5 tea/in those cups

6 cups/in front of that kettle
7 chocolate/behind that book
8 teapots/in that cupboard
9 cars/in front of that building
10 coffee/on the table

Lesson 45　The boss's letter　老板的信

Listen to the tape then answer this question.
Why can't Pamela type the letter?
听录音，然后回答问题。帕梅拉为什么无法打信?

THE BOSS : Can you come here a minute
　　　　　 please, Bob?

BOB : 　　　Yes, sir?

THE BOSS : Where's Pamela?

BOB : 　　　She's next door.
　　　　　 She's in her office, sir.

THE BOSS : Can she type
　　　　　 this letter for me?
　　　　　 Ask her please.

BOB : 　　　Yes, sir.

BOB : 　　　Can you type this letter
　　　　　 for the boss please, Pamela?

PAMELA : 　Yes, of course I can.

BOB : 　　　Here you are.

PAMELA : 　Thank you, Bob.

PAMELA : 　Bob!

BOB : 　　　Yes?
　　　　　 What's the matter?

PAMELA : 　I can't type this letter.

PAMELA : 　I can't read it!
　　　　　 The boss's handwriting is terrible!

New words and expressions 生词和短语

can /kæn/ *modal verb* 能够
boss /bɒs/ *n.* 老板, 上司
minute /'mɪnɪt/ *n.* 分（钟）

ask /ɑːsk/ *v.* 请求, 要求
handwriting /'hænd,raɪtɪŋ/ *n.* 书写
terrible /'terɪbəl/ *adj.* 糟糕的, 可怕的

Notes on the text 课文注释

1 Can you come here a minute please, Bob?
句中的 can 是情态动词, 表示"能力"。情态动词的否定式由情态动词加 not 构成; 疑问句中将情态动词置于句首, 后接句子的主语和主要谓语动词。
句中 a minute 作时间状语, 当"一会儿"讲。

2 next door, 隔壁。

3 boss's, 老板的。这种所有格的形式已在第 11 课的课文注释中讲过。请注意它的发音是 /'bɒsɪs/。

参考译文

老　板：请你来一下好吗, 鲍勃?
鲍　勃：什么事, 先生?

老　板：帕梅拉在哪儿?
鲍　勃：她在隔壁, 在她的办公室里, 先生。

老　板：她能为我打一下这封信吗? 请问问她。
鲍　勃：好的, 先生。

鲍　勃：请你把这封信给老板打一下可以吗, 帕梅拉?
帕梅拉：可以, 当然可以。

鲍　勃：给你。
帕梅拉：谢谢你, 鲍勃。

帕梅拉：鲍勃!
鲍　勃：怎么了? 怎么回事?
帕梅拉：我打不了这封信。

帕梅拉：我看不懂这封信, 老板的书写太糟糕了!

Lesson 46   Can you ... ? 你能⋯⋯吗?

 Listen to the tape and answer the questions.
听录音,然后回答这个问题 。

1,000

a thousand

I can put my hat on,

but I can't put my coat on.

5,000

five thousand

I can see that aeroplane,

but I can't see a bird.

10,000

ten thousand

I can paint this bookcase,

but I can't paint this room.

100,000

a hundred thousand

I can lift that chair,

but I can't lift this table.

210,000

two hundred and ten thousand

I can read this book,

but I can't read that magazine.

350,000

three hundred and fifty thousand

I can jump off this box,

but I can't jump off that wall.

500,000

five hundred thousand

I can make cakes,

but I can't make biscuits.

1,000,000

a million

I can put the vase on this table,

but I can't put it on that shelf.

New words and expressions 生词和短语

lift /lɪft/ v. 拿起, 搬起, 举起

biscuit /'bɪskɪt/ n. 饼干

cake /keɪk/ n. 饼, 蛋糕

Written exercises 书面练习

A Rewrite these sentences.

模仿例句改写以下句子。

Examples:

He is taking his book. *He can take his book.*

She is putting on her coat. *She can put on her coat.*

1 They are typing these letters.
2 She is making the bed.
3 You are swimming across the river.
4 We are coming now.
5 We are running across the park.
6 He is sitting on the grass.
7 I am giving him some chocolate.

B Write questions and answers using *I, he, she, it, we* or *they.*

模仿例句写出相应的对话, 选用 I, he, she, it, we 或 they 等代词。

Examples:

Can you put on your coat?

Yes, I can.

What can you do?

I can put on my coat.

Can you and Sam listen to the radio?

Yes, we can.

What can you and Sam do?

We can listen to the radio.

1 Can you type this letter?
2 Can Penny wait for the bus?
3 Can Penny and Jane wash the dishes?
4 Can George take these flowers to her?
5 Can the cat drink its milk?
6 Can you and Sam paint this bookcase?
7 Can you see that aeroplane?
8 Can Jane read this book?

Lesson 47　A cup of coffee　一杯咖啡

Listen to the tape then answer this question. How does Ann like her coffee?
听录音, 然后回答问题 。安想要什么样的咖啡?

CHRISTINE : Do you like coffee, Ann?

ANN :　　　Yes, I do.

1

CHRISTINE : Do you want a cup?

ANN :　　　Yes, please, Christine.

2

CHRISTINE : Do you want any sugar?

ANN :　　　Yes, please.

3

CHRISTINE : Do you want any milk?

ANN :　　　No, thank you.

　　　　　I don't like milk in my coffee.

　　　　　I like black coffee.

4

CHRISTINE : Do you like biscuits?

ANN :　　　Yes, I do.

5

CHRISTINE : Do you want one?

ANN :　　　Yes, please.

6

New words and expressions 生词和短语

like /laɪk/ v. 喜欢, 想要

want /wɒnt/ v. 想

Notes on the text 课文注释

1   Do you want a cup?
    句中的 a cup 后面省略了 of coffee 。英语中的动词主要有及物动词和不及物动词两大类, 及物动词的后面要有名词或名词性短语做宾语。like 和 want 都是及物动词 。

2   Yes, I do.
    是一种简略回答 。完整的回答是： Yes, I like coffee. 句中的 do 是助动词, 用来替代动词, 常用于简略答语中 。

3   black coffee 是指不加牛奶或咖啡伴侣的咖啡, 加牛奶的咖啡叫 white coffee 。

4   Do you want one?
    句中不定代词 one 是指 biscuit, 以免重复 。

参考译文

克里斯廷：你喜欢咖啡吗, 安?
    安：是的, 我喜欢 。

克里斯廷：你想要一杯吗?
    安：好的, 请来一杯, 克里斯廷 。

克里斯廷：你要放些糖吗?
    安：好的, 请放一些 。

克里斯廷：要放些牛奶吗?
    安：不了, 谢谢 。我不喜欢咖啡中放牛奶, 我喜欢清咖啡 。

克里斯廷：你喜欢饼干吗?
    安：是的, 我喜欢 。

克里斯廷：你想要一块吗?
    安：好的, 请来一块 。

Lesson 48 Do you like . . . ? 你喜欢……吗?
Do you want . . . ? 你想要……吗?

Listen to the tape and answer the questions.
听录音并回答问题 。

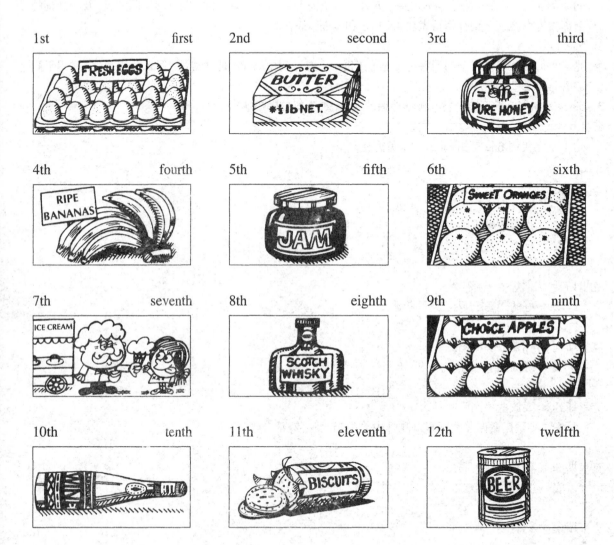

1st   first   FRESH EGGS

2nd   second   BUTTER ※¼ lb NET.

3rd   third   PURE HONEY

4th   fourth   RIPE BANANAS

5th   fifth   JAM

6th   sixth   SWEET ORANGES

7th   seventh   ICE CREAM

8th   eighth   SCOTCH WHISKY

9th   ninth   CHOICE APPLES

10th   tenth   WINE

11th   eleventh   BISCUITS

12th   twelfth   BEER

New words and expressions 生词和短语

fresh /freʃ/ adj. 新鲜的

egg /eg/ n. 鸡蛋

butter /'bʌtə/ n. 黄油

pure /pjʊə/ adj. 纯净的

honey /'hʌni/ n. 蜂蜜

ripe /raɪp/ adj. 成熟的

banana /bə'nɑːnə/ n. 香蕉

jam /dʒæm/ n. 果酱

sweet /swiːt/ adj. 甜的

orange /'ɒrɪndʒ/ n. 橙

Scotch whisky /'skɒtʃ-'wɪski/ 苏格兰威士忌

choice /tʃɔɪs/ adj. 上等的, 精选的

apple /'æpl/ n. 苹果

wine /waɪn/ n. 酒, 果酒

beer /bɪə/ n. 啤酒

blackboard /'blækbɔːd/ n. 黑板

Written exercises 书面练习

A Complete these sentences using *off, over, between, along, in front of, behind, under* or *across.*

完成以下句子, 用 *off, over, between, along, in front of, behind, under* 或 *across* 等介词或介词短语填空 。

1 The aeroplane is flying _____ the village.

2 The ship is going _____ the bridge.

3 The children are swimming _____ the river.

4 Two cats are running _____ the wall.

5 The boy is jumping _____ the branch.

6 The girl is sitting _____ her mother and her father.

7 The teacher is standing _____ the blackboard.

8 The blackboard is _____ the teacher.

B Answer these questions.

模仿例句回答问题, 注意可数名词与不可数名词的区别 。

Examples :

Do you like eggs?

Yes, I do.

I like eggs, but I don't want one.

Do you like butter?

Yes, I do.

I like butter, but I don't want any.

1 Do you like honey?

2 Do you like bananas?

3 Do you like jam?

4 Do you like oranges?

5 Do you like ice cream?

6 Do you like whisky?

7 Do you like apples?

8 Do you like wine?

9 Do you like biscuits?

10 Do you like beer?

Lesson 49   At the butcher's 在肉店

Listen to the tape then answer this question. What does Mr. Bird like?
听录音，然后回答问题 。伯德先生喜欢什么？

BUTCHER :   Do you want any meat today,
             Mrs. Bird?
MRS. BIRD : Yes, please.

BUTCHER :   Do you want beef or lamb?
MRS. BIRD : Beef, please.

BUTCHER :   This lamb's very good.
MRS. BIRD : I like lamb,
             but my husband doesn't.

BUTCHER :   What about some steak?
             This is a nice piece.
MRS. BIRD : Give me that piece, please.

MRS. BIRD : And a pound of mince, too.

BUTCHER :   Do you want a chicken, Mrs. Bird?
             They're very nice.
MRS. BIRD : No, thank you.

MRS. BIRD : My husband likes steak,
             but he doesn't like chicken.
BUTCHER :   To tell you the truth, Mrs. Bird,
             I don't like chicken either!

New words and expressions 生词和短语

butcher /'bʊtʃə/ n. 卖肉者

meat /miːt/ n. （食用）肉

beef /biːf/ n. 牛肉

lamb /læm/ n. 羔羊肉

husband /'hʌzbənd/ n. 丈夫

steak /steɪk/ n. 牛排

mince /mɪns/ n. 肉馅

chicken /'tʃɪkən/ n. 鸡

tell /tel/ v. 告诉

truth /truːθ/ n. 实情

either /'aɪðə/ adv. 也（用于否定句）

Notes on the text 课文注释

1 Do you want beef or lamb?
  是选择疑问句, 本句有两项选择, 第一选择 beef 念升调, lamb 则读降调 。

2 I like lamb, but my husband doesn't.
  句中的 doesn't 后面省略了 like lamb 。用 but 连接的并列句, 在后一分句中可以省略与前一分句
  中相同的谓语动词和宾语 。

3 To tell you the truth （或 To tell the truth）, 意思是: "老实说", "说实话" 。

4 I don't like chicken either.
  either 当 "也（不）" 讲, 用在否定句中 。肯定句和疑问句中可用too, 在第 7 课和第 31 课中已出现这
  样的句子 。

参考译文

肉　　商: 您今天要买点肉吗, 伯德夫人?
伯德夫人: 是的, 我买一点 。

肉　　商: 您要牛肉还是要羔羊肉?
伯德夫人: 请给我牛肉 。

肉　　商: 这羔羊肉很好 。
伯德夫人: 我喜欢羔羊肉, 可我丈夫不喜欢 。

肉　　商: 来点牛排吗? 这块很好 。
伯德夫人: 就请给我那块吧 。

伯德夫人: 再来一磅肉馅 。

肉　　商: 您要买只鸡吗, 伯德夫人? 这些鸡很好 。
伯德夫人: 不要了, 谢谢 。

伯德夫人: 我丈夫喜欢牛排, 但他不喜欢鸡 。
肉　　商: 说老实话, 伯德夫人, 我也不喜欢鸡 。

Lesson 50　He likes . . .　他喜欢……

But he doesn't like . . .　但是他不喜欢……

Listen to the tape and answer the questions.
听录音并回答问题 。

13th　　　　　　thirteenth

14th　　　　　　fourteenth

15th　　　　　　fifteenth

16th　　　　　　sixteenth

17th　　　　　　seventeenth

18th　　　　　　eighteenth

19th　　　　　　nineteenth

20th　　　　　　twentieth

21st　　　　　　twenty-first

22nd　　　　　　twenty-second
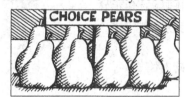

23rd　　　　　　twenty-third

24th　　　　　　twenty-fourth

New words and expressions 生词和短语

tomato /tə'mɑ:təʊ/ n. 西红柿

potato /pə'teɪtəʊ/ n. 土豆

cabbage /'kæbɪdʒ/ n. 卷心菜

lettuce /'letɪs/ n. 莴苣

pea /piː/ n. 豌豆

bean /biːn/ n. 豆角

pear /peə/ n. 梨

grape /greɪp/ n. 葡萄

peach /piːtʃ/ n. 桃

Written exercises 书面练习

A Complete these sentences using *am not, aren't, isn't, can't, don't* or *doesn't*.
完成以下句子, 用 *am not, aren't, isn't, can't, don't* 或 *doesn't* 填空 。

1 He likes coffee, but I _____ .

2 She likes tea, but he _____ .

3 He is eating some bread, but she _____ .

4 She can type very well, but he _____ .

5 They are working hard, but we _____ .

6 He is reading a magazine, but I _____ .

B Answer these questions using *I, he* or *she*.
模仿例句回答以下问题, 选用 *I, he* 或 *she* 。

Examples :

Does Penny like tomatoes?

Yes, she does.
She likes tomatoes, but she doesn't want any.

Do you like potatoes?

Yes, I do.
I like potatoes, but I don't want any.

1 Does Sam like cabbage?

2 Does Sam like lettuce?

3 Do you like peas?

4 Does Mrs. White like beans?

5 Do you like bananas?

6 Does Mr. Jones like oranges?

7 Does George like apples?

8 Does Elizabeth like pears?

9 Do you like grapes?

10 Does Carol like peaches?

Lesson 51   A pleasant climate 宜人的气候

Listen to the tape then answer this question. Does it ever snow in Greece?
听录音, 然后回答问题。希腊下过雪吗?

HANS :   Where do you come from?

DIMITRI : I come from Greece.

HANS :   What's the climate like

in your country?

DIMITRI : It's very pleasant.

HANS :   What's the weather like in spring?

DIMITRI : It's often windy in March.

It's always warm in April and May,

but it rains sometimes.

HANS :   What's it like in summer?

DIMITRI : It's always hot

in June, July and August.

The sun shines every day.

HANS :   Is it cold or warm in autumn?

DIMITRI : It's always warm

in September and October.

It's often cold in November

and it rains sometimes.

HANS :   Is it very cold in winter?

DIMITRI : It's often cold

in December, January and February.

It snows sometimes.

New words and expressions 生词和短语

Greece /griːs/ *n.* 希腊

climate /'klaɪmɪt/ *n.* 气候

country /'kʌntri/ *n.* 国家

pleasant /'plezənt/ *adj.* 宜人的

weather /'weðə/ *n.* 天气

spring /sprɪŋ/ *n.* 春季

windy /'wɪndi/ *adj.* 有风的

warm /wɔːm/ *adj.* 温暖的

rain /reɪn/ *v.* 下雨

sometimes /'sʌmtaɪmz/ *adv.* 有时

summer /'sʌmə/ *n.* 夏天

autumn /'ɔːtəm/ *n.* 秋天

winter /'wɪntə/ *n.* 冬天

snow /snəʊ/ *v.* 下雪

January /'dʒænjuəri/ *n.* 1月

February /'februəri/ *n.* 2月

March /mɑːtʃ/ *n.* 3月

April /'eɪprəl/ *n.* 4月

May /meɪ/ *n.* 5月

June /dʒuːn/ *n.* 6月

July /dʒʊ'laɪ/ *n.* 7月

August /'ɔːgəst/ *n.* 8月

September /sep'tembə/ *n.* 9月

October /ɒk'təʊbə/ *n.* 10月

November /nəʊ'vembə/ *n.* 11月

December /dɪ'sembə/ *n.* 12月

Notes on the text 课文注释

1 Where do you come from?

用于问对方是哪儿的人, 在第7课中出现过一个类似的句子。

2 What's the climate like in your country?

句中like 是介词, 不是动词, 它的宾语是what。

参考译文

汉　　斯：你是哪国人?

迪米特里：我是希腊人。

汉　　斯：你们国家的气候怎么样?

迪米特里：气候非常宜人。

汉　　斯：春季的天气怎么样?

迪米特里：3 月里常常刮风。4 月和5 月的天气总是暖洋洋的, 但有时下雨。

汉　　斯：夏季的天气如何呢?

迪米特里：6 月、7 月和8 月的天气总是炎热的, 每天都出太阳。

汉　　斯：秋季的天气是冷还是暖呢?

迪米特里：9月和10月总是很暖和, 11月常常很冷, 而且有时下雨。

汉　　斯：冬季的天气很冷吗?

迪米特里：12月、1 月和2月常常很冷, 有时还下雪。

Lesson 52   What nationality are they?   他们是哪国人？
Where do they come from?   他们来自哪个国家？

 Listen to the tape and answer the questions.
听录音并回答问题。

20th

I'm American.

I come from the U.S.

21st

He's Brazilian.

He comes from Brazil.

22nd

She's Dutch.

She comes from Holland

23rd

We're English.

We come from England.

24th

They're French.

They come from France.

25th

You're German.

You come from Germany

26th

He's Greek.

He comes from Greece.

27th

You're Italian.

You come from Italy.

28th

We're Norwegian.

We come from Norway.

29th

They're Russian.

They come from Russia.

30th

She's Spanish.

She comes from Spain.

31st

I'm Swedish.

I come from Sweden.

New words and expressions 生词和短语

the U.S. 美国
Brazil /brəˈzıl/ n. 巴西
Holland /ˈhɒlənd/ n. 荷兰
England /ˈıŋglənd/ n. 英国
France /ˈfrɑːns/ n. 法国
Germany /ˈdʒɜːməni/ n. 德国

Italy /ˈıtəli/ n. 意大利
Norway /ˈnɔːweı/ n. 挪威
Russia /ˈrʌʃə/ n. 俄罗斯
Spain /speın/ n. 西班牙
Sweden /ˈswiːdn/ n. 瑞典

Note on the text 课文注释

the U.S. 与 the U.S.A. 是 the United States of America 的缩写, 用的是两或三个首字母, 即美利坚合众国。

Written exercises 书面练习

A Complete these sentences.
　模仿例句完成以下句子。

Example :

I come from England, but Stella _____ from Spain.

I come from England, but Stella comes from Spain.

1 We come from Germany, but Dimitri _____ from Greece.
2 I like cold weather, but he _____ warm weather.
3 He comes from the U.S., but she _____ from England.
4 She doesn't like the winter, but she _____ the summer.
5 I come from Norway, but you _____ from Spain.
6 Stella comes from Spain, but Hans and Karl _____ from Germany.
7 We don't come from Spain. We _____ from Brazil.

B Write questions and answers.
　模仿例句提问并回答。

Example :

he/(Brazil)/the U.S.
Where does he come from?
Does he come from Brazil?
No, he doesn't come from Brazil. He comes from the U.S.
What nationality is he?
He's American.

1 she/(England)/the U.S.
2 they/(France)/England
3 he/(France)/Germany
4 he/(Italy)/Greece

5 they/(Greece)/Italy
6 they/(Brazil)/Norway
7 they/(Norway)/Greece
8 she/(Italy)/Spain

9 she/(Norway)/France
10 he/(the U.S.)/Brazil

Lesson 53   An interesting climate 有趣的气候

Listen to the tape then answer this question.
What is the favourite subject of conversation in England?
听录音, 然后回答问题 。在英国最受欢迎的话题是什么?

HANS : Where do you come from?

JIM :   I come from England.

HANS : What's the climate like
    in your country?

JIM :   It's mild,
    but it's not always pleasant.

1

JIM :   The weather's often cold in the North
    and windy in the East.
    It's often wet in the West
    and sometimes warm in the South.

2

HANS : Which seasons do you like best?

JIM :   I like spring and summer.
    The days are long
    and the nights are short.
    The sun rises early
    and sets late.

3

JIM :   I don't like autumn and winter.
    The days are short
    and the nights are long.
    The sun rises late
    and sets early.
    Our climate is not very good,
    but it's certainly interesting.
    It's our favourite subject
    of conversation.

4

New words and expressions 生词和短语

mild /maɪld/ *adj.* 温和的, 温暖的
always /'ɔːlweɪz/ *adv.* 总是
north /nɔːθ/ *n.* 北方
east /iːst/ *n.* 东方
wet /wet/ *adj.* 潮湿的
west /west/ *n.* 西方
south /saʊθ/ *n.* 南方
season /'siːzən/ *n.* 季节
best /best/ *adv.* 最

night /naɪt/ *n.* 夜晚
rise /raɪz/ *v.* 升起
early /'ɜːli/ *adv.* 早
set /set/ *v.* （太阳）落下去
late /leɪt/ *adv.* 晚, 迟
interesting /'ɪntrɪstɪŋ/ *adj.* 有趣的, 有意思的
subject /'sʌbdʒɪkt/ *n.* 话题
conversation /ˌkɒnvə'seɪʃən/ *n.* 谈话

Note on the text 课文注释

in the North = in the north of England
North的第一个字母大写, 是因为它单独使用, 特指英国的北部。

参考译文

汉斯: 你是哪国人?
吉姆: 我是英国人。
汉斯: 你们国家的气候怎么样?
吉姆: 气候温和, 但也不总是宜人的。

吉姆: 北部的天气常常寒冷, 东部则常常刮风。
　　　西部常下雨, 南部有时则很暖和。

汉斯: 你最喜欢哪些季节?
吉姆: 我最喜欢春季和夏季。因为此时白天长而夜晚短, 太阳升得早而落得晚。

吉姆: 我不喜欢秋季和冬季。因为此时白天短而夜晚长, 太阳升得迟而落得早。
　　　虽然我们国家的气候并不很好, 但确实很有意思。天气是我们最喜欢谈论的话题。

Lesson 54　What nationality are they?　他们是哪国人?
Where do they come from?　他们来自哪个国家?

 Listen to the tape and answer the questions.
听录音并回答问题。

20th

I'm Australian.

I come from Australia.

30th

He's Austrian.

He comes from Austria.

40th

He's Canadian.

He comes from Canada.

50th

We're Chinese.

We come from China.

60th

You're Finnish.

You come from Finland.

70th

She's Indian.

She comes from India.

80th

You're Japanese.

You come from Japan.

90th

I'm Korean.

I come from Korea.

100th

We're Nigerian.

We come from Nigeria.

101st

They're Polish.

They come from Poland.

102nd

She is Thai.

She comes from Thailand.

103rd

She's Turkish.

She comes from Turkey.

New words and expressions 生词和短语

Australia /ɒsˈtreɪljə/ *n.* 澳大利亚
Australian /ɒsˈtreɪljən/ *n.* 澳大利亚人
Austria /ˈɒstriə/ *n.* 奥地利
Austrian /ˈɒstriən/ *n.* 奥地利人
Canada /ˈkænədə/ *n.* 加拿大
Canadian /kəˈneɪdiən/ *n.* 加拿大人
China /ˈtʃaɪnə/ *n.* 中国
Finland /ˈfɪnlənd/ *n.* 芬兰
Finnish /ˈfɪnɪʃ/ *n.* 芬兰人
India /ˈɪndiə/ *n.* 印度
Indian /ˈɪndiən/ *n.* 印度人

Japan /dʒəˈpæn/ *n.* 日本
Nigeria /naɪˈdʒɪəriə/ *n.* 尼日利亚
Nigerian /naɪˈdʒɪəriən/ *n.* 尼日利亚人
Turkey /ˈtɜːki/ *n.* 土耳其
Turkish /ˈtɜːkɪʃ/ *n.* 土耳其人
Korea /kəˈriə/ *n.* 韩国
Polish /ˈpəʊlɪʃ/ *n.* 波兰人
Poland /ˈpəʊlənd/ *n.* 波兰
Thai /taɪ/ *n.* 泰国人
Thailand /ˈtaɪlənd/ *n.* 泰国

Written exercises 书面练习

A Write questions and answers.
模仿例句写出与下列句子相对应的疑问句和否定句 。

Example :

The sun rises early.
Does the sun rise early?
The sun doesn't rise early.

1 The sun sets late.
2 He likes ice cream.

3 Mrs. Jones wants a biscuit.
4 Jim comes from England.

B Write questions and answers using these words.
模仿例句提问并回答 。

Example :

he/Brazil
Where does he come from? Is he Brazilian?
Yes. He's Brazilian. He comes from Brazil.

1 he/Australia
2 he/Austria
3 he/Canada
4 they/China
5 he/Finland

6 she/India
7 they/Japan
8 they/Nigeria
9 she/Turkey
10 she/Korea

Lesson 55　The Sawyer family　索耶一家人

Listen to the tape then answer this question.
When do the children do their homework?
听录音,然后回答问题 。孩子们什么时候做功课?

The Sawyers live at 87 King Street.

1

In the morning, Mr. Sawyer goes to work
and the children go to school.
Their father takes them to school every day.

2

Mrs. Sawyer stays at home every day.
She does the housework.

3

She always eats her lunch at noon.

4

In the afternoon,
she usually sees her friends.
They often drink tea together.

5

In the evening,
the children come home from school.
They arrive home early.

6

Mr. Sawyer comes home from work.
He arrives home late.

7

At night,
the children always do their homework.
Then they go to bed.
Mr. Sawyer usually reads his newspaper,
but sometimes he and his wife watch television.

8

New words and expressions 生词和短语

live /lɪv/ v. 住, 生活
stay /steɪ/ v. 呆在, 停留
home /həʊm/ n. 家; adv. 在家, 到家
housework /'haʊswɜːk/ n. 家务
lunch /lʌntʃ/ n. 午饭
afternoon /ˌɑːftə'nuːn/ n. 下午

usually /'juːʒʊəli/ adv. 通常
together /tə'geðə/ adv. 一起
evening /'iːvnɪŋ/ n. 晚上
arrive /ə'raɪv/ v. 到达
night /naɪt/ n. 夜间

Notes on the text 课文注释

1 the Sawyers 是指索耶一家。在英文中, 姓氏后面加-s, 前面加定冠词 the, 用来指一家人, 特别是丈夫和妻子。
2 go to school, 上学, 请注意 school 前不带任何冠词。
3 at noon 指 "正午", 也叫 midday。请注意本课中表示时间的不同短语: in the morning/afternoon/evening, at noon/night。
4 They arrive home early.
   在本句中 home 和 early 都是副词, 下文中的 home 和 late 也是副词。
5 at night, 在夜里。

参考译文

索耶一家住在国王街 87 号。

早上, 索耶先生去上班, 孩子们去上学。父亲每天送孩子们去上学。

索耶夫人每天呆在家里。她料理家务。

她总是在正午吃午饭。

下午, 她总是会见她的朋友。她们经常在一起喝茶。

傍晚, 孩子们放学回家。他们到家很早。

索耶先生下班回家。他到家很晚。

晚上, 孩子们总是做作业, 然后去睡觉。索耶先生总是读报纸, 但有时和他的妻子一起看电视。

Lesson 56　What do they usually do?　他们通常做什么？

Listen to the tape and answer the questions.
听录音并回答问题。

every day	in the morning	at noon
	in the afternoon	at night
	in the evening	

1st

dusts

2nd

makes

3rd

shaves

4th

listen

21st

cleans

22nd

go

23rd

washes

24th

type

31st

drinks

32nd

watch

33rd

eats

34th

reads

Written exercises 书面练习

A Complete these sentences using –s or –es.
完成以下句子, 根据需要在动词后面加上 –s 或 –es 。

Example :

She wash _____ the dishes every day.
She washes the dishes every day.

1 The children go _____ to school in the morning.
2 Their father take _____ them to school.
3 Mrs. Sawyer stay _____ at home.
4 She do _____ the housework.
5 She always eat _____ her lunch at noon.

B Write questions and answers.
模仿例句提问并回答 。

Example :

she/morning   often/dust/the cupboard
What does she do in the morning?
She often dusts the cupboard in the morning.

  1 she/morning　　　　always/make/the bed
  2 he/morning　　　　always/shave
  3 they/evening　　　　sometimes/listen to/the stereo
  4 he/every day　　　　always/clean/the blackboard
  5 they/night　　　　always/go/to bed early
  6 she/every day　　　　usually/wash/the dishes
  7 they/afternoon　　　　usually/type/some letters
  8 it/every day　　　　usually/drink/some milk
  9 they/evening　　　　sometimes/watch/television
10 she/noon　　　　always/eat/her lunch
11 he/evening　　　　often/read/his newspaper

Lesson 57 An unusual day 不平常的一天

Listen to the tape then answer this question.
What is Mr. Sawyer doing tonight?
听录音，然后回答问题。索耶先生今晚在做什么？

It is eight o'clock.
The children go to school by car
every day,
but today,
they are going to school on foot.

It is ten o'clock.
Mrs. Sawyer usually stays at home
in the morning,
but this morning,
she is going to the shops.

It is four o'clock.
In the afternoon,
Mrs. Sawyer usually drinks tea
in the living room.
But this afternoon,
she is drinking tea in the garden.

It is six o'clock.
In the evening,
the children usually do their homework,
but this evening,
they are not doing their homework.
At the moment,
they are playing in the garden.

It is nine o'clock.
Mr. Sawyer usually reads his newspaper
at night.
But he's not reading his newspaper tonight.
At the moment,
he's reading an interesting book.

New words and expressions 生词和短语

o'clock /ə'klɒk/ *adv.* 点钟

shop /ʃɒp/ *n.* 商店

moment /'məʊmənt/ *n.* 片刻, 瞬间

Notes on the text 课文注释

1   It is eight o'clock. 现在是 8 点钟。在英语中常用 it 来指时间、天气、温度或距离。这种 it 被称作 "虚主语"。

2   by car, 乘汽车。on foot, 步行。这两个状语短语均用来表示方式。

3   at the moment, 指眼前, "此刻"。

参考译文

现在是 8 点钟。孩子们每天都乘小汽车去上学, 而今天, 他们正步行去上学。

现在是 10 点钟。上午, 索耶夫人通常是呆在家里的, 但今天上午, 她正去商店买东西。

现在是 4 点钟。下午, 索耶夫人通常是在客厅里喝茶, 但今天下午, 她正在花园里喝茶。

现在是 6 点钟。晚上, 孩子们通常是做作业, 而今天晚上, 他们没做作业。此刻, 他们正在花园里玩。

现在是 9 点钟。索耶先生通常是在晚上看报, 但今天晚上他没看报。此刻, 他正在看一本有趣的书。

Lesson 58　What's the time?　几点钟？

 Listen to the tape and answer the questions.
听录音并回答问题。

1st 2nd 3rd 4th 5th 6th

7th 8th 9th 10th 11th 12th

They usually . . . but today, they are . . . 他们通常……，但是今天他们正……

13th

He usually shaves at
seven o'clock every day,

14th

but today, he . . .

15th

She usually drinks tea in the morning,

16th

but this morning, she . . .

17th

They usually play in the
garden in the afternoon,

18th

but this afternoon, they . . .

19th

I usually cook a meal in the evening,

20th

but this evening, I . . .

21st

We usually watch television at night,

22nd

but tonight, we . . .

115

Written exercises 书面练习

A Complete these sentences.
模仿例句完成以下句子。

Example :

He usually shaves at 7.00 o'clock,
but today, he _____ at 8.00.

He usually shaves at 7.00 o'clock,
but today, he is shaving at 8.00.

1 She usually drinks tea in the morning, but this morning, she _____ coffee.
2 They usually play in the garden in the afternoon, but this afternoon, they _____ in the park.
3 He usually washes the dishes at night, but tonight he _____ clothes.

B Write questions and answers following the pattern in the example.
模仿例句提问并回答。

Examples :

they/every day   go/to school by car
What do they usually do every day?
They usually go to school by car every day.

today   go/to school on foot
What are they doing today?
They are going to school on foot today.

1 she/morning   drink/tea
   morning   drink/coffee
2 they/afternoon   play/in the garden
   afternoon   swim/in the river
3 I/evening   cook/a meal
   evening   read/a book
4 we/night   watch/television
   tonight   listen to/the stereo

Lesson 59 Is that all? 就这些吗？

Listen to the tape then answer this question. Does the lady buy any chalk?
听录音，然后回答问题。这位女士有没有买粉笔?

LADY :	I want some envelopes, please.	1
SHOP ASSISTANT :	Do you want the large size or the small size?	
LADY :	The large size, please.	

LADY :	Do you have any writing paper?	2
SHOP ASSISTANT :	Yes, we do.	

SHOP ASSISTANT :	I don't have any small pads. I only have large ones. Do you want a pad?	3
LADY :	Yes, please.	

LADY :	And I want some glue.	4
SHOP ASSISTANT :	A bottle of glue.	

LADY :	And I want a large box of chalk, too.	5
SHOP ASSISTANT :	I only have small boxes. Do you want one?	
LADY :	No, thank you.	

SHOP ASSISTANT :	Is that all?	6
LADY :	That's all, thank you.	

SHOP ASSISTANT :	What else do you want?	7
LADY :	I want my change.	

New words and expressions 生词和短语

envelope /ˈenvələʊp/ n. 信封
writing paper /ˈraɪtɪŋ-ˈpeɪpə/ 信纸
shop assistant /ˈʃɒp-əˈsɪstənt/ 售货员
size /saɪz/ n. 尺寸, 尺码, 大小

pad /pæd/ n. 信笺簿
glue /gluː/ n. 胶水
chalk /tʃɔːk/ n. 粉笔
change /tʃeɪndʒ/ n. 零钱, 找给的钱

Notes on the text 课文注释

1 Do you want the large size or the small size?
这句话是选择疑问句, 逗号前的 size 读升调, 后者读降调 。

2 I only have large ones.
句中的 ones 指 pads 。

3 What else do you want? 您还要什么吗? 其中的 What else ...? 可以看作是表示疑问的一个短语, 意思是："还有什么吗"?

参考译文

女　士： 请给我拿几个信封 。
售货员： 您要大号的还是小号的?
女　士： 请拿大号的 。

女　士： 您有信纸吗?
售货员： 有 。

售货员： 我没有小本的信纸, 只有大本的 。您要一本吗?
女　士： 好, 请拿一本 。

女　士： 我还要些胶水 。
售货员： 一瓶胶水 。

女　士： 我还要一大盒粉笔 。
售货员： 我只有小盒的 。您要一盒吗?
女　士： 不了, 谢谢 。

售货员： 就要这些吗?
女　士： 就这些, 谢谢 。

售货员： 您还要什么吗?
女　士： 我要找的零钱 。

Lesson 60　What's the time?　几点钟？

 Listen to the tape and answer the questions.
听录音并回答问题。

1st 　2nd 　3rd 　4th 　5th 　6th

7th 　8th 　9th 　10th 　11th 　12th

Do you have any . . . ?　你有……吗？

13th
cheese

14th
butter

15th
eggs

16th
jam

17th
honey

18th
bread

19th
biscuits

20th
potatoes

21st
tomatoes

22nd
peas

23rd
beans

24th
cabbages

25th
lettuces

26th
bananas

27th
grapes

28th
peaches

29th
steak

30th
mince

31st
chicken

32nd
whisky

33rd
beer

34th
wine

35th
tobacco

36th
soap

119

Written exercises 书面练习

A Rewrite these sentences using -s or -es where necessary.

　　根据需要为以下句子中用斜体书写的名词加上 -s 或 -es, 或保持原形 。

Examples :

I don't have any *banana*, but I have some *peach*.

I don't have any bananas, but I have some peaches.

I don't have any *coffee*, but I have some *milk*.

I don't have any coffee, but I have some milk.

1 I don't have any *grape*, but I have some *peach*.
2 I don't have any *tomato*, but I have some *potato*.
3 I don't have any *mince*, but I have some *steak*.
4 I don't have any *glue* , but I have some *ink*.
5 I don't have any *envelope*, but I have some *writing paper*.

B Answer these questions beginning with *I, we* or *they.*

　　模仿例句回答问题, 选用 *I, we* 或 *they* 。

Example :

Do you have any butter?　　　　/cheese

I don't have any butter, but I have some cheese.

1 Do you have any honey?　　　　　　/jam
2 Do you and Penny have any beans?　　/potatoes
3 Do Penny and Sam have any wine?　　/beer
4 Do you and Sam have any bread?　　　/biscuits
5 Do Sam and Penny have any grapes?　/bananas
6 Do you have any mince?　　　　　　/steak
7 Do the children have any butter?　　/eggs
8 Do you have any lettuces?　　　　　/cabbages
9 Do you and Penny have any beans?　　/peas

Lesson 61 A bad cold 重感冒

Listen to the tape then answer this question. What is good news for Jimmy?
听录音, 然后回答问题。吉米有什么好消息?

MR. WILLIAMS : Where's Jimmy?

MRS. WILLIAMS : He's in bed.

MR. WILLIAMS : What's the matter with him?

MRS. WILLIAMS : He feels ill.

MR. WILLIAMS : He looks ill.

MRS. WILLIAMS : We must call the doctor.

MR. WILLIAMS : Yes, we must.

MR. WILLIAMS : Can you remember
the doctor's telephone number?

MRS. WILLIAMS : Yes.
It's 09754.

DOCTOR : Open your mouth, Jimmy.
Show me your tongue.
Say, 'Ah'.

MR. WILLIAMS : What's the matter with him,
doctor?

DOCTOR : He has a bad cold,
Mr. Williams,
so he must stay in bed
for a week.

MRS. WILLIAMS : That's good news for Jimmy.

DOCTOR : Good news?
Why?

MR. WILLIAMS : Because he doesn't like school!

New words and expressions 生词和短语

feel /fiːl/ *v.* 感觉

look /lʊk/ *v.* 看（起来）

must /mʌst/ *modal verb* 必须

call /kɔːl/ *v.* 叫，请

doctor /'dɒktə/ *n.* 医生

telephone /'telɪfəʊn/ *n.* 电话

remember /rɪ'membə/ *v.* 记得，记住

mouth /maʊθ/ *n.* 嘴

tongue /tʌŋ/ *n.* 舌头

bad /bæd/ *adj.* 坏的，严重的

cold /kəʊld/ *n.* 感冒

news /njuːz/ *n.* 消息

Notes on the text 课文注释

1 What's the matter with him? 他怎么啦?

What's the matter with ...? 常用来询问人或事物的状况, 常作 "是否有问题?" "是否有麻烦" 讲。

2 feel ill, 觉得病了, feel 是系动词, ill 是表语。注意 feel ill 和 look ill 在意思上的区别; 前者指自我感觉, 后者指外表形象。

3 It's 09754. 其中 It's 指 "电话号码是"。

4 have a bad cold, 得了重感冒。

5 That's good news 中的 news 是不可数名词, 不是复数形式。

6 Good news? 是省略句, 完整的句子应为 Is it good news?

参考译文

威廉斯先生： 吉米在哪儿?

威廉斯夫人： 他躺在床上。

威廉斯先生： 他怎么啦?

威廉斯夫人： 他觉得不舒服。

威廉斯先生： 他看上去是病了。

威廉斯夫人： 我们得去请医生。

威廉斯先生： 是的, 一定得请。

威廉斯先生： 你还记得医生的电话号码吗?

威廉斯夫人： 记得。是09754。

医　　生： 把嘴张开, 吉米。让我看看你的舌头。说 "啊 ——"

威廉斯先生： 他得了什么病, 医生?

医　　生： 他得了重感冒, 威廉斯先生, 因此他必须卧床一周。

威廉斯夫人： 对吉米来说, 这可是个好消息。

医　　生： 好消息? 为什么?

威廉斯先生： 因为他不喜欢上学。

Lesson 62　What's the matter with them?　他们怎么啦？
What must they do?　他们该怎么办？

 Listen to the tape and answer the questions.
听录音并回答问题 。

41st

She has a headache.

So she must take an aspirin.

52nd

George has an earache.

So he must see a doctor.

63rd

He has a toothache.

So he must see a dentist.

74th

Jane has a stomach ache.

So she must take some medicine.

85th

Sam has a temperature.

So he must go to bed.

96th

Dave has flu.

So he must stay in bed.

107th

Jimmy has measles.

So we must call the doctor.

118th

Susan has mumps.

So we must call the doctor.

New words and expressions 生词和短语

headache /'hedeɪk/ *n.* 头痛

aspirin /'æsprɪn/ *n.* 阿斯匹林 .

earache /'ɪəreɪk/ *n.* 耳痛

toothache /'tuːθeɪk/ *n.* 牙痛

dentist /'dentɪst/ *n.* 牙医

stomach ache /'stʌmək-eɪk/ 胃痛

medicine /'medɪsɪn/ *n.* 药

temperature /'tempərətʃə/ *n.* 温度

flu /fluː/ *n.* 流行性感冒

measles /'miːzəlz/ *n.* 麻疹

mumps /mʌmps/ *n.* 腮腺炎

Notes on the text 课文注释

1 take an aspirin 相当于 have an aspirin, 服（吃）一片阿斯匹林 。

2 have a temperature, 发烧 。

Written exercises 书面练习

A Rewrite these sentences using *He*.
　　改写下列句子, 用 *He* 作主语 。

Examples :

I have a headache.　*He has a headache.*

I must stay at home.　*He must stay at home.*

1 I have a cold .　　　　　He ＿＿＿＿＿＿　　4 I feel ill.　　　　　　　＿＿＿＿＿＿＿

2 I can't go to work.　　　＿＿＿＿＿＿＿　　5 I must see a doctor.　　＿＿＿＿＿＿＿

3 I am not well.　　　　　＿＿＿＿＿＿＿　　6 I do not like doctors.　＿＿＿＿＿＿＿

B Write sentences like those in the example.
　　模仿例句完成以下句子 。

Example :

Jimmy/(a stomach ache)/a headache/take an aspirin

What's the matter with Jimmy?

Does he have a stomach ache?

No, he doesn't have a stomach ache.

He has a headache.

So he must take an aspirin.

1 Elizabeth/(an earache)/a headache/take an aspirin

2 George/(a headache)/an earache/see a doctor

3 Jim/(a stomach ache)/a toothache/see a dentist

4 Jane/(a toothache)/a stomach ache/take some medicine

5 Sam/(a stomach ache)/a temperature/go to bed

6 Dave/(a headache)/flu/stay in bed

7 Jimmy/(a headache)/measles/we . . . call the doctor

8 Susan/(an earache)/mumps/we . . . call the doctor

Lesson 63 Thank you, doctor. 谢谢你，医生 。

Listen to the tape then answer this question. Who else is in bed today? Why? 听录音，然后回答问题 。还有谁今天也卧床休息? 为什么?

DOCTOR :	How's Jimmy today?	
MRS. WILLIAMS :	Better. Thank you, doctor.	1
DOCTOR :	Can I see him please, Mrs. Williams?	
MRS. WILLIAMS :	Certainly, doctor.	
	Come upstairs.	

DOCTOR :   You look very well, Jimmy.
You are better now,
but you mustn't get up yet.
You must stay in bed
for another two days.

2

DOCTOR :   The boy mustn't
go to school yet, Mrs. Williams.
And he mustn't eat rich food.

MRS. WILLIAMS : Does he have a temperature, doctor?

DOCTOR :   No, he doesn't.

MRS. WILLIAMS : Must he stay in bed?

DOCTOR :   Yes.
He must remain in bed
for another two days.
He can get up
for about two hours each day,
but you must keep the
room warm.

3

DOCTOR :   Where's Mr. Williams this evening?

MRS. WILLIAMS : He's in bed, doctor.
Can you see him please?
He has a bad cold, too!

4

New words and expressions 生词和短语

better /'betə/ *adj.* 形容词 well 的比较级

certainly /'sɜːtnli/ *adv.* 当然

get up 起床

yet /jet/ *adv.* 还, 仍

rich /'rɪtʃ/ *adj.* 油腻的

food /fuːd/ *n.* 食物

remain /rɪ'meɪn/ *v.* 保持, 继续

Notes on the text 课文注释

1　He's better.

在英文中, 如果将一个人或物等与另一个人或物等进行比较, 就可以用比较级。在这句话中, 威廉斯夫人是把吉米今天的状况和前几天相比。形容词 well 的比较级形式不规则, 意思是 "健康状况有所好转"。

2　come upstairs, 上楼, 此处 upstairs 是副词。

3　… you mustn't get up yet.

yet 这个词一般用于否定句。get up 表示起床, 在英语中有不少动词常与介词或副词连用, 组成一个词组, 称为动词短语, 如 get up 就是一个动词短语。

4　for another two days,

for 引导的表示时间的短语往往可以译作 "达", "计"。本课中 for about two hours each day 可译为 "每天可达两小时"。each day 是 "每天" 的意思。

5　keep the room warm, 使房间保持暖和。

参考译文

医　　　生: 吉米今天怎么样了?

威廉斯夫人: 他好些了。谢谢您, 医生。

医　　　生: 我可以看看他吗, 威廉斯夫人?

威廉斯夫人: 当然可以, 医生。上楼吧。

医　　　生: 你看上去很好, 吉米。你现在好些了, 但你还不应该起床。你必须再卧床两天。

医　　　生: 这孩子还不能去上学, 威廉斯夫人, 而且不能吃油腻的食物。

威廉斯夫人: 他还发烧吗, 医生?

医　　　生: 不, 他不发烧了。

威廉斯夫人: 他还必须卧床吗?

医　　　生: 是的, 他还必须卧床两天。他每天可以起来两个小时, 但您必须保持房间温暖。

医　　　生: 威廉斯先生今晚去哪儿了?

威廉斯夫人: 他在床上呢, 医生。您能看看他吗? 他也得了重感冒!

Lesson 64   Don't . . . ! 不要……!
You mustn't . . . ! 你不应该……!

 Listen to the tape and answer the questions.
听录音并回答问题 。

110

. . . take any
aspirins!

221

. . . take this
medicine!

332

. . . call the
doctor!

443

. . . play with
matches!

554

. . . talk in the
library!

665

. . . make a noise!

776

. . . drive so
quickly!

887

. . . lean out of
the window!

998

. . . break that vase!

New words and expressions 生词和短语

play /pleɪ/ v. 玩

match /mætʃ/ n. 火柴

talk /tɔːk/ v. 谈话

library /'laɪbrəri/ n. 图书馆

drive /draɪv/ v. 开车

so /səʊ/ adv. 如此地

quickly /'kwɪkli/ adv. 快地

lean out of 身体探出

break /breɪk/ v. 打破

noise /nɔɪz/ n. 喧闹声

Notes on the text 课文注释

1 play with matches, 玩火柴。

2 make a noise 指"弄出噪音","发出响声"。

Written exercises 书面练习

A Rewrite these sentences using *Jimmy*.
   改写以下句子,用 *Jimmy* 作主语。

Example :

I mustn't take any aspirins.

Jimmy mustn't take any aspirins.

1 I am better now but I mustn't get up yet.

2 I have a cold and I must stay in bed.

3 I can get up for two hours each day.

4 I often read in bed.

5 I listen to the stereo, too.

6 I don't feel ill now.

B Complete these sentences.
   模仿例句完成以下句子。

Example :

_____ eat rich food!

Don't eat rich food!

You mustn't eat rich food!

1 _____ take any aspirins!

2 _____ take this medicine!

3 _____ call the doctor!

4 _____ play with matches!

5 _____ talk in the library!

6 _____ make a noise!

7 _____ drive so quickly!

8 _____ lean out of the window!

9 _____ break that vase!

Lesson 65 Not a baby 不是小孩子

Listen to the tape then answer this question.
Does Jill take the key to the front door?
听录音, 然后回答问题。吉尔有没有拿到大门的钥匙?

FATHER :   What are you going to do
           this evening, Jill?

JILL :   I'm going to meet some friends, Dad.

FATHER :   You mustn't come home late.
           You must be home at half past ten.

JILL :   I can't get home so early, Dad!

JILL :   Can I have the key
           to the front door, please?

FATHER :   No, you can't.

MOTHER :   Jill's eighteen years old, Tom.
           She's not a baby.
           Give her the key.
           She always comes home early.

FATHER :   Oh, all right!

FATHER :   Here you are.
           But you mustn't come home
           after a quarter past eleven.
           Do you hear?

JILL :   Yes, Dad.

JILL :   Thanks, Mum.

MOTHER :   That's all right.
           Goodbye.
           Enjoy yourself!

JILL :   We always enjoy ourselves, Mum.
           Bye-bye.

New words and expressions 生词和短语

Dad /dæd/ *n.* 爸（儿语）

key /kiː/ *n.* 钥匙

baby /'beɪbi/ *n.* 婴儿

hear /hɪə/ *v.* 听见

enjoy /ɪn'dʒɔɪ/ *v.* 玩得快活

yourself /jɔː'self/ *pron.* 你自己

ourselves /ˌaʊə'selvz/ *pron.* 我们自已

mum /mʌm/ *n.* 妈妈

Notes on the text 课文注释

1 the key to the front door,

to the front door 是介词短语, 作定语, 修饰 key 。

2 a quarter past eleven, 11点1刻, past 是介词 。

3 Enjoy yourself! 好好玩吧 。在 enjoy 这个动词后面往往有一个反身代词, 如 yourself, ourselves, himself, herself 等 。

参考译文

父亲：今晚你打算干什么, 吉尔?
吉尔：我打算去看几个朋友, 爸爸 。

父亲：你不准回家太晚, 你必须在10点半到家 。
吉尔：这么早我到不了家, 爸爸!

吉尔：我能带上前门的钥匙吗?
父亲：不行, 你不能带 。

母亲：吉尔都18岁了, 汤姆 。她不是小孩子了 。把钥匙给她吧 。她总是早早回家的 。
父亲：那么, 好吧!

父亲：拿去 。但你不能超过11点1刻回家 。听见了吗?
吉尔：听见了, 爸爸 。

吉尔：谢谢, 妈妈 。
母亲：不用谢 。再见 。好好玩吧!
吉尔：我们总是玩得很开心的, 妈妈 。再见 。

Lesson 66　What's the time?　几点钟？

 Listen to the tape and answer the questions.
听录音并回答问题。

1st 　2nd 　3rd 　4th 　5th 　6th

7th 　8th 　9th 　10th 　11th 　12th

When's your birthday?　你的生日是哪一天？

How old are you?　你多大了？

		JULY			
S		7	14	21	28
M	1	8	15	22	29
TU	2	9	16	23	30
W	3	10	17	24	31
TH	4	11	18	25	
F	5	12	19	26	
S	6	13	20	27	

Enjoy yourself!　你好好玩吧！

13th

Enjoy yourself!

I always enjoy myself.

14th

We're enjoying ourselves.

They're enjoying themselves.

15th

He's enjoying himself.

16th

She's enjoying herself.

131

New words and expressions 生词和短语

myself /maɪˈself/ *pron.* 我自己

himself /hɪmˈself/ *pron.* 他自己

themselves /ðəmˈselvz/ *pron.* 他们自己

herself /hɜːˈself/ *pron.* 她自己

Written exercises 书面练习

A Complete these sentences using *in, at* or *from*.
用 *in, at* 或 *from* 完成以下句子。

1 I am going to see him _____ ten o'clock.

2 It often rains _____ November.

3 Where do you come _____ ? I come _____ France.

4 I always go to work _____ the morning.

5 What's the climate like _____ your country?

6 It's cold _____ winter and hot _____ summer.

B Answer these questions using *I/you/he/she/we/they* and . . . *o'clock, a quarter to . . . ,*
   past . . . , half past . . .
   模仿例句回答问题。

Example :

When must you come home? (1.00)

I must come home at one o'clock.

1 When must she go to the library? (1.15)

2 When must you and Sam see the dentist? (3.45)

3 When must you type this letter? (2.00)

4 When must Sam and Penny see the boss? (1.30)

5 When must George take his medicine? (3.15)

6 When must Sophie arrive in London? (2.30)

7 When must I catch the bus? (3.30)

8 When must you arrive there? (3.00)

9 When must they come home? (2.15)

10 When must you meet Sam? (1.45)

11 When must he telephone you? (2.45)

Lesson 67   The weekend 周末

Listen to the tape then answer this question.
What are the Johnsons going to do at the weekend?
听录音,然后回答问题 。约翰逊夫妇周末准备做什么?

MRS. JOHNSON :   Hello.

Were you at the butcher's?

MRS. WILLIAMS : Yes, I was.

Were you at the butcher's, too?

MRS. JOHNSON :   No, I wasn't.

I was at the greengrocer's.

How's Jimmy today?

MRS. WILLIAMS : He's very well, thank you.

MRS. JOHNSON :   Was he absent from school last week?

MRS. WILLIAMS : Yes, he was.

He was absent on Monday, Tuesday,

Wednesday and Thursday.

How are you all keeping?

MRS. JOHNSON :   Very well, thank you.

We're going to spend three days

in the country.

We're going to stay at my mother's

for the weekend.

MRS. WILLIAMS : Friday, Saturday and Sunday

in the country!

Aren't you lucky!

New words and expressions 生词和短语

greengrocer /ˈgriːnˌgrəʊsə/ n. 蔬菜水果零售商
absent /ˈæbsnt/ adj. 缺席的
Monday /ˈmʌndi/ n. 星期一
Tuesday /ˈtjuːzdi/ n. 星期二
Wednesday /ˈwenzdi/ n. 星期三
Thursday /ˈθɜːzdi/ n. 星期四
keep /kiːp/ v. （身体健康）处于（状况）

spend /spend/ v. 度过
weekend /ˈwiːkend/ n. 周末
Friday /ˈfraɪdi/ n. 星期五
Saturday /ˈsætədi/ n. 星期六
Sunday /ˈsʌndi/ n. 星期日
country /ˈkʌntri/ n. 乡村
lucky /ˈlʌki/ adj. 幸运的

Notes on the text 课文注释

1 在英文表示某一种商店的短语中, 往往可以把 shop 这个词省略, 如课文中的 the butcher's (shop) 和 the greengrocer's (shop) 。类似的例子还有 the hairdresser's (shop), the stationer's (shop), the doctor's (office), my mother's (house) 等 。

2 在英文中, 过去发生的而现在已经结束的动作要用一般过去时来表示 。"是" (be) 动词的过去式不规则, 第一, 第三人称单数用 was, 其他情况用 were 。

3 How are you all keeping?
这是一句问候对方身体如何的话 。

4 for the weekend 是指整个周末这几天的时间, 而 at the weekend 是强调时间的某一点 。

5 Aren't you lucky!
这句话是否定疑问句形式的感叹句, 为的是加强语气 。尽管形式上是否定的, 但却表示强有力的肯定 。

参考译文

约翰逊夫人：您好 。刚才您在肉店里吗?
威廉斯夫人：是的, 我在肉店里 。您也在肉店里吗?
约翰逊夫人：不, 我不在 。我在蔬菜水果店里 。吉米今天怎么样?
威廉斯夫人：他很好, 谢谢您 。
约翰逊夫人：上星期他没上学吧?
威廉斯夫人：是的, 他没上学 。他星期一、星期二、星期三和星期四没去上学 。你们身体都好吗?
约翰逊夫人：很好, 谢谢您 。我们打算到乡下去三天, 在我母亲家度周末 。
威廉斯夫人：星期五、星期六和星期日在乡下过! 你们真幸运啊!

Lesson 68　What's the time?　几点钟?

 Listen to the tape and answer the questions.
听录音并回答问题。

1st 2nd 3rd 4th 5th 6th

7th 8th 9th 10th 11th 12th

Where were you on . . . ? ……你在什么地方?

When were you at . . . ? 你什么时候在……?

Sunday, January 1st

church

Monday, February 2nd

school

Tuesday, March 3rd

the office

Wednesday, April 4th

the butcher's

Thursday, May 5th

the hairdresser's

Friday, June 6th

the baker's

Saturday, July 7th

the dairy

Sunday, August 8th

home

Monday, September 9th

the grocer's

Tuesday, October 10th

the greengrocer's

New words and expressions 生词和短语

church /tʃɜːtʃ/ n. 教堂

dairy /'deəri/ n. 乳品店

baker /'beɪkə/ n. 面包师傅

grocer/'grəʊsə/ n. 食品杂货商

Written exercises 书面练习

A Complete these sentences using *the* where necessary.
  完成以下句子, 必要时填上定冠词 *the* 。

1 I was at _____ church on Sunday.

2 I was at _____ office on Monday.

3 My son was at _____ school on Tuesday.

4 My wife was at _____ butcher's on Wednesday.

5 She was at _____ grocer's on Thursday.

6 My daughter was in _____ country on Friday.

7 I was at _____ home on Saturday.

B Write questions and answers using *he/she* and *at/on*.
  模仿例句提问并回答 。

Example :

he/church/Sunday

When was he at church?

He was at church on Sunday.

1 Tom/the hairdresser's/Thursday

2 Mrs. Jones/the butcher's/Wednesday

3 he/home/Sunday

4 Penny/the baker's/Friday

5 Mrs. Williams/the grocer's/Monday

6 Nicola/the office/Tuesday

Lesson 69 The car race 汽车比赛

 Listen to the tape then answer this question.
Which car was the winner in 1995?
听录音，然后回答问题。哪辆车在1995年的比赛中获胜？

There is a car race
near our town every year.
In 1995,
there was a very big race.

There were hundreds of people there.
My wife and I were at the race.
Our friends Julie and Jack
were there, too.
You can see us in the crowd.
We are standing on the left.

There were twenty cars in the race.
There were English cars, French cars,
German cars, Italian cars,
American cars and Japanese cars.

It was an exciting finish.
The winner was Billy Stewart.
He was in car number fifteen.
Five other cars were just behind him.

On the way home,
my wife said to me,
'Don't drive so quickly!
You're not Billy Stewart!'

New words and expressions 生词和短语

year /jɪə/ *n.* 年
race /reɪs/ *n.* 比赛
town /taʊn/ *n.* 城镇
crowd /kraʊd/ *n.* 人群
stand /stænd/ *v.* 站立
exciting /ɪkˈsaɪtɪŋ/ *adj.* 使人激动的

just /dʒʌst/ *adv.* 正好, 恰好
finish /ˈfɪnɪʃ/ *n.* 结尾, 结束
winner /ˈwɪnə/ *n.* 获胜者
behind /bɪˈhaɪnd/ *prep.* 在……之后
way /weɪ/ *n.* 路途

Notes on the text 课文注释

1 hundreds of . . ., 数以百计的……, 用来表示不确定数量的复数形式。
2 On the way home, 在回家的途中。on the way 是指"在……的途中"。

参考译文

在我们镇子附近每年都有一场汽车比赛。1995 年举行了一次盛大的比赛。

许许多多的人都去了赛场。我和我的妻子也去了。我们的朋友朱莉和杰克也去了。你可以在人群中看到我们。我们站在左面。

有20 辆汽车参加比赛。有英国、法国、德国、意大利、美国和日本的汽车。

比赛的结尾是激动人心的。获胜者是比利·斯图尔特。他在第 15 号车里, 其他 5 辆汽车紧跟在他后面。

在回家的途中, 我妻子对我说: "别开得这样快! 你可不是比利·斯图尔特!"

Lesson 70　When were they there? 他们是什么时候在那里的?

 Listen to the tape and answer the questions.
听录音并回答问题。

ON

Monday	Tuesday	Wednesday	Thursday	Friday	Saturday
STATIONER	GREENGROCER	HAIRDRESSER	BUTCHER	GROCER	DAIRY

At: _____

ON

Jan. 21st	Feb. 22nd	March 23rd	April 24th	May 25th	June 26th

At: _____

IN

July	August	September	October	November	December
AUSTRALIA	AUSTRIA	CANADA	CHINA	DENMARK	FINLAND

In: _____

IN

1985	1987	1990	1994	1996
INDIA	POLAND	TURKEY	JAPAN	NIGERIA

In: _____

New words and expressions 生词和短语

stationer /'steɪʃənə/ *n.* 文具商

Denmark /'denmɑːk/ *n.* 丹麦

Written exercises 书面练习

A Complete these sentences using *at, on* or *in*.
完成以下句子,用适当的介词填空 。

1 We were _____ the stationer's _____ Monday.
2 We were there _____ four o'clock.
3 They were _____ Australia _____ September.
4 They were there _____ spring.
5 _____ November 25th, they were _____ Canada.
6 They were there _____ 1990.

B Write questions and answers using *we/they* and *at/in/on*.
模仿例句提问并回答, 选用 *we* 或 *they* 作主语, 介词可选用 *at, in* 或 *on* 。

Examples :

Sam and Penny/the stationer's /Monday
Where were Sam and Penny on Monday?
They were at the stationer's on Monday.

you and Penny/Australia/July
Where were you and Penny in July?
We were in Australia in July.

1 you and Susan/the office/March 23rd
2 Sam and Penny/India/1986
3 you and Penny/the baker's/Saturday
4 Sam and Penny/Canada/1993

5 you and Penny/Austria/August
6 Sam and Penny/home/May 25th
7 you and Penny/Finland/December
8 you and Sam/school/February 22nd

Lesson 71　He's awful!　他讨厌透了!

Listen to the tape then answer this question.
How did Pauline answer the telephone at nine o'clock?
听录音, 然后回答问题 。波琳在9点接电话时是如何说的?

JANE :　What's Ron Marston like, Pauline?

PAULINE :　He's awful!

He telephoned me

four times yesterday,

and three times

the day before yesterday.

PAULINE :　He telephoned the office

yesterday morning

and yesterday afternoon.

My boss answered the telephone.

JANE :　What did your boss say to him?

PAULINE :　He said, 'Pauline is typing letters.

She can't speak to you now!'

PAULINE :　Then I arrived home

at six o'clock yesterday evening.

He telephoned again.

But I didn't answer the phone!

JANE :　Did he telephone again last night?

PAULINE :　Yes, he did.

He telephoned at nine o'clock.

JANE :　What did you say to him?

PAULINE :　I said, 'This is Pauline's mother.

Please don't telephone

my daughter again!'

JANE :　Did he telephone again?

PAULINE :　No, he didn't!

1

2

3

4

5

6

7

New words and expressions 生词和短语

awful /'ɔːfəl/ *adj.* 让人讨厌的，坏的

telephone /'telɪfəʊn/ *v. & n.* 打电话；电话

time /taɪm/ *n.* 次（数）

answer /'ɑːnsə/ *v.* 接（电话）

last /lɑːst/ *adj.* 最后的，前一次的

phone /fəʊn/ *n.* 电话 (= telephone)

again /ə'gen/ *adv.* 又一次地

say /seɪ/ (said /sed/) *v.* 说

Notes on the text 课文注释

1　He telephoned me four times yesterday. 他昨天给我打了 4 次电话。be 动词以外的动词在过去时中一般有两种形式。规则动词一般是在动词后面加 -ed, 如 answer/answered; 以 -e 结尾的规则动词加 -d, 如 telephone/telephoned, arrive/arrived。另一部分动词的过去式拼写不规则，因此称为不规则动词, 如 say/said, do/did。从本课开始, 单词表中的不规则动词除列出原形外, 还将在括弧中列出过去式的拼写和读音。

2　一般过去时的句子中常常有表示过去某一时刻的时间状语, 如本课中的 yesterday（昨天）, the day before yesterday（前天）, yesterday morning（昨天上午）, yesterday afternoon（昨天下午）, yesterday evening（昨天晚上）, last night（昨夜）。

参考译文

简：波琳, 朗·马斯顿是怎样一个人?

波琳：他讨厌透了! 他昨天给我打了 4 次电话, 前天打了 3 次。

波琳：他昨天上午和下午把电话打到了我的办公室, 是我的老板接的。

简：你老板是怎么对他说的?

波琳：他说：“波琳正在打信, 她现在不能同你讲话!”

波琳：后来, 我昨晚 6 点钟回到家。他又打来电话, 但我没接。

简：他昨天夜里又打电话了吗?

波琳：是的, 打了。他在 9 点钟又打来了电话。

简：你对他怎么说的?

波琳：我说：“我是波琳的母亲。请不要再给我女儿打电话了!”

简：他又打了没有?

波琳：没有!

Lesson 72　When did you . . . ?　你什么时候……?

 Listen to the tape and answer the questions.
听录音并回答问题。

TODAY	YESTERDAY	THE DAY BEFORE YESTERDAY
this morning	yesterday morning	the day before yesterday in the morning
this afternoon	yesterday afternoon	the day before yesterday in the afternoon
this evening	yesterday evening	the day before yesterday in the evening
tonight	last night	the night before last

1st

aired

2nd

cleaned

3rd

opened

4th

sharpened

5th

turned on

6th

listened

7th

boiled

8th

arrived

9th

played

10th

stayed

11th

shaved

12th

climbed

13th

telephoned

14th

called

15th

emptied

Written exercises 书面练习

A Complete these sentences.
　　模仿例句完成以下句子。

Example :

She is airing the room now. She _____ it yesterday.
She aired it yesterday.

1　It is raining now. It _____ yesterday.
2　It is snowing now. It _____ yesterday.
3　He is boiling some eggs. He _____ some yesterday.
4　We are enjoying our lunch. We _____ it yesterday, too.

B Write questions and answers.
　　模仿例句提问并回答。

Example :

she/air the room/yesterday
What did she do yesterday?
She aired the room yesterday.

1　they/clean their shoes/yesterday
2　he/open the box/last night
3　they/sharpen their pencils/this morning
4　she/turn on the television/this evening
5　she/listen to the radio/last night
6　she/boil an egg/yesterday morning
7　they/play a game/yesterday afternoon
8　he/stay in bed/the day before yesterday/in the morning
9　she/telephone her husband/yesterday evening
10　she/call the doctor/the night before last

Can you do this test?
你能完成以下测试吗？

I   Dictation.

听写。

II   Look at this:

阅读以下例句：

I am tired.   *He is tired.*

Write these again. Begin each sentence with *He*.

改写下面的句子，用 *He* 作句子的主语。

1   I must call the doctor.   _____

2   I am going to telephone him.   _____

3   I can go with her.   _____

4   I have a new car.   _____

5   I come from America.   _____

6   I am American.   _____

7   I like ice cream.   _____

8   I want a newspaper.   _____

9   I was at school yesterday.   _____

10   I don't live here.   _____

III   Look at this:

阅读以下例句：

There is a pencil on the desk.
There are some pencils on the desk.

Write these again. Begin each sentence with *There are ...*

改写下面的句子，将 *There are* 置于句首。

1   *There is a watch* on the table.   6   *There is a peach* on the desk.

2   *There is a knife* near that tin.   7   *There is a passport* on the shelf.

3   *There is a policeman* in the kitchen.   8   *There is a fish* in the cupboard.

4   *There is a cup* on the table.   9   *There is a tree* in the garden.

5   *There is a letter* on the shelf.   10   *There is a boat* on the river.

IV   Put in *a, some* or *any*:
      用 *a, some* 或 *any* 填空：

1   I have _____ new car.
2   There are _____ clouds in the sky.
3   There is _____ milk in the bottle.
4   Is there _____ chocolate on the shelf?
5   There is _____ bar of chocolate on
    the table.

6   I want _____ loaf of bread, please.
7   Do you want _____ bread?
8   No, I don't want _____ bread.
9   I want _____ tea.
10 I want _____ biscuits, too.

V   Put in *in, at, from* or *on*:
      用 *in, at, from* 或 *on* 填空：

1   He is going to telephone _____ five o'clock.
2   My birthday is _____ May 21st.
3   It is always cold _____ February.
4   She isn't French. She comes _____ Spain.
5   My father was there _____ 1942.
6   Were you _____ school yesterday?
7   He doesn't live here. He lives _____ England.
8   They always do their homework _____ the evening.
9   Can you come _____ Monday?
10 She's not here. She's _____ the butcher's.

VI   Put in *across, over, between, off, along, in, on, into, out of,* or *under*:
      用 *across, over, between, off, along, in, on, into, out of* 或 *under* 填空：

1   The aeroplane is flying _____ the village.
2   The ship is going _____ the bridge.
3   The boy is swimming _____ the river.
4   Two cats are running _____ the wall.
5   My books are _____ the shelf.
6   The bottle of milk is _____ the refrigerator.
7   The boy is jumping _____ the branch.
8   Mary is sitting _____ her mother and her father.
9   It is 9.0 o'clock. The children are going _____ class.
10 It is 4.0 o'clock. The children are coming _____ class.

VII   Look at this:

阅读以下例句：

> Take ...   He is *taking* his book.

Do these in the same way:

模仿例句完成以下句子：

1   Make ...   She is _____ the bed.
2   Swim ...   They are _____ acoss the river.
3   Shine ...   The sun is _____
4   Shave ...   My father is _____
5   Run ...   They are _____ across the park.
6   Sit ...   She is _____ in an armchair.
7   Type ...   We are _____ letters.
8   Put ...   He is _____ on his coat.
9   Come ...   I am _____
10 Give ...   I am _____ it to him.

VIII Look at this:

阅读以下例句：

> | | He is sitting in an armchair. |
> |---|---|
> | QUESTION: | *Is he sitting in an armchair?* |
> | QUESTION: | Where *is he sitting?* |
> | NEGATIVE: | *He isn't sitting in an armchair.* |

Do these in the same way:

模仿例句提问，并作出否定的回答：

1   He can come now.

Q: _____

Q: When _____

N: _____

2   There is a newspaper on the desk.

Q: _____

Q: What _____

N: _____

3   He wants a new car.

Q: _____

Q: What _____

N: _____

4   He is going to come now.

Q: _____

Q: When _____

N: _____

5   They like ice cream.

Q: _____

Q: What _____

N: _____

7   They must go home now.

Q: _____

Q: When _____

N: _____

9   He has a headache.

Q: _____

Q: What _____

N: _____

6   He comes from Germany.

Q: _____

Q: Where _____

N: _____

8   He feels ill.

Q: _____

Q: How _____

N: _____

10   He cleaned his shoes.

Q: _____

Q: When _____

N: _____

Lesson 73　The way to King Street　到国王街的走法

 Listen to the tape then answer this question.
Why did the man need a phrasebook?
听录音，然后回答问题。为什么这位男士需要一本常用语手册？

Last week Mrs. Mills went to London.
She does not know London very well,
and she lost her way.

1

Suddenly, she saw a man
near a bus stop.
'I can ask him the way,'
she said to herself.

2

'Excuse me,' she said.
'Can you tell me the way
to King Street, please?'

3

The man smiled pleasantly.
He did not understand English!
He spoke German.
He was a tourist.

4

Then he put his hand
into his pocket,
and took out a phrasebook.

5

He opened the book
and found a phrase.
He read the phrase slowly.
'I am sorry,' he said.
'I do not speak English.'

6

New words and expressions 生词和短语

week /wiːk/ *n.* 周
London /'lʌndən/ *n.* 伦敦
suddenly /'sʌdnli/ *adv.* 突然地
bus stop /'bʌs-stɒp/ 公共汽车站
smile /smaɪl/ *v.* 微笑
pleasantly /'plesəntli/ *adv.* 愉快地
understand /ˌʌndə'stænd/ (understood /ˌʌndə'stʊd/)
    v. 懂, 明白

speak /spiːk/ (spoke /spəʊk/) *v.*
    讲, 说
hand /hænd/ *n.* 手
pocket /'pɒkɪt/ *n.* 衣袋
phrasebook /'freɪzbʊk/ *n.* 短语手册, 常用语手册
phrase /'freɪz/ *n.* 短语
slowly /'sləʊli/ *adv.* 缓慢地

Notes on the text 课文注释

1 . . . , and she lost her way. ……因此她迷路了。
    句中的 and 当"所以"讲, 表示结果。

2 she said to herself, 她心中暗想。

参考译文

上星期米尔斯夫人去了伦敦。她对伦敦不很熟悉, 因此迷了路。

突然, 她在公共汽车站附近看到一个男人。"我可以向他问路。"她想。

"对不起, 您能告诉我到国王街怎么走吗?"她说。

这人友好地笑了笑。他不懂英语! 他讲德语。他是个旅游者。

然后他把手伸进了衣袋, 掏出了一本常用语手册。

他翻开书找到了一条短语。他缓慢地读着短语。

"很抱歉!"他说,"我不会讲英语。"

Lesson 74　What did they do?　他们干了什么？

 Listen to the tape and answer the questions.
听录音并回答问题 。

101

He shaved hurriedly
this morning and
cut himself badly.

102

He took a cake
and ate it quickly.

103

I gave him a glass of water
and he drank it thirstily.

104

I met her in the street
the day before yesterday
and she greeted me warmly.

105

The bus went slowly
yesterday afternoon
and we arrived home late.

106

They worked very hard
this morning.

107

We enjoyed ourselves
very much last night.

108

He swam very well this afternoon.

New words and expressions 生词和短语

hurriedly /'hʌridli/ *adv.* 匆忙地

cut /kʌt/ (cut) *v.* 割, 切

thirstily /'θɜːstili/ *adv.* 口渴地

go /gəʊ/ (went /went/) *v.* 走

greet /griːt/ *v.* 问候, 打招呼

Written exercises 书面练习

A Look at this.

注意下面的词 。

quick — quickly; thirsty — thirstily; careful — carefully

Example :

She smiled _____ . (pleasant)

She smiled pleasantly.

Complete these sentences.

模仿例句完成以下句子 。

1 He read the phrase _____ . (slow)

2 He worked _____ . (lazy)

3 He cut himself _____ . (bad)

4 He worked _____ . (careful)

5 The door opened _____ . (sudden)

B Look at this table:

注意下表 :

	does not know		very hard
	read		hurriedly
	smiled		slowly
He	went	a glass of water	very well
She	shaved	the phrase	thirstily
We	drank	me	warmly
The bus	greeted	London	pleasantly
	worked		very much
	enjoyed ourselves		

Now write eight sentences.

模仿下面的例句, 从上面的表格中选出恰当的词和词组, 写出8句话 。

Example:

He read the phrase slowly.

Lesson 75　Uncomfortable shoes 不舒适的鞋子

 Listen to the tape then answer this question.
What's wrong with the fashionable shoes?
听录音，然后回答问题 。这些时髦的鞋有什么毛病?

LADY :	Do you have any shoes like these?
SHOP ASSISTANT :	What size?
LADY :	Size five.
SHOP ASSISTANT :	What colour?
LADY :	Black.
SHOP ASSISTANT :	I'm sorry.
	We don't have any.
LADY :	But my sister bought this pair
	last month.
SHOP ASSISTANT :	Did she buy them here?
LADY :	No, she bought them
	in the U.S.
SHOP ASSISTANT :	We had some shoes like those
	a month ago,
	but we don't have any now.
LADY :	Can you get a pair for me, please?
SHOP ASSISTANT :	I'm afraid that I can't.
	They were in fashion last year
	and the year before last.
	But they're not in fashion
	this year.

1

SHOP ASSISTANT :	These shoes are in fashion now.
LADY :	They look very uncomfortable.
SHOP ASSISTANT :	They *are* very uncomfortable.
	But women always wear
	uncomfortable shoes!

2

New words and expressions 生词和短语

ago /əˈɡəʊ/ adv. 以前
buy /baɪ/ (bought /bɔːt/) v. 买
pair /peə/ n. 双, 对

fashion /ˈfæʃən/ n. （服装的）流行式样
uncomfortable /ʌnˈkʌmftəbəl/ adj. 不舒服的
wear /weə/ (wore /wɔː/) v. 穿着

Notes on the text 课文注释

1 like these 是介词短语作定语, 修饰 shoes 。意思是 "像这样的鞋子"。
2 We don't have any.
   any 后面省略了 black shoes 。
3 ago 放在表示时间长度的短语的后面, 常与表示一般过去时的动词连用 。如 a month ago （一个月之前）。
4 in fashion, 流行的, 时髦的 。
5 I'm afraid ... 我恐怕…… 。

参考译文

女　士：像这样的鞋子你们有吗?
售货员：什么尺码的?
女　士：5 号的 。
售货员：什么颜色?
女　士：黑的 。
售货员：对不起, 我们没有 。
女　士：但是, 我姐姐上个月买到了这样的一双 。
售货员：她是在这儿买的吗?
女　士：不 。她是在美国买的 。
售货员：一个月前我们有这样的鞋, 但是现在没有了 。
女　士：您能为我找一双吗?
售货员：恐怕不行 。这鞋在去年和前年时兴, 而今年已不流行了 。

售货员：现在流行的是这种鞋子 。
女　士：这种鞋子看上去很不舒服 。
售货员：的确很不舒服 。可是女人们总是穿不舒服的鞋子!

Lesson 76　When did you . . . ?　你什么时候……?

 Listen to the tape and answer the questions.
听录音并回答问题。

this week	last week	the week before last
this month	last month	the month before last
this year	last year	the year before last

a minute		two minutes
an hour		five hours
a day	AGO	three days	AGO
a week		two weeks
a month		four months
a year		six years

109

looked
at a photograph

110

jumped
off the wall

111

walked
across the park

112

washed
his hands

113

worked
in an office

114

asked
a question

115

typed
those letters

116

watched
television

117

talked
to the salesman

118

thanked
her father

119

dusted
the cupboard

120

painted
that bookcase

121

waited
at the bus stop

122

wanted
a car like that one

123

greeted
her

Written exercises 书面练习

A Rewrite these sentences.
   模仿例句将以下句子改成过去时。

Example :

She *goes* to town every day. *She went to town yesterday.*

1 She *meets* her friends every day.
2 They *drink* some milk every day.
3 He *swims* in the river every day.
4 She *takes* him to school every day.
5 He *cuts* himself every morning.

B Write questions and answers.
   模仿例句提问并回答。

Example :

look at that photograph/an hour ago
When did you look at that photograph?
I looked at that photograph an hour ago.

1 walk across the park/last week
2 wash your hands/a minute ago
3 work in an office/the year before last
4 ask a question/five minutes ago
5 type those letters/a month ago
6 watch television/every day this week

7 talk to the shop assistant/last month
8 thank your father/an hour ago
9 dust the cupboard/three days ago
10 paint that bookcase/the year before last
11 want a car like that one/a year ago
12 greet her/a minute ago

Lesson 77　　Terrible toothache　要命的牙痛

 Listen to the tape then answer this question.
What time of day is it, do you think? How do you know?
听录音, 然后回答问题 。你认为现在是几点钟? 你怎么知道的?

NURSE :　　　Good morning, Mr. Croft.

MR. CROFT :　Good morning, nurse.

　　　　　　I want to see the dentist, please.

NURSE :　　　Do you have an appointment?

MR. CROFT :　No, I don't.

NURSE :　　　Is it urgent?

MR. CROFT :　Yes, it is.

　　　　　　It's very urgent.

　　　　　　I feel awful.

　　　　　　I have a terrible toothache.

NURSE :　　　Can you come at 10 a.m.

　　　　　　on Monday, April 24th?

MR. CROFT :　I must see the dentist now, nurse.

NURSE :　　　The dentist is very busy

　　　　　　at the moment.

　　　　　　Can you come at 2 p.m.?

MR. CROFT :　That's very late.

　　　　　　Can the dentist see me now?

NURSE :　　　I'm afraid that he can't, Mr. Croft.

　　　　　　Can't you wait till this afternoon?

MR. CROFT :　I can wait, but my toothache can't!

New words and expressions 生词和短语

appointment /əˈpɔɪntmənt/ n. 约会, 预约

urgent /ˈɜːdʒənt/ adj. 紧急的, 急迫的

till /tɪl/ prep. 直到……为止

Notes on the text 课文注释

1 Can't you wait till this afternoon?

这是情态动词的否定疑问句, 表示请求。

2 a.m., "上午", p.m. 是指 "下午"。10 a.m., 上午10点, 2 p.m., 下午两点。

参考译文

护　　　　士：早上好, 克罗夫特先生。

克罗夫特先生：早上好, 护士。我想见牙科医生。

护　　　　士：您约好了吗?

克罗夫特先生：没有。

护　　　　士：急吗?

克罗夫特先生：是的, 很急。我难受极了, 牙痛得要命。

护　　　　士：您在4月24日星期一上午10点钟来可以吗?

克罗夫特先生：我必须现在就见牙科医生, 护士。

护　　　　士：牙科医生这会儿很忙。您下午两点钟来行吗?

克罗夫特先生：那就太晚了。牙科医生现在能给我看一下吗?

护　　　　士：恐怕不能, 克罗夫特先生。您就不能等到今天下午吗?

克罗夫特先生：我倒是可以等。可是我的牙痛等不了啊!

Lesson 78   When did you . . . ? 你什么时候……?

Listen to the tape and answer the questions.
听录音并回答问题 。

AT:

ON: Sunday   Monday   Tuesday   Wednesday   Thursday   Friday   Saturday

IN: January   February   March   April   May   June
       July   August   September   October   November   December

IN: 1988   1989   1990   1991   1992   1993   1994   1995   1996   1997

ON: July 1st   Aug. 2nd   Sept. 3rd   4th Oct.   5th Nov.   6th Dec.

159

Written exercises 书面练习

A Complete these sentences.
把下列句子改写成过去时 。

Example :

She goes to town every day. She *went* to town yesterday.

1   She buys a new car every year. She _____ a new car last year.
2   She airs the room every day. She _____ it this morning.
3   He often loses his pen. He _____ his pen this morning.
4   She always listens to the news. She _____ to the news yesterday.
5   She empties this basket every day. She _____ it yesterday.

B Answer these questions.
模仿例句回答以下问题, 注意时间状语的变化 。

Examples:

It's eight o'clock. When did you see him?
(half an hour ago)
I saw him at half past seven.

It's Friday. When did she go to London?
(the day before yesterday)
She went to London on Wednesday.

It's June. When did Mr. Jones buy that car?
(last month)
He bought that car in May.

1   It's 1997. When did you paint this room?
    (last year)
2   It's 5th January. When did she meet him?
    (two months ago)
3   It's a quarter past eleven. When did they arrive?
    (half an hour ago)
4   It's Sunday. When did he lose his pen?
    (yesterday)

Lesson 79   Carol's shopping list 卡罗尔的购物单

 Listen to the tape then answer this question. What is Carol not going to buy? 听录音，然后回答问题 。卡罗尔不准备买什么？

TOM :   What are you doing, Carol?

CAROL : I'm making a shopping list, Tom.

1

TOM :   What do we need?

CAROL : We need a lot of things this week.

2

CAROL : I must go to the grocer's.

We haven't got much tea or coffee,

and we haven't got any sugar or jam.

3

TOM :   What about vegetables?

CAROL : I must go to the greengrocer's.

We haven't got many tomatoes,

but we've got a lot of potatoes.

4

CAROL : I must go to the butcher's, too.

We need some meat.

We haven't got any meat at all.

5

TOM :   Have we got any beer and wine?

CAROL : No, we haven't.

And I'm not going to get any!

6

TOM :   I hope that you've got some money.

CAROL : I haven't got much.

TOM :   Well, I haven't got much either!

7

New words and expressions 生词和短语

shopping /'ʃɒpɪŋ/ *n.* 购物
list /lɪst/ *n.* 单子
vegetable /'vedʒtəbəl/ *n.* 蔬菜
need /niːd/ *v.* 需要

hope /həʊp/ *v.* 希望
thing /θɪŋ/ *n.* 事情
money /'mʌni/ *n.* 钱

Notes on the text 课文注释

1 make a shopping list, 写一张采购物品的单子。
2 a lot of 当"许多"讲, 既可用在可数名词前, 又能用在不可数名词前, 一般用于肯定句。
3 We haven't got any meat at all. 我们一点肉也没有了。
   at all 这个词组用在否定句中, 表示"丝毫"、"一点"、"根本"的意思, 有强调作用。
   have got 与 have ("有") 同义。
4 many 和 much 均可译成"许多", 但用法不同: many 主要用于疑问句和否定句中, 放在可数名词之前, 如 many tomatoes; much 用于疑问句和否定句中, 放在不可数名词之前, 如 much tea, much money。

参考译文

汤　姆: 卡罗尔, 你在干什么?
卡罗尔: 我在写购物单, 汤姆。

汤　姆: 我们都需要什么?
卡罗尔: 这星期我们需要很多东西。

卡罗尔: 我得去一下食品店。我们的茶叶和咖啡不多了, 糖和果酱也没有了。

汤　姆: 蔬菜呢?
卡罗尔: 我还得到蔬菜水果店去一下。我们的番茄不多了, 但土豆还有不少。

卡罗尔: 我还要到肉店去一下。我们需要些肉。我们一点肉也没有了。

汤　姆: 我们还有啤酒和葡萄酒吗?
卡罗尔: 没有了。不过, 我不打算去买!

汤　姆: 我希望你还有钱。
卡罗尔: 我的钱不多了。
汤　姆: 唉, 我也不多了!

Lesson 80 I must go to the . . . 我必须去……

 Listen to the tape and answer the questions.
听录音并回答问题。

GROCER'S to get some GROCERIES:

120	121	122	123	124	125

cheese   eggs   butter   honey   jam   biscuits

GREENGROCER'S to get some FRUIT and VEGETABLES:

226	227	228	229	230	231

pears   oranges   bananas   beans   peas   cabbages

BUTCHER'S to get some MEAT:

332	333	334	335	336

lamb   beef   steak   mince   chicken

NEWSAGENT'S to get some STATIONERY:

437	438	439	440	441

glue   envelopes   writing paper   newspapers   magazines

BAKER'S to get some: CHEMIST'S to get some:

543	544	545	546

bread   cakes   aspirins   medicine

New words and expressions 生词和短语

groceries /'grəʊsəriz/ n. 食品杂货
fruit /fruːt/ n. 水果
stationery /'steɪʃənəri/ n. 文具

newsagent /'njuːz,eɪdʒənt/ n. 报刊零售人
chemist /'kemɪst/ n. 药剂师

Written exercises 书面练习

A Rewrite these sentences.
模仿例句改写以下句子。

Examples :

I don't have any eggs. *I haven't got many eggs.*
He doesn't have any coffee. *He hasn't got much coffee.*

1 I don't have any butter.
2 You don't have any envelopes.
3 We don't have any milk.
4 She doesn't have any biscuits.
5 They don't have any stationery.

B Make two statements for each question, as in the examples.
模仿例句用两种方式回答以下每个问题。

Examples :

Have you got any cheese?   (grocer's)
I need a lot of cheese. I haven't got much.
I must go to the grocer's to get some cheese.

Has he got any envelopes?   (newsagent's)
He needs a lot of envelopes. He hasn't got many.
He must go to the newsagent's to get some envelopes.

1 Have they got any bread?   (baker's)
2 Has she got any eggs?   (grocer's)
3 Have they got any magazines?   (newsagent's)
4 Have you got any beef?   (butcher's)
5 Has she got any butter?   (grocer's)
6 Have they got any bananas?   (greengrocer's)
7 Has he got any medicine?   (chemist's)

Lesson 81 Roast beef and potatoes 烤牛肉和土豆

Listen to the tape then answer this question. Why is Carol disappointed?
听录音，然后回答问题。为什么卡罗尔感到失望？

SAM : Hi, Carol!
        Where's Tom?
CAROL : He's upstairs.
        He's having a bath.

CAROL : Tom!
TOM :   Yes?
CAROL : Sam's here.
TOM :   I'm nearly ready.

TOM :   Hello, Sam.
        Have a cigarette.
SAM :   No, thanks, Tom.
TOM :   Have a glass of whisky then.
SAM :   OK. Thanks.

TOM :   Is dinner ready, Carol?
CAROL : It's nearly ready.
        We can have dinner at seven o'clock.

TOM :   Sam and I had lunch together today.
        We went to a restaurant.
CAROL : What did you have?
TOM :   We had roast beef
        and potatoes.

CAROL : Oh!
TOM :   What's the matter, Carol?
CAROL : Well, you're going to have
        roast beef and potatoes again tonight!

New words and expressions 生词和短语

bath /bɑːθ/ *n.* 洗澡

nearly /'nɪəli/ *adv.* 几乎, 将近

ready /'redi/ *adj.* 准备好的, 完好的

dinner /'dɪnə/ *n.* 正餐, 晚餐

restaurant /'restərɒnt/ *n.* 饭馆, 餐馆

roast /rəʊst/ *adj.* 烤的

Notes on the text 课文注释

1 在第 13 课中我们见到了这样的句子: Come upstairs ... , 其中的 upstairs 表示动作的方向。本课中的 He's upstairs. 则表示他的方位, 其中的 upstairs 可译为 "在楼上"。

2 He's having a bath. 他正在洗澡。在本课中, 动词 have 后面接名词或名词短语, 有 "进行"、"从事" 的意思, 如 have a bath, have a cigarette, have a glass of whisky, have dinner, have lunch 等。

参考译文

萨　姆：你好, 卡罗尔! 汤姆在哪儿?

卡罗尔：他在楼上。他正在洗澡。

卡罗尔：汤姆!

汤　姆：什么事?

卡罗尔：萨姆来了。

汤　姆：我马上就好。

汤　姆：你好, 萨姆。请抽烟。

萨　姆：不, 谢谢, 汤姆。

汤　姆：那么, 来杯威士忌吧。

萨　姆：好的, 谢谢。

汤　姆：卡罗尔, 饭好了吗?

卡罗尔：马上就好。7 点钟我们可以吃饭。

汤　姆：我和萨姆今天一起吃的午饭。我们去了一家饭店。

卡罗尔：你们吃什么?

汤　姆：我们吃的是烤牛肉和土豆。

卡罗尔：噢!

汤　姆：怎么了, 卡罗尔?

卡罗尔：唉, 今晚你们又要吃烤牛肉和土豆了!

Lesson 82 I had ... 我吃（喝、从事）了……

 Listen to the tape and answer the questions.
听录音并回答问题。

760

breakfast

870

lunch

980

tea

1,010

dinner

1,020

a meal

1,030

a swim

1,040

a bath

1,050

a haircut

1,060

a lesson

1,070

a party

1,080

a holiday

1,090

a good time

New words and expressions 生词和短语

breakfast /'brekfəst/ *n.* 早饭

haircut /'heəkʌt/ *n.* 理发

party /'pɑːti/ *n.* 聚会

holiday /'hɒlɪdi/ *n.* 假日

Written exercises 书面练习

A Rewrite these sentences using *drank, enjoyed yourself, are eating, went for, ate* or *take.*
模仿例句完成以下句子, 选用 *drank, enjoyed yourself, are eating, went for, ate* 或 *take* 。

Example:

I *had* a cup of coffee. I *drank* a cup of coffee.

1 They *had* a meal at a restaurant. They _____ a meal at a restaurant.
2 We *had* a holiday last month. We _____ a holiday last month.
3 *Have* a biscuit. _____ a biscuit.
4 You *had a good time*. You _____ .
5 They *are having* their lunch. They _____ their lunch.
6 I *had* a glass of milk. I _____ a glass of milk.

B Answer these questions using *going to have, having, must have* or *had.*
模仿例句回答以下问题, 选用恰当的动词和动词时态 。

Example:

What is he going to do? (a glass of whisky)

He's going to have a glass of whisky.

1	What are they going to do?	(breakfast)
2	What are they doing?	(lunch)
3	What must he do?	(tea)
4	What did they do?	(dinner)
5	What must they do?	(a meal)
6	What is he going to do?	(a swim)
7	What is he doing?	(a bath)
8	What did he do?	(a haircut)
9	What are they doing?	(a lesson)
10	What did they do?	(a party)
11	What must they do?	(a holiday)
12	What are they going to do?	(a good time)

Lesson 83　Going on holiday　度假

Listen to the tape then answer this question.
Where did Sam go for his holiday this year?
听录音, 然后回答问题 。今年萨姆去了什么地方度假?

CAROL : Hello, Sam.
Come in.

TOM : Hi, Sam.
We're having lunch.
Do you want to have lunch with us?

SAM : No, thank you, Tom.
I've already had lunch.
I had lunch at half past twelve.

CAROL : Have a cup of coffee then.

SAM : I've just had a cup, thank you.
I had one after my lunch.

TOM : Let's go into the living room, Carol.
We can have our coffee there.

CAROL : Excuse the mess, Sam.
This room's very untidy.
We're packing our suitcases.
We're going to leave tomorrow.
Tom and I are going to have a holiday.

SAM : Aren't you lucky!

TOM : When are you going to
have a holiday, Sam?

SAM : I don't know.
I've already had my holiday this year.

CAROL : Where did you go?

SAM : I stayed at home!

New words and expressions 生词和短语

mess /mes/ *n.* 杂乱, 凌乱

pack /pæk/ *v.* 打包, 装箱

suitcase /'suːtkeɪs/ *n.* 手提箱

leave /liːv/ (left /left/, left) *v.* 离开

already /ɔːl'redi/ *adv.* 已经

Notes on the text 课文注释

1 在英语中, 现在完成时主要用于以下两种情况: (1)表示在过去不确定的时间里发生的并与现在有着某种联系的动作; (2)表示开始于过去并持续到现在的动作。本课中萨姆的 3 句话属于第一种情况, 正是因为他吃了饭、喝过了咖啡、也休过假, 因此他谢绝了汤姆的邀请, 并表示今年已无可能再次休假。现在完成时是由 have 的现在式加上过去分词组成。规则动词的过去分词与过去式相同, 而不规则动词的过去分词则无统一的规律可言。从本课起不规则动词后还将列出其过去分词的拼写和读音。

2 I've already had lunch. 注意 already 的语序。在一般情况下, 它跟在助动词后面。

3 Excuse the mess. 意思是: "乱七八糟, 请原谅。"

4 have a holiday, 度假。

have 在不同词组中, 意思不同。如: have lunch, 吃午饭; have a cup of coffee, 喝杯咖啡。

5 stay at home, 呆在家里, 注意名词 home 之前不加任何冠词。在诸如 go home, arrive home 的短语中, home 是副词。

参考译文

卡罗尔: 你好, 萨姆。进来吧。

汤　姆: 你好, 萨姆。我们正在吃午饭, 你跟我们一起吃午饭好吗?

萨　姆: 不, 汤姆, 谢谢。我已经吃过饭了。我在12 点半吃的。

卡罗尔: 那么喝杯咖啡吧。

萨　姆: 我刚喝了一杯, 谢谢。我是在饭后喝的。

汤　姆: 我们到客厅里去吧, 卡罗尔。我们可以在那里喝咖啡。

卡罗尔: 屋子很乱, 请原谅, 萨姆。房间里乱七八糟。我们正在收拾行李箱。明天我们就要走了。我和汤姆准备去度假。

萨　姆: 你们真幸运!

汤　姆: 萨姆, 你准备什么时候去度假?

萨　姆: 我不知道。今年我已度过假了。

卡罗尔: 你去哪儿了?

萨　姆: 我呆在家里了!

Lesson 84 Have you had . . . ? 你已经……了吗？

Listen to the tape and answer the questions.
听录音并回答问题 。

1,000	2,000	3,000	4,000	5,000
fruit	bananas	oranges	peaches	apples

6,000	7,000	8,000	9,000	10,000
vegetables	lettuce	cabbage	peas	beans

11,000	12,000	13,000	14,000	15,000
meat	beef	lamb	steak	chicken

16,000	17,000	18,000	19,000	20,000
milk	tea	coffee	wine	beer

Written exercises 书面练习

A Write responses using *some* or *one*.
  模仿例句写出对应的回答, 选用 *some* 或 *one* 。

Examples:

Have some coffee. *I've already had some.*
Have a banana.   *I've already had one.*

1 Have some beer.
2 Have an apple.
3 Have a peach.
4 Have some milk.
5 Have a glass of water.
6 Have a biscuit.
7 Have some cheese.

B Answer these questions.
  模仿例句回答以下问题 。

Example:

Have you had any vegetables or fruit? (I)
I haven't had any vegetables.
I've just had some fruit.

1 Has he had any beans or peas?   (He)
2 Have they had any tea or coffee?   (They)
3 Have you had any apples or peaches?   (I)
4 Have you had any cabbage or lettuce?   (I)
5 Has she had any beer or wine?   (She)
6 Has he had any lamb or beef?   (He)
7 Have they had any tea or milk?   (They)
8 Has she had any meat or vegetables?   (She)
9 Have you had any chicken or steak?   (I)
10 Have they had any bananas or oranges?   (They)

Lesson 85 Paris in the spring 巴黎之春

 Listen to the tape then answer this question.
At what time of year did Ken visit Paris?
听录音，然后回答问题。肯是在什么季节访问巴黎的？

GEORGE : Hello, Ken.

KEN : Hi, George.

GEORGE : Have you just been to the cinema?

KEN : Yes, I have.

GEORGE : What's on?

KEN : 'Paris in the Spring'.

GEORGE : Oh, I've already seen it.

I saw it

on television last year.

It's an old film, but it's very good.

KEN : Paris is a beautiful city.

GEORGE : I've never been there.

Have you ever been there, Ken?

KEN : Yes, I have.

I was there in April.

GEORGE : Paris in the spring, eh?

KEN : It was spring,

but the weather was awful.

It rained all the time.

GEORGE : Just like London!

New words and expressions 生词和短语

Paris /'pærɪs/ *n.* 巴黎

cinema /'sɪnɪmə/ *n.* 电影院

film /fɪlm/ *n.* 电影

beautiful /'bjuːtɪfəl/ *adj.* 漂亮的

city /'sɪti/ *n.* 城市

never /'nevə/ *adv.* 从来没有

ever /'evə/ *adv.* 在任何时候

Notes on the text 课文注释

1 have been to ...，到过…… 。 "到过那里" 则说 have been there 。注意，在这里我们讲 to the cinema, 同时也说 to the park, 但在第 55 课中，我们有 to work, to school 的短语。在名词 school, work, church 之前不加定冠词 the 。

2 What's on? 上演什么电影?

3 eh /eɪ/, 感叹词, 在此表示疑问。读升调。

4 all the time, 一直, 始终。

5 Just like London!
这是省略句, 完整的句子为 Paris was just like London 。其中的 just 有 "正好"、"恰恰是" 的意思。而在第 3 行的 Have you just been to ... 中 just 是指时间, 有 "刚才" 的意思。

参考译文

乔治：你好, 肯 。

肯：你好, 乔治 。

乔治：你刚去过电影院吗?

肯：是的, 我刚去过 。

乔治：上映什么片子?

肯：《巴黎之春》 。

乔治：噢, 我已看过了 。我是去年在电视上看的 。这是部老片子, 但很好 。

肯：巴黎是座美丽的城市 。

乔治：我从未去过 。肯, 你去过吗 ?

肯：是的, 我去过 。4 月份我在那儿 。

乔治：那是巴黎之春, 是吗?

肯：是春天, 但天气太糟了 。一直在下雨 。

乔治：就像伦敦一样!

Lesson 86   What have you done? 你已经做了什么？

 Listen to the tape and answer the questions.
听录音并回答问题 。

1st	2nd	3rd	4th	5th

aired	cleaned	opened	sharpened	turned on

6th	7th	8th	9th

listened to	boiled	answered	emptied

10th	11th	12th	13th

asked	typed	washed	walked

14th	15th
painted	dusted

Written exercises 书面练习

A Look at these two sentences.

注意以下两个例句 。

She has already aired the room.
She aired it this morning.

In which of these sentences can we put *has*?

在下面的句子中有一般过去时和现在完成时两种不同的时态 。选出现在完成
时的句子, 并填上 *has* 。

1 She _____ just boiled an egg.
2 She _____ boiled it a minute ago.
3 She _____ never been to China, but he was there in 1992.
4 He _____ already painted that bookcase.
5 He _____ painted it a week ago.
6 She _____ emptied the basket this morning.
7 He _____ just dusted the cupboard.

B Rewrite these sentences.

模仿例句改写以下祈使句 。

Example:

Air the room!   (this morning)
I've already aired the room.
I aired the room this morning.

1   Clean your shoes!   (last night)
2   Open the window!   (an hour ago)
3   Sharpen your pencil!   (a minute ago)
4   Turn on the television!   (ten minutes ago)
5   Boil the milk!   (yesterday morning)
6   Empty the basket!   (yesterday)
7   Ask a question!   (two minutes ago)
8   Type that letter!   (this morning)
9   Wash your hands!   (five minutes ago)
10 Walk across the park!   (an hour ago)
11 Paint that bookcase!   (a year ago)
12 Dust the cupboard!   (this afternoon)

Lesson 87　A car crash　车祸

 Listen to the tape then answer this question.
Can the mechanics repair Mr. Wood's car?
听录音, 然后回答问题。修理工能否修复伍德先生的汽车?

MR. WOOD :　Is my car ready yet?

ATTENDANT :　I don't know, sir.

　　　　　　　What's the number

　　　　　　　of your car?

MR. WOOD :　It's LFZ 312 G.

ATTENDANT :　When did you bring it to us?

MR. WOOD :　I brought it here three days ago.

ATTENDANT :　Ah yes, I remember now.

MR. WOOD :　Have your mechanics finished yet?

ATTENDANT :　No, they're still working on it.

　　　　　　　Let's go into the garage

　　　　　　　and have a look at it.

1

ATTENDANT :　Isn't that your car?

MR. WOOD :　Well, it *was* my car.

ATTENDANT :　Didn't you have a crash?

MR. WOOD :　That's right.

　　　　　　　I drove it into a lamp-post.

　　　　　　　Can your mechanics repair it?

ATTENDANT :　Well,

　　　　　　　they're trying to repair it, sir.

　　　　　　　But to tell you the truth,

　　　　　　　you need a new car!

2

New words and expressions 生词和短语

attendant /əˈtendənt/ n. 接待员

bring /brɪŋ/ (brought /brɔːt/, brought) v. 带来, 送来

garage /ˈɡærɑːʒ/ n. 车库, 汽车修理厂

crash /kræʃ/ n. 碰撞

lamp-post /ˈlæmp-pəust/ n. 灯杆, 路灯柱

repair /rɪˈpeə/ v. 修理

try /traɪ/ v. 努力, 设法

Notes on the text 课文注释

1 在英文中可以用一般疑问句的否定形式来表示期待、请求或希望得到肯定的答复, 如课文中的 Isn't that your car? 和 Didn't you have a crash?

2 Well, it *was* my car.
   well 是感叹词。在这里表示"哎"。*was* 用斜体, 表示"过去是, 现在不是了"。*was* 要重读。

3 drive into 是"撞到……"的意思。

4 they're trying to repair it, 他们正在设法修理。try 后面常接 to + 动词不定式。

参考译文

伍德先生：我的汽车修好了吗?

服 务 员：我不知道, 先生。您的汽车牌号是多少?

伍德先生：是LFZ312G。

服 务 员：您什么时候送来的?

伍德先生：3 天前。

服 务 员：啊, 是的, 我现在记起来了。

伍德先生：你们的机械师修好了吗?

服 务 员：没有, 他们还在修呢。我们到车库去看一下吧。

服 务 员：这不是您的车吗?

伍德先生：唔, 这曾是我的车。

服 务 员：您不是出车祸了吧?

伍德先生：是啊。我把汽车撞在路灯柱上了。你们的机械师能修好吗?

服 务 员：啊, 他们正设法修呢, 先生。不过说实在的, 您需要一辆新车了!

Lesson 88　Have you . . . yet?　你已经……了吗?

 Listen to the tape and answer the questions.
听录音并回答问题。

1

Have you met Mrs. Jones yet?

Yes, I have.

When did you meet her?

I met her two weeks ago.

2

Has the boss left yet?

Yes, he has.

When did he leave?

He left ten minutes ago.

3

Have you had breakfast yet?

Yes, we have.

When did you have it?

We had it at half past seven.

4

Has she found her pen yet?

Yes, she has.

When did she find it?

She found it an hour ago.

Study these verbs.
记住以下不规则动词的过去式和过去分词。

buy	bought	bought	lose	lost	lost
find	found	found	make	made	made
get	got	got	meet	met	met
have	had	had	send	sent	sent
hear	heard	heard	sweep	swept	swept
leave	left	left	tell	told	told

Written exercises 书面练习

A Write questions and answers.

模仿例句就以下句子提问, 并作出否定的回答。

Example:

He bought a house last year.
QUESTION: *Did he buy a house last year?*
NEGATIVE: *He didn't buy a house last year.*

1 He found his pen a minute ago.
2 He got a new television last week.
3 We heard the news on the radio.
4 They left this morning.
5 He lost his umbrella yesterday.
6 I swept the floor this morning.

B Write questions and answers.

模仿例句提问并回答。

Example:

they/buy a new house/two weeks ago
Have they bought a new house yet?
Yes, they have already bought a new house.
When did they buy a new house?
They bought a new house two weeks ago.

1 he/meet Mrs. Jones/two weeks ago
2 the boss/leave/ten minutes ago
3 he/have breakfast/at half past seven
4 she/find her pen/an hour ago
5 he/get a television/two weeks ago
6 she/hear the news/yesterday
7 she/make the bed/this morning
8 he/send the letter/the day before yesterday
9 she/sweep the floor/yesterday morning
10 she/tell him the truth/last night

Lesson 89   For sale 待售

 Listen to the tape then answer this question. Why couldn't Nigel decide? 听录音, 然后回答问题 。为什么奈杰尔作不了决定?

NIGEL : Good afternoon.

I believe that

this house is for sale.

IAN :   That's right.

NIGEL : May I have a look at it, please?

IAN :   Yes, of course.

Come in.

NIGEL : How long have you lived here?

IAN :   I've lived here for twenty years.

NIGEL : Twenty years!

That's a long time.

IAN :   Yes, I've been here since 1976.

NIGEL : Then why do you want to sell it?

IAN :   Because I've just retired.

I want to buy

a small house in the country.

NIGEL : How much does this house cost?

IAN :   £68,500.

NIGEL : That's a lot of money!

IAN :   It's worth every penny of it.

NIGEL : Well, I like the house,

but I can't decide yet.

My wife must see it first.

IAN :   Women always have

the last word.

New words and expressions 生词和短语

believe /bɪˈliːv/ v. 相信, 认为
may /meɪ/ modal verb (用于请求许可)可以
how long 多长
since /sɪns/ prep. 自从
why /waɪ/ adv. 为什么
sell /sel/ (sold /səʊld/, sold) v. 卖, 出售

because /bɪˈkɒz/ conj. 因为
retire /rɪˈtaɪə/ v. 退休
cost /kɒst/ (cost, cost) v. 花费
pound /paʊnd/ n. 英镑 (£)
worth /wɜːθ/ prep. 值……钱
penny /ˈpeni/ n. 便士

Notes on the text 课文注释

1 for sale, 供出售, 待售。

2 May I …? 是一种比较正式的表示请求的句型。其中的 may 有"请求允许"的意思。

3 It's worth every penny of it.
有强调的意思, 后面的一个 it 是指刚才提到的那笔钱。全句的意思是: "你支付出的每一个便士都是划算的", 可以译成: "它确实值这么多钱。"

4 I can't decide yet. 我还不能决定。句中的 yet 常用在否定句中, 表示"迄今仍未"的意思。

5 My wife must see it first. 我的妻子必须先来看一看。其中的 must 当"必须"讲。

6 have the last word, 最后拍板。

参考译文

奈杰尔: 下午好。我想这房子是要出售的吧!
伊　恩: 是的。
奈杰尔: 我可以看一看吗?
伊　恩: 可以, 当然可以。请进。

奈杰尔: 您在这里住了多长时间?
伊　恩: 我在这里已经住了20 年了。
奈杰尔: 20年! 这个时间可不短。
伊　恩: 是啊, 从1976年起我就住在这里。
奈杰尔: 那么, 您为什么要卖掉它呢?
伊　恩: 因为我刚退休。我想在乡下买幢小房子。
奈杰尔: 这座房子卖多少钱?
伊　恩: 68,500英镑。
奈杰尔: 那可真是一大笔钱呢!
伊　恩: 它确确实实值这么多钱。
奈杰尔: 啊, 我喜欢这房子, 但我还不能决定。我妻子必须先来看一看。
伊　恩: 女人总是最后说了算的。

Lesson 90　Have you . . . yet?　你已经……了吗？

 Listen to the tape and answer the questions.
听录音并回答问题。

1

Have you read this book yet?

Yes, I have.

When did you read it?

I read it last year.

2

Have you done your homework yet?

Yes, I have.

When did you do it?

I did it half an hour ago.

3

Has he gone yet?

Yes, he has.

When did he go?

He went an hour ago.

4

Has she spoken to him yet?

Yes, she has.

When did she speak to him?

She spoke to him yesterday.

Study these verbs.
记住以下不规则动词的过去式和过去分词。

cut	cut	cut	do	did	done	eat	ate	eaten
put	put	put	come	came	come	go	went	gone
read	read	read	give	gave	given	rise	rose	risen
set	set	set	swim	swam	swum	see	saw	seen
shut	shut	shut	take	took	taken	speak	spoke	spoken

Written exercises 书面练习

A Write questions and answers.
   模仿例句就以下句子提问，并作出否定的回答。

Example:

He read this book last week.
QUESTION: *Did he read this book last week?*
NEGATIVE: *He didn't read this book last week.*

1 The sun set at twenty past seven.
2 He ate his lunch at one o'clock.
3 They did their homework last night.
4 He came by car this morning.
5 The sun rose at half past five.
6 We swam across the river yesterday.

B Answer these questions.
   模仿例句回答以下问题。

Examples:

Did you read this book last week?
Yes, I read this book last week.

What about Penny?
She hasn't read this book yet.

1 Did you do your homework last night?
   What about Tom?
2 Did Mrs. Jones go to the butcher's this morning?
   What about Mrs. Williams?
3 Did you speak to him yesterday?
   What about Susan?
4 Did George swim across the river an hour ago?
   What about Sam?
5 Did you see that film yesterday?
   What about Sam and Penny?
6 Did Tim take off his shoes a minute ago?
   What about Frank?

Lesson 91　Poor Ian! 可怜的伊恩!

Listen to the tape then answer this question. Who wanted to sell the house?
听录音,然后回答问题。谁想卖房?

CATHERINE : Has Ian sold his house yet?

JENNY : Yes, he has.

He sold it last week.

CATHERINE : Has he moved to his new house yet?

JENNY : No, not yet.

He's still here.

He's going to move tomorrow.

CATHERINE : When? Tomorrow morning?

JENNY : No. Tomorrow afternoon.

I'll miss him.

He has always been a good neighbour.

LINDA : He's a very nice person.

We'll all miss him.

CATHERINE : When will the new people

move into this house?

JENNY : I think that they'll move in

the day after tomorrow.

LINDA : Will you see Ian today, Jenny?

JENNY : Yes, I will.

LINDA : Please give him my regards.

CATHERINE : Poor Ian!

He didn't want to leave this house.

JENNY : No, he didn't want to leave,

but his wife did!

New words and expressions 生词和短语

still /stɪl/ adv. 还，仍旧
move /muːv/ v. 搬家
miss /mɪs/ v. 想念，思念
neighbour /'neɪbə/ n. 邻居

person /'pɜːsən/ n. 人
people /'piːpəl/ n. 人们
poor /pʊə/ adj. 可怜的

Notes on the text 课文注释

1　No, not yet. 不，还没有 。
　　这是简略回答，完整的回答是 He hasn't moved to his new house yet.
2　He's a very nice person. 他是一个非常好的人 。person 是指人 。当需要表示复数形式时，往往用 people 这个词 。如后面的一句话 When will the new people move into this house?
3　Please give him my regards. 请代我问候他 。
4　No, he didn't want to leave ... 是对上一句话的证实 。由于上一句话中用了否定形式，因此，在证实时句中的动词不可模仿前一句话的形式，而要根据事实来决定 。但在译成汉语时，No 就要译成肯定的意思，如："是的，他不想离开 。"

参考译文

凯瑟琳：伊恩已把他的房子卖掉了吗?
詹　尼：是的，卖掉了 。他上星期卖掉的 。
凯瑟琳：他已经迁进新居了吗?
詹　尼：不，还没有 。他仍在这里 。他打算明天搬家 。
凯瑟琳：什么时候? 明天上午吗?
詹　尼：不，明天下午 。我会想念他的 。他一直是个好邻居 。
琳　达：他是个非常好的人，我们大家都会想念他的 。
凯瑟琳：新住户什么时候搬进这所房子?
詹　尼：我想他们将在后天搬进来吧 。
琳　达：詹尼，您今天会见到伊恩吗?
詹　尼：是的，我会见到他 。
琳　达：请代我问候他 。
凯瑟琳：可怜的伊恩! 他本不想离开这幢房子 。
詹　尼：是啊，他是不想离开，可是他妻子要离开 。

Lesson 92　When will . . . ? 什么时候要……?

 Listen to the tape and answer the questions.
听录音并回答问题。

TODAY	TOMORROW	THE DAY AFTER TOMORROW
this morning	tomorrow morning	the day after tomorrow in the morning
this afternoon	tomorrow afternoon	the day after tomorrow in the afternoon
this evening	tomorrow evening	the day after tomorrow in the evening
tonight	tomorrow night	the night after next

1st

rain

2nd

snow

3rd

leave

4th

get up

5th

arrive

6th

finish work

7th

have a holiday

8th

drive home

9th

have a haircut

10th

telephone me

11th

have a shave

12th

pack his bags

13th

sweep the floor

14th

paint this room

15th

repair my car

16th

make an
appointment

Written exercises 书面练习

A Rewrite these sentences.
   模仿例句改写以下句子 。

Example:

It will rain tomorrow.
It'll rain tomorrow.

1 *He will* arrive tomorrow morning.
2 *She will* come this evening.
3 *It will* snow tonight.
4 *He will* not believe me.

B Rewrite these sentences.
   模仿例句确认以下的每一句话 。

Example:

It rained yesterday.
Yes, and it will rain tomorrow, too.

1 It snowed yesterday.
2 He got up late yesterday.
3 He arrived late yesterday.
4 He finished work late yesterday.
5 She drove to London yesterday.
6 She telephoned him yesterday.
7 He had a shave yesterday.
8 She swept the floor yesterday.

Lesson 93   Our new neighbour 我们的新邻居

 Listen to the tape then answer this question. Why is Nigel a lucky man?
听录音，然后回答问题 。为什么说奈杰尔很幸运?

Nigel is our new next-door neighbour.
He's a pilot.

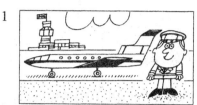

He was in the R.A.F.

He will fly to New York next month.

The month after next he'll fly to Tokyo.

At the moment, he's in Madrid.
He flew to Spain a week ago.

He'll return to London
the week after next.

He's only forty-one years old,
and he has already been
to nearly every country in the world.

Nigel is a very lucky man.
But his wife isn't very lucky.
She usually stays at home!

189

New words and expressions 生词和短语

pilot /'paɪlət/ *n.* 飞行员
return /rɪ'tɜːn/ *v.* 返回
New York /'njuː-'jɔːk/ *n.* 纽约

Tokyo /'təʊkɪəʊ/ *n.* 东京
Madrid /mə'drɪd/ *n.* 马德里
fly /flaɪ/ (flew /fluː/, flown /fləʊn/) *v.* 飞行

Notes on the text 课文注释

1 next-door neighbour, 隔壁邻居 。next-door 是一个复合词, 作定语 。
2 the R.A.F. = the Royal Air Force, 英国皇家空军 。
3 He is only forty-one years old, and he has . . .
    本句中的 and 相当于 but (而……), 起转折作用 。

参考译文

奈杰尔是我们新搬来的隔壁邻居 。他是个飞行员 。

他曾在皇家空军任职 。

下个月他将飞往纽约 。

再下个月他将飞往东京 。

现在他在马德里 。他是一星期以前飞到西班牙的 。

再下个星期他将返回伦敦 。

他只有41岁, 但他却去过世界上几乎每一个国家 。

奈杰尔是个很幸运的人 。但他的妻子运气不很好 。她总是呆在家里!

Lesson 94　When did you/will you go to ...?
你过去／将在什么时候去……？

 Listen to the tape and answer the questions.
听录音并回答问题。

last week	this week	next week	the week after next
last month	this month	next month	the month after next
last year	this year	next year	the year after next

1

Athens

2

Beijing

3

Berlin

4

Bombay

5

Geneva

6

London

7

Madrid

8

Moscow

9

New York

10

Paris

11
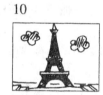
Rome

12

Seoul

13

Stockholm

14

Sydney

15

Tokyo

New words and expressions 生词和短语

Athens /'æθɪnz/ n. 雅典

Berlin /bɜː'lɪn/ n. 柏林

Bombay /bɒm'beɪ/ n. 孟买

Geneva /dʒɪ'niːvə/ n. 日内瓦

Moscow /'mɒskəʊ/ n. 莫斯科

Rome /rəʊm/ n. 罗马

Seoul /səʊl/ n. 首尔

Stockholm /'stɒkhəʊm/ n. 斯德哥尔摩

Sydney /'sɪdni/ n. 悉尼

Written exercises 书面练习

A Rewrite these sentences using *will*.
   模仿例句改写以下句子, 用上*will* 。

Example:

He went to Beijing last year.

He will go to Beijing next year.

1 He went to New York last week.
2 She went to Sydney last month.
3 I went to Paris the year before last.
4 We went to Stockholm last year.
5 They went to Geneva the week before last.

B Answer these questions.
   模仿例句回答以下问题 。

Example:

Will you go to Athens next week?   (Beijing)

No, I won't go to Athens next week. I'll go to Beijing.

1 Will Helen return to Geneva next year?   (Bombay)
2 Will you fly to London tomorrow?   (Geneva)
3 Will you and Tom go to Madrid next year?   (London)
4 Will Tom arrive from Moscow next month?   (Madrid)
5 Will Carol and Helen stay in New York next month?   (Moscow)

Lesson 95　Tickets, please. 请把车票拿出来。

Listen to the tape then answer this question.
Why did George and Ken miss the train?
听录音,然后回答问题 。为什么乔治和肯误了火车?

GEORGE :　　　Two return tickets to London, please.
　　　　　　What time will the next train leave?

ATTENDANT :　At nineteen minutes past eight.

GEORGE :　　　Which platform?

ATTENDANT :　Platform Two.
　　　　　　Over the bridge.

KEN :　　　What time will the next train leave?

GEORGE :　At eight nineteen.

KEN :　　　We've got plenty of time.

GEORGE :　It's only three minutes to eight.

KEN :　　　Let's go and have a drink.
　　　　　There's a bar
　　　　　next door to the station.

GEORGE :　We had better
　　　　　go back to the station now, Ken.

PORTER :　　Tickets, please.

GEORGE :　　We want to catch
　　　　　　the eight nineteen to London.

PORTER :　　You've just missed it!

GEORGE :　　What!
　　　　　　It's only eight fifteen.

PORTER :　　I'm sorry, sir.
　　　　　　That clock's ten minutes slow.

GEORGE :　　When's the next train?

PORTER :　　In five hours' time!

193

New words and expressions 生词和短语

return /rɪ'tɜːn/ n. 往返
train /treɪn/ n. 火车
platform /'plætfɔːm/ n. 站台
plenty /'plenti/ n. 大量

bar /baː/ n. 酒吧
station /'steɪʃən/ n. 车站, 火车站
porter /'pɔːtə/ n. 乘务员
catch /kætʃ/ (caught /kɔːt/, caught) v. 赶上
miss /mɪs/ v. 错过

Notes on the text 课文注释

1 return ticket, 往返票 。
2 next door to . . ., 与……相邻, 在……隔壁 。
3 had better 相当于情态动词, 当 "最好" 讲, 用于指现在和将要做的事情 。各种人称后面的形式相同,
   简写作 'd better 。后面接动词原形 。
4 catch the eight nineteen to London,
   这里的 eight nineteen 是指 8 点 19 分的火车, to London 是表示火车的行车方向 。
5 in five hours' time, 5 小时之后 。
   这里的介词 in 是 "在……之后" 的意思, 复数名词 hours 后面用所有格, 直接加表示所有格的
   撇号就可以, 不必再加-s 。

参考译文

乔　治：买两张到伦敦的往返票 。下一班火车什么时候开?
售票员：8 点 19 分 。

乔　治：在哪个站台?
售票员：2 号站台 。过天桥 。

　肯：下一班火车什么时候开?
乔　治：8 点 19 分 。
　肯：我们的时间还很宽裕 。

乔　治：现在才 7 点 57 分 。
　肯：让我们去喝点东西吧, 车站旁有一个酒吧 。

乔　治：肯, 我们现在最好回到车站去 。

乘务员：请出示车票 。
乔　治：我们要乘 8 点 19 分的车去伦敦 。
乘务员：你们刚好错过了那班车 。

乔　治：什么! 现在只有 8 点 15 分 。
乘务员：对不起, 先生, 那个钟慢了 10 分钟 。
乔　治：下一班车是什么时候?
乘务员：5个小时以后!

Lesson 96 What's the exact time? 确切的时间是几点？

Listen to the tape and answer the questions.
听录音并回答问题。

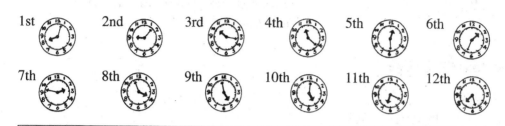

1st 2nd 3rd 4th 5th 6th

7th 8th 9th 10th 11th 12th

a minute/two minutes		a minute's/two minutes'	
an hour/two hours		an hour's/two hours'	
a day/two days	AGO IN	a day's/two days'	TIME
a week/two weeks		a week's/two weeks'	
a month/two months		a month's/two months'	
a year/two years		a year's/two years'	

When did he/will he go to ...? 他曾／将在什么时候去……？

1 Athens 2 Beijing 3 Berlin 4 Bombay 5 Geneva

6 London 7 Madrid 8 Moscow 9 New York 10 Paris

11 Rome 12 Seoul 13 Stockholm 14 Sydney 15 Tokyo

Written exercises 书面练习

A Rewrite these sentences using *had better*.
   用 *had better* 来改写以下句子：

Example:

We must go back to the station.
We had better go back to the station.

1 I must stay here.
2 We must wait for him.
3 You must call a doctor.
4 They must go home.
5 She must hurry.
6 You must be careful.

B Answer these questions using *'ll*.
   模仿例句回答以下问题，用上 *'ll*。

Examples:

I went to Beijing a year ago. What about you?
a year's time
I'll go to Beijing in a year's time.
Tom flew to Stockholm two weeks ago. What about Pamela?
two weeks' time
She'll fly to Stockholm in two weeks' time.
Dave and Alan returned to Tokyo two days ago. What about you and Jean?
two days' time
We'll return to Tokyo in two days' time.

1 I went to Sydney a month ago. What about you?
   a month's time
2 A train left for Geneva an hour ago. What about the next one?
   an hour's time
3 Carol flew to Beijing two days ago. What about you?
   two days' time
4 Tom and Mary went to London an hour ago. What about you and Jean?
   an hour's time

Lesson 97　A small blue case　一只蓝色的小箱子

Listen to the tape then answer this question. Does Mr. Hall get his case back?
听录音，然后回答问题。霍尔先生有没有要回他的箱子？

MR. HALL :　　I left a suitcase
　　　　　　　on the train to London
　　　　　　　the other day.

ATTENDANT :　Can you describe it, sir?

MR. HALL :　　It's a small blue case
　　　　　　　and it's got a zip.
　　　　　　　There's a label on the handle
　　　　　　　with my name and address on it.

ATTENDANT :　Is this case yours?

MR. HALL :　　No, that's not mine.

ATTENDANT :　What about this one?
　　　　　　　This one's got a label.

MR. HALL :　　Let me see it.

ATTENDANT :　What's your name and address?

MR. HALL :　　David Hall,
　　　　　　　83, Bridge Street.

ATTENDANT :　That's right.
　　　　　　　D. N. Hall,
　　　　　　　83, Bridge Street.

ATTENDANT :　Three pounds fifty pence, please.

MR. HALL :　　Here you are.

ATTENDANT :　Thank you.

MR. HALL :　　Hey!

ATTENDANT :　What's the matter?

MR. HALL :　　This case doesn't belong to me!
　　　　　　　You've given me the wrong case!

New words and expressions 生词和短语

leave /liːv/ (left /left/, left) v. 遗留
describe /dɪˈskraɪb/ v. 描述
zip /zɪp/ n. 拉链
label /ˈleɪbəl/ n. 标签

handle /ˈhændl/ n. 提手, 把手
address /əˈdres/ n. 地址
pence /pens/ n. penny 的复数形式
belong /bɪˈlɒŋ/ v. 属于

Notes on the text 课文注释

1 the other day, 几天前 。

2 It's got a zip.
   句中的 it's = it has, 不是 it is 。

3 Is this case yours? 这箱子是您的吗? 其中的 yours 是表示所有格的代词, 所有格代词不能用于名词之前, 在句中一般要重读 。

4 83, Bridge Street, 大桥街 83号 。
   在英文中书写地址时, 要把门牌号放在街名的前面 。

5 Hey! 感叹词, 用来表示惊讶、疑问或用以引起注意 。

参考译文

霍尔先生： 几天前我把一只手提箱忘在开往伦敦的火车上了 。
服 务 员： 先生, 您能描述一下它是什么样子的吗?

霍尔先生： 是只蓝色的小箱子, 上面有拉链 。箱把上有个标签, 上面写着我的姓名和住址 。

服 务 员： 这箱子是您的吗?
霍尔先生： 不, 那不是我的 。

服 务 员： 这只是不是? 这只箱子有个标签 。
霍尔先生： 让我看看 。

服 务 员： 您的姓名和住址?
霍尔先生： 大卫·霍尔, 大桥街 83 号 。
服 务 员： 那就对了 。D. N. 霍尔, 大桥街 83 号 。

服 务 员： 请付 3 英镑 50 便士 。
霍尔先生： 给您 。
服 务 员： 谢谢您 。

霍尔先生： 嗨!
服 务 员： 怎么回事?
霍尔先生： 这箱子不是我的! 您给错了!

Lesson 98　Whose is it?　它是谁的？
Whose are they?　它们是谁的？

Listen to the tape and answer the questions.
听录音并回答问题 。

Does this belong to me?	Is this mine?
Does this belong to you?	Is this yours?
Does this belong to him?	Is this his?
Does this belong to her?	Is this hers?
Do these belong to us?	Are these ours?
Do these belong to you?	Are these yours?
Do these belong to them?	Are these theirs?

1

2

3

4

5

6

7

8

9

10

11

12

Written exercises 书面练习

A Complete these sentences.
模仿例句完成以下句子, 选用适当的所有格代词 。

Example:

This dress belongs to my sister. It *is hers*.

1   These things belong to my husband. They _____ .
2   This coat belongs to me. It _____ .
3   These shoes belong to my wife. They _____ .
4   These books belong to my brother and me. They _____ .
5   These pens belong to Tom and Jill. The pens _____ .
6   This suitcase belongs to you. It _____ .

B Answer these questions.
模仿例句回答以下问题 。

Examples:

Are these your keys?
Yes, they're mine. They belong to me.

Is this John's letter?
Yes, it's his. It belongs to him.

Are these my clothes?
Yes, they're yours. They belong to you.

1   Is this Jane's passport?
2   Are these their tickets?
3   Is this your watch?
4   Are these her flowers?
5   Is this my boat?
6   Is this Jim's phrasebook?
7   Are these hammers Frank's and Gary's?
8   Is this our car?
9   Are these the children's pens?

Lesson 99 Ow! 啊哟!

Listen to the tape then answer this question.
Must Andy go to see the doctor?
听录音,然后回答问题 。安迪需要去看医生吗?

ANDY : Ow!　　　　　　　　　　　　　　　1

LUCY : What's the matter, Andy?　　　　　2
ANDY : I slipped and fell downstairs.

LUCY : Have you hurt yourself?　　　　　　3
ANDY : Yes, I have.
I think that
I've hurt my back.

LUCY : Try and stand up.　　　　　　　　4
Can you stand up?
Here.
Let me help you.

ANDY : I'm sorry, Lucy.　　　　　　　　5
I'm afraid that
I can't get up.

LUCY : I think that　　　　　　　　　　6
the doctor had better see you.
I'll phone Dr. Carter.

LUCY : The doctor says that　　　　　　7
he will come at once.
I'm sure that
you need an X-ray, Andy.

New words and expressions 生词和短语

ow /aʊ/ *int.* 哎哟

slip /slɪp/ *v.* 滑倒

fall /fɔːl/ (fell /fel/, fallen /'fɔːlən/) *v.* 落下, 跌倒

downstairs /ˌdaʊn'steəz/ *adv.* 下楼

hurt /hɜːt/ (hurt, hurt) *v.* 伤, 伤害, 疼痛

back /bæk/ *n.* 背

stand up /'stænd-'ʌp/ 起立, 站起来

help /help/ *v.* 帮助

at once 立即

sure /ʃɔː/ *adj.* 一定的, 确信的

X-ray /'eks-reɪ/ *n.* X 光透视

Notes on the text 课文注释

1 fell downstairs, 从楼梯上摔下来。
downstairs 是副词, 修饰 fell, 作状语。

2 Try and stand up. 试着站起来。在英语中, 常用 and 把两个动词连接在一起, 如第 13 课的 come upstairs and see it. 这种句子往往用来鼓励某种动作。

3 Here 在这里是感叹词, 意思是 "来" 或 "喂", 引起别人注意。

4 Let me help you. 让我来帮你。其中 let 有 "允许" 的意思。注意在 let 后面要加不带 to 的动词不定式。

5 The doctor says that he will come at once.
在英文中如果要把某人所说的话告诉另一个人, 要用间接引语。间接引语不用引号, 往往在引语前加 that 等引导词。

参考译文

安迪: 啊哟!

露西: 怎么了, 安迪?
安迪: 我滑了一跤, 从楼梯上摔下来了。

露西: 你摔伤了没有?
安迪: 是啊, 摔伤了。我想我把背摔坏了。

露西: 试试站起来。你能站起来吗? 来, 让我帮你。
安迪: 对不起, 露西, 恐怕我站不起来。

露西: 我想最好请医生来给你看一下。我去给卡特医生打电话。

露西: 医生说他马上就来。安迪, 我看你需要做一次 X 光透视。

Lesson 100 He says that . . . She says that . . . They say that . . .

他/她/他们说……

Listen to the tape and answer the questions.

听录音并回答问题。

He	says thinks believes knows understands is afraid is sorry is sure	that he	is … feels … has (got) … needs … wants … can … must … will …

is/are
feel(s)

1	2	3	4

tired	thirsty	cold	ill

has/have
(got)

5	6	7	8
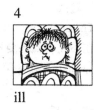			
a cold	a headache	an earache	a toothache

need(s)
want(s)

9	10	11	12

a haircut	a licence	an X-ray	some money

can
must
will

13	14	15	16
wait	catch	repair	sell

New words and expressions 生词和短语

licence /'laisəns/ *n.* 执照

Written exercises 书面练习

A Rewrite these sentences.
　模仿例句把下列句子改写成间接引语。

Examples:

He is drinking his milk. *He says that he is drinking his milk.*

1　She has found her pen.
2　They must remain here.
3　He remembers you.
4　She doesn't speak English.
5　They're washing the dishes.

B Answer these questions.
　模仿例句用间接引语回答以下问题。

Examples:

What's the matter with him?　(feel/tired)
He says that he feels tired.

What do they want?　　　(some/money)
They say that they want some money.

1	What's the matter with him?	(feel/ill)
2	What's the matter with her?	(have got/a headache)
3	What does he want?	(a haircut)
4	What's the matter with them?	(are/thirsty)
5	What's the matter with them?	(have/a toothache)
6	What does she need?	(a licence)
7	What does he want?	(an X-ray)
8	What's the matter with her?	(is/cold)
9	What's the matter with him?	(have got/a cold)
10	What's the matter with him?	(have/an earache)

Lesson 101　A card from Jimmy　吉米的明信片

 Listen to the tape then answer this question. Does Grandmother seem pleased to get a card from Jimmy? Why/Why not?

听录音，然后回答问题。收到吉米寄来的一张明信片，祖母是否显得高兴？为什么？

GRANDMOTHER : Read Jimmy's card to me please, Penny.

PENNY : 'I have just arrived in Scotland
and I'm staying at a Youth Hostel.'

GRANDMOTHER : Eh?

PENNY : He says he's just arrived in Scotland.
He says he's staying at a Youth Hostel.
You know he's a member of the Y.H.A.

GRANDMOTHER : The what?

PENNY : The Y.H.A., Mum.
The Youth Hostels Association.

GRANDMOTHER : What else does he say?

PENNY : 'I'll write a letter soon.
I hope you are all well.'

GRANDMOTHER : What?
Speak up, Penny.
I'm afraid I can't hear you.

PENNY : He says he'll write a letter soon.
He hopes we are all well.
'Love, Jimmy.'

GRANDMOTHER : Is that all?
He doesn't say very much, does he?

PENNY : He can't write very much
on a card, Mum.

New words and expressions 生词和短语

Scotland /'skɒtlənd/ *n.* 苏格兰（英国）

card /kɑːd/ *n.* 明信片

youth /juːθ/ *n.* 青年

hostel /'hɒstl/ *n.* 招待所, 旅馆

association /əˌsəʊsi'eɪʃən/ *n.* 协会

soon /suːn/ *adv.* 不久

write /raɪt/ (wrote /rəʊt/, written /'rɪtn/) *v.* 写

Notes on the text 课文注释

1　"I have just arrived in Scotland . . . a Youth Hostel."
　　这是一个直接引语的例子。直接引语是英文中用书面语的形式来表示口语的方式, 实际讲的话要放在引号之间, 句尾的标点符号也要放在引号之内。

2　the Y.H.A. = the Youth Hostels Association
　　青年招待所协会。简称Y.H.A。a Youth Hostel 是一种为参加野外探险度假活动的青年人提供廉价住宿的招待所。这种青年招待所实行会员制, 首先要加入Y.H.A.才有资格享受这种待遇。

3　speak up, 大声地说。

4　Love, Jimmy. 爱你们的吉米。
　　Yours, Jimmy（你的, 吉米）。这是亲人朋友间通信时常用的结束语。

5　He doesn't say very much, does he?
　　这是英文中的反意疑问句, 它是由两部分组成的, 前面是一个陈述句, 逗号之后是一个简略问句。反意疑问句可以用来确认自己的判断, 获取真实的信息, 还可以用来表示惊讶、愤怒等感情。如果前一部分陈述句是肯定形式, 简略问句就要用否定形式; 如果前一部分是否定形式, 后一部分则用肯定形式。

参考译文

祖母： 请把吉米的明信片念给我听听, 彭妮。

彭妮： "我刚到苏格兰, 我现住在一家青年招待所。"

祖母： 什么?

彭妮： 他说他刚到苏格兰。他说他现住在一家青年招待所。您知道, 他是Y.H.A.的一个成员。

祖母： 什么?

彭妮： Y.H.A, 妈妈。青年招待所协会。

祖母： 他还说了些什么?

彭妮： "我很快会写信的。祝你们大家身体都好。"

祖母： 什么? 彭妮, 大声一点。我可听不见你念的。

彭妮： 他说他很快会写信的。他祝我们大家身体好。"爱你们的吉米。"

祖母： 就这些吗? 他没写多少, 是吗?

彭妮： 在明信片上他写不了很多, 妈妈。

Lesson 102   He says he . . . She says she . . . They say they . . .
他／她／他们说他／她／他们……

Listen to the tape and answer the questions.
听录音并回答问题。

	says		is . . .
	thinks		feels . . .
	believes		has (got) . . .
He	knows	**he**	needs . . .
	hopes		wants . . .
	is afraid		can . . .
	is sorry		must . . .
	is sure		will . . .

is/are
feel(s)

1	2	3	4
tired	thirsty	cold	ill

has/have
(got)

5	6	7	8
a cold	a headache	an earache	a toothache

need(s)
want(s)

9	10	11	12
a haircut	a licence	an X-ray	some money

can
must
will

13	14	15	16
wait	catch	repair	sell

Written exercises 书面练习

A Rewrite these sentences.
模仿例句把下列句子改写成间接引语。

Example:

He is drinking his milk.

He says he has drunk his milk.

1 She is shutting the door.
2 He is putting on his coat.
3 He is reading this magazine.
4 They are speaking to the boss.
5 The sun is rising.

B Look at this table.
注意以下表格。

		cold
		a bus
		a haircut
	has got	tired
	feels	a cold
He says he	will sell	thirsty
	needs	an X-ray
	must wait for	an earache
		his house
		ill

Now write nine sentences.
利用上表中的短语,模仿例句写出9句话。

Example:

He says he feels ill.

Lesson 103 The French test 法语考试

 Listen to the tape then answer this question. How long did the exam last?
听录音, 然后回答问题 。考试持续了多长时间?

GARY :   How was the exam, Richard?

RICHARD : Not too bad.

               I think I passed in

               English and Mathematics.

               The questions were very easy.

               How about you, Gary?

GARY :   The English and Maths papers

               weren't easy enough for me.

               I hope I haven't failed.

RICHARD : I think I failed the French paper.

               I could answer sixteen of the questions.

               They were very easy.

               But I couldn't answer the rest.

               They were too difficult for me.

GARY :   French tests are awful, aren't they?

RICHARD : I hate them.

               I'm sure I've got a low mark.

GARY :   Oh, cheer up!

               Perhaps we didn't do too badly.

               The guy next to me

               wrote his name

               at the top of the paper.

RICHARD : Yes?

GARY :   Then he sat there

               and looked at it for three hours!

He didn't write a word!

New words and expressions 生词和短语

exam /ɪɡ'zæm/ n. 考试

pass /pɑːs/ v. 及格, 通过

mathematics /ˌmæθə'mætɪks/ (maths /mæθs/ 是缩写)
    n. 数学

question /'kwestʃən/ n. 问题

easy /'iːzi/ adj. 容易的

enough /ɪ'nʌf/ adv. 足够地

paper /'peɪpə/ n. 考卷

fail /feɪl/ v. 未及格, 失败

answer /'ɑːnsə/ v. 回答

mark /mɑːk/ n. 分数

rest /rest/ n. 其他的东西

difficult /'dɪfɪkəlt/ adj. 困难的

hate /heɪt/ v. 讨厌

low /ləʊ/ adj. 低的

cheer /tʃɪə/ v. 振作, 振奋

guy /ɡaɪ/ n. 家伙, 人

top /tɒp/ n. 上方, 顶部

Notes on the text 课文注释

1 I think I passed in English and Mathematics. 我想我的英语和数学及格了。如果说通过某一个考试, 直接用动词 pass; 如果说通过某一科目, 则用 pass in。

2 the English and Maths papers, 英文和数学卷子。

   paper 这个词当 "试卷" 讲时, 是可数名词。

3 How about . . .? ……怎么样?

   用于征求他人意见或询问情况。

4 easy enough for me, 是指对我来说不难, 我可以完成和通过。而 too difficult for me 是指对我来说太难了, 无法完成和通过。

5 cheer up, 振作起来。

参考译文

加   里: 考试考得怎样, 理查德?

理查德: 不算太坏, 我想我的英语和数学及格了。题目很容易。加里, 你怎么样?

加   里: 英语和数学试题对我来说不那么容易。我希望别不及格。

理查德: 我想我的法语及不了格, 我能回答其中的16道题。这些题很容易。

      但我回答不出其余的题。那些题对我来说太难了。

加   里: 法语考试太可怕了, 你说呢?

理查德: 我讨厌法语考试。我的成绩肯定很低。

加   里: 啊, 别灰心! 或许我们考得还不太糟。坐在我旁边的那个人只在试卷顶端写了自己的名字。

理查德: 是吗?

加   里: 然后他就坐在那儿, 对着考卷看了3个小时, 一个字也没写!

Lesson 104 Too, very, enough 太、非常、足够

 Listen to the tape and answer the questions.
听录音并回答问题。

> I could answer the questions.
> They were very easy.
> I couldn't answer the questions.
> They were too difficult.
> The questions were easy enough for me to answer.
> The questions were too difficult for me to answer.

A

B

C

D

answer all the questions

answer all the questions

easy

difficult

clever

stupid

E

F

G

H

buy the car

eat the cakes

cheap

expensive

fresh

stale

I

J

K

L

hear the stereo

climb the wall

loud

low

low

high

M

N

O

P

eat the pear

eat the orange

soft

hard

sweet

sour

New words and expressions 生词和短语

clever /'klevə/ *adj.* 聪明的
stupid /'stjuːpɪd/ *adj.* 笨的
cheap /tʃiːp/ *adj.* 便宜的
expensive /ɪk'spensɪv/ *adj.* 贵的
fresh /freʃ/ *adj.* 新鲜的
stale /steɪl/ *adj.* 不新鲜的, 变味的
low /ləʊ/ *adj.* 低的, 矮的

loud /laʊd/ *adj.* 大声的
high /haɪ/ *adj.* 高的
hard /haːd/ *adj.* 硬的
sweet /swiːt/ *adj.* 甜的
soft /sɒft/ *adj.* 软的
sour /saʊə/ *adj.* 酸的

Written exercises 书面练习

A Complete these sentences using *too, very* or *enough*.
  完成以下句子, 用 *too, very* 或 *enough* 填空。

1 I couldn't speak to the boss. He was _____ busy.
2 I couldn't go out. It was _____ cold for me to go out.
3 I could answer all the questions. They were _____ easy.
4 Is that suitcase light _____ for you to carry?
5 Is your brother old _____ to be a member of our association?
6 They couldn't see that film. They were _____ young.

B Answer these questions.
  模仿例句回答以下问题。

Examples:

Could he answer all the questions? (Yes/easy)
Yes, he could. They were easy enough for him to answer.
Could he answer all the questions? (No/difficult)
No, he couldn't. They were too difficult for him to answer.

1	Could he buy the car?	(Yes/cheap)
2	Could he buy the car?	(No/expensive)
3	Could they eat the cakes?	(Yes/fresh)
4	Could they eat the cakes?	(No/stale)
5	Could they hear the stereo?	(Yes/loud)
6	Could they hear the stereo?	(No/low)
7	Could he climb the wall?	(Yes/low)
8	Could he climb the wall?	(No/high)
9	Could she eat the pear?	(Yes/soft)
10	Could she eat the pear?	(No/hard)
11	Could she eat the orange?	(Yes/sweet)
12	Could she eat the orange?	(No/sour)

Lesson 105 Full of mistakes 错误百出

 Listen to the tape then answer this question. What was Sandra's present?
听录音, 然后回答问题 。给桑德拉的礼物是什么?

THE BOSS : Where's Sandra, Bob?

I want her.

BOB : Do you want to speak to her?

THE BOSS : Yes, I do.

I want her to come to my office.

Tell her to come at once.

SANDRA : Did you want to see me?

THE BOSS : Ah, yes, Sandra.

How do you spell 'intelligent'?

Can you tell me?

SANDRA : I-N-T-E-L-L-I-G-E-N-T.

THE BOSS : That's right.

You've typed it with only one 'L'.

This letter's full of mistakes.

I want you to type it again.

SANDRA : Yes, I'll do that.

I'm sorry about that.

THE BOSS : And here's a little present for you.

SANDRA : What is it?

THE BOSS : It's a dictionary.

I hope it'll help you.

New words and expressions 生词和短语

spell /spel/ (spelt /spelt/, spelt) v. 拼写

intelligent /ɪnˈtelɪdʒənt/ adj. 聪明的, 有智慧的

mistake /mɪˈsteɪk/ n. 错误

present /ˈprezənt/ n. 礼物

dictionary /ˈdɪkʃənəri/ n. 词典

Notes on the text 课文注释

1 Do you want to speak to her?

在这句话中, to speak 是动词 want 的宾语, 而这个结构 —— 动词原形前加 to —— 在英文中被称为动词不定式。本课用动词不定式作宾语的例句还有:

I want her to come to my office;

Tell her to come at once;

Did you want to see me;

I want you to type it again 等。

2 full of . . ., 充满了……。

3 And here's . . . 。

这里 and 表示承上启下, 使上下文紧密联系, 当 "于是"、"因此" 讲。

参考译文

老　板: 鲍勃, 桑德拉在哪儿? 我要找她。

鲍　勃: 您要同她谈话吗?

老　板: 是的, 我要她到我的办公室来。叫她马上就来。

桑德拉: 您找我吗?

老　板: 啊, 是的, 桑德拉。"intelligent" 怎样拼写? 你能告诉我吗?

桑德拉: I — N — T — E — L — L — I — G — E — N — T。

老　板: 对的。但你只打了 1 个 "L"。这封信里错误百出。我要你重打一遍。

桑德拉: 是, 我重打。对此我感到很抱歉。

老　板: 这里有一件小礼物送你。

桑德拉: 是什么?

老　板: 是本词典。我希望它能对你有所帮助。

Lesson 106　I want you/him/her/them to . . .
　　　　　　　　我要你／他／她／他们……
　　　　　　　　Tell him/her/them to . . .
　　　　　　　　告诉他／她／他们……

 Listen to the tape and answer the questions.
听录音并回答问题。

K

carry it

L

correct it

M

listen to it

N

describe it

O

move it

P

try it

Q

finish it

R

keep it

I don't want you/him/her/them to . . . 我不要你／他／她／他们……
Tell him/her/them not to . . . 告诉他／她／他们不要……

S

hurt yourself

T

slip

U

fall

V

miss it

W

break it

X

drive it

Y

lose it

Z

cut yourself

New words and expressions 生词和短语

carry /'kæri/ v. 带
keep /ki:p/ v. 保存, 保留

correct /kə'rekt/ v. 改正, 纠正

Written exercises 书面练习

A Rewrite these sentences.
　模仿例句将以下祈使句改写成带有动词不定式的陈述句:

Example:

Please repair it. *I want you to repair it.*

1 Please spell it.　　　　3 Please wear it.　　　　5 Please tell them.
2 Please telephone him.　　4 Please ask her.　　　　6 Please help us.

B Write questions and answers.
　模仿例句改写以下句子。

Example:

Type it again!
What do you want me to do? I want you to type it again.

1 Carry it!　　　3 Listen to it!　　　5 Move it!　　　7 Finish it!
2 Correct it!　　4 Describe it!　　　6 Try it!　　　　8 Keep it!

C Rewrite these sentences.
　模仿例句改写以下句子, 注意不定式的否定形式。

Example:

Don't type it again! (He/her)
He is telling her not to type it again. He doesn't want her to type it again.

1 Don't hurt yourself! (She/him)　　3 Don't fall! (She/him)　　　5 Don't break it! (She/him)
2 Don't slip! (She/him)　　　　　　4 Don't miss it! (She/them)　　6 Don't drive it! (He/her)

D Answer these questions.
　模仿例句回答以下问题。

Example:

Why is he speaking to her? (type it again)　　*Because he doesn't want her to type it again.*

1 Why is she speaking to him? (hurt himself)　　4 Why is she speaking to them? (miss it)
2 Why is she speaking to him? (slip)　　　　　　5 Why is she speaking to him? (break it)
3 Why is she speaking to him? (fall)　　　　　　6 Why is he speaking to her? (drive it)

Lesson 107   It's too small.   太小了。

Listen to the tape then answer this question.
What kind of dress does the lady want?
听录音，然后回答问题。这位女士想要什么样的服装？

ASSISTANT : Do you like this dress, madam?

LADY :   I like the colour very much.

It's a lovely dress,

but it's too small for me.

ASSISTANT : What about this one?

It's a lovely dress.

It's very smart.

Short skirts are in fashion now.

Would you like to try it?

LADY :   All right.

LADY :   I'm afraid this green dress

is too small for me as well.

It's smaller than the blue one.

LADY :   I don't like the colour either.

It doesn't suit me at all.

I think the blue dress is prettier.

LADY :   Could you show me

another blue dress?

I want a dress like that one,

but it must be my size.

ASSISTANT : I'm afraid I haven't got a larger dress.

This is the largest dress in the shop.

New words and expressions 生词和短语

madam /'mædəm/ *n.* 夫人, 女士（对妇女的尊称）

smart /smɑːt/ *adj.* 漂亮的

as well /əz-'wel/ 同样

suit /suːt/ *v.* 适于

pretty /'prɪti/ *adj.* 漂亮的

Notes on the text 课文注释

1 madam, 是对妇女的一种尊称, 服务行业的人员常用此称呼; 同时, 对于不知姓名的女士也可以用此来表示尊重。这个单词也可拼作 ma'am /mæm/。

2 Would you like . . . ? 你愿意……吗? 用来表示委婉的请求或提议。

3 It's smaller than the blue one. 它比那套蓝色的小一些。
在英文中, 当我们把一个人或物与另一个人或物进行比较时, 就要用形容词的比较级。大多数单音节的形容词的比较级是在原级后面加上 -er, 如 small — smaller, large — larger; 有些以 -y 结尾的双音节形容词, 如果 -y 前面是一个辅音字母, 变比较级时就要把 -y 先变为 -i, 然后再加 -er, 如 pretty — prettier。
如果在句子中提到了对比的双方, 就必须在比较级后面加上 than, 如 It's smaller than the blue one. 如果形容词比较级所指很清楚, 比较级也可以独立存在, 如 I haven't got a larger dress.

4 Could you . . . ?
用在表示请求, 比 Can you . . . ? 更婉转客气。
例: Could you tell me the way to the post office?
请你告诉我去邮局怎么走好吗?

5 This is the largest dress in the shop. 这是店里最大的一件衣服。
句中使用了形容词的最高级, 它是在形容词原级后面加上-est, 在最高级形容词之前要加定冠词 the。
最高级用在将一个人或物与其他一个以上的人或物作比较时。

参考译文

店员: 夫人, 您喜欢这件衣服吗?
女士: 我很喜欢这颜色。这是件漂亮的衣服, 可是对我来说太小了。

店员: 这件怎么样? 这是件漂亮的衣服, 它很时髦。短裙现在正流行。您要试一试吗?
女士: 好吧。

女士: 恐怕这件绿色的我穿着也太小了。它比那件蓝色的还要小。

女士: 我也不喜欢这种颜色。这颜色我穿根本不合适。我认为那件蓝色的更漂亮些。

女士: 您能再给我看一件蓝色的吗? 我想要一件和那件一样的, 但必须是我的尺寸。

店员: 恐怕没有更大的了。这是店里最大的一件。

Lesson 108　How do they compare? 比一比

 Listen to the tape and answer the questions.
听录音并回答问题 。

A

Sophie is tall.

B

Paul is taller
than Sophie.

C

Hans is the tallest
student in our class.

D

It is hot today.

E

It was hotter
yesterday. .

F

The day before yesterday
was the hottest day
in the year.

G

There was a large
crowd at the race
last year.

H

This year the
crowd is larger.

I

It is the largest
crowd I have ever seen.

J

The brown suitcase
is heavy.

K

The blue suitcase
is heavier than
the brown one.

L

The green suitcase is
the heaviest of them all.

Written exercises 书面练习

A Look at these words.
注意这些形容词的比较级形式。

cold — colder; nice — nicer; hot — hotter; heavy — heavier.

Now complete these sentences.
模仿例句完成以下句子。

Example:

It is warm today, but it was _____ yesterday.
It is warm today, but it was warmer yesterday.

1 It is cool today, but it was _____ yesterday.
2 It is wet today, but it was _____ yesterday.
3 He's late again today, but he was _____ yesterday.
4 This test is easy, but that one is _____ .
5 This bookcase is large, but that one is _____ .

B Write new sentences.
模仿例句改写以下句子。

Example:

I am very young.
I am younger than you are.
I am the youngest in the class.

1 I am very old.   3 I am very lazy.   5 I am very lucky.   7 I am very thin.
2 I am very tall.   4 I am very heavy.   6 I am very fat.   8 I am very big.

C Write new sentences.
模仿例句改写以下句子。

Example:

This policeman is tall.
But that policeman is taller.
He is the tallest policeman I have ever seen.

1 This street is clean.   3 This river is long.   5 This knife is blunt.
2 This man is old.   4 This woman is short.   6 This car is cheap.

Lesson 109 A good idea 好主意

 Listen to the tape then answer this question.
What does Jane have with her coffee?
听录音, 然后回答问题。喝咖啡时简吃了什么?

CHARLOTTE : Shall I make some coffee, Jane?

JANE : That's a good idea, Charlotte.

CHARLOTTE : It's ready.
Do you want any milk?

JANE : Just a little, please.

CHARLOTTE : What about some sugar?
Two teaspoonfuls?

JANE : No, less than that.
One and a half teaspoonfuls, please.
That's enough for me.

JANE : That was very nice.

CHARLOTTE : Would you like some more?

JANE : Yes, please.

JANE : I'd like a cigarette, too.
May I have one?

CHARLOTTE : Of course.
I think there are a few in that box.

JANE : I'm afraid it's empty.

CHARLOTTE : What a pity!

JANE : It doesn't matter.

CHARLOTTE : Have a biscuit instead.
Eat more and smoke less!

JANE : That's very good advice!

New words and expressions 生词和短语

idea /aɪ'dɪə/ n. 主意

a little 少许（用于不可数名词之前）

teaspoonful /'tiːspuːnfʊl/ n. 一满茶匙

less /les/ adj. （little 的比较级）较少的, 更小的

a few /ə-'fjuː/ 几个（用于可数名词之前）

pity /'pɪti/ n. 遗憾

instead /ɪn'sted/ adv. 代替

advice /əd'vaɪs/ n. 建议, 忠告

Notes on the text 课文注释

1 less than that, 意思是"比那稍微少一些", 其中的 that 指上文中的 two teaspoonfuls 。

2 I'd = I would；I'd like . . . , 我想要…… 。

3 What a pity! 真遗憾。英语中常用"What a + 可数名词"和"What + 不可数名词"的结构来表示感叹 。

参考译文

夏洛特： 我来煮点咖啡好吗, 简?

简 ： 这是个好主意, 夏洛特 。

夏洛特： 咖啡好了, 你要放点奶吗?

简 ： 请稍加一点 。

夏洛特： 加些糖怎么样? 两茶匙行吗?

简 ： 不, 再少一些 。请放一勺半 。那对我已足够了 。

简 ： 太好了 。

夏洛特： 你再来点儿吗?

简 ： 好的, 请再来一点 。

简 ： 我还想抽支烟 。可以给我一支吗?

夏洛特： 当然可以 。我想那个盒子里有一些 。

简 ： 恐怕盒子是空的 。

夏洛特： 真遗憾!

简 ： 没关系 。

夏洛特： 那就吃块饼干吧 。多吃点儿, 少抽点儿!

简 ： 这是极好的忠告啊!

Lesson 110　How do they compare? 比一比

 Listen to the tape and answer the questions.
听录音并回答问题 。

I

Have you got any chocolate?

I haven't got much.

J

I've got more than you have.

K

I've got the most.

L

Have you got any chocolate?

I've got very little.

M

I've got less than you have.

N

I've got the least.

O

Have you made any mistakes?

I haven't made many.

P

I've made more than you
have.

Q

I've made the most.

R

Have you made any mistakes?

I've made very few.

S

I've made fewer than you
have.

T

I've made the fewest.

U

You must see my new car.

It's very good.

V

This one's better.

W

This one's the best
I've ever seen.

X

You mustn't go to that restaurant.

It's very bad.

Y

This one's worse.

Z

This one's the worst
I've ever seen.

New words and expressions 生词和短语

most /məʊst/ *adj.* （many, much 的最高级）最多的
least /liːst/ *adj.* （little 的最高级）最小的, 最少的
best /best/ *adj.* （good 的最高级）最好的

worse /wɜːs/ *adj.* （bad 的比较级）更坏的
worst /wɜːst/ *adj.* （bad 的最高级）最坏的

Written exercises 书面练习

A Complete these sentences using *much, many, less* or *fewer*.
　　完成以下句子, 用 *much, many, less* 或 *fewer* 填空。

1 I haven't got any pens. I haven't got _____ either.
2 I've got some money. I've got _____ than you have.
3 I haven't got any money. I haven't got _____ either.
4 I've got some books. I've got _____ than you have.

B Answer these questions.
　　模仿例句回答以下问题。

Examples:

Have you got any coffee? — *I haven't got much coffee. I've got very little.*
Have you got any biscuits? — *I haven't got many biscuits. I've got very few.*

1 Have you got any jam?　　　3 Have you got any oranges?　　5 Have you got any meat?
2 Have you got any potatoes?　4 Have you got any vegetables?　6 Have you got any money?

C Write new sentences.
　　模仿例句将以下句子改成比较级。

Example:

I've got some coffee.
I've got more coffee than you have.

1 I've got some soap.　　　3 I've got some books.　　5 I've got some eggs.
2 I've got some fruit.　　　4 I've got some presents.　6 I've got some stationery.

D Write new sentences.
　　模仿例句改写以下句子。

Examples:

I've got some coffee. — *I've got less coffee than you have. I've got the least.*
I've got some biscuits. — *I've got fewer than you have. I've got the fewest.*

1 I've got some jam.　　　3 I've got some vegetables.　　5 I've got some meat.
2 I've got some potatoes.　4 I've got some oranges.　　　6 I've got some money.

Lesson 111   The most expensive model 最昂贵的型号

Listen to the tape then answer this question.
Can Mr. Frith buy the television on instalments? How does it work?
听录音, 然后回答问题 。弗里斯先生可以用分期付款的方式购买电视机
吗? 如何操作呢?

MR. FRITH :   I like this television very much.
              How much does it cost?
ASSISTANT : It's the most expensive model
              in the shop.
              It costs five hundred pounds.

MRS. FRITH : That's too expensive for us.
              We can't afford all that money.

ASSISTANT : This model's less expensive
              than that one.
              It's only three hundred pounds.
              But, of course,
              it's not as good as the expensive one.

MR. FRITH :   I don't like this model.
              The other model's more expensive,
              but it's worth the money.

MR. FRITH :   Can we buy it on instalments?
ASSISTANT : Of course.
              You can pay a deposit of thirty pounds,
              and then fourteen pounds a month
              for three years.

MR. FRITH :   Do you like it, dear?
MRS. FRITH : I certainly do,
              but I don't like the price.
              You always want the best,
              but we can't afford it.
              Sometimes you think
              you're a millionaire!
MR. FRITH :   Millionaires don't buy things
              on instalments!

225

New words and expressions 生词和短语

model /'mɒdl/ *n.* 型号, 式样
afford /ə'fɔːd/ *v.* 付得起（钱）
deposit /dɪ'pɒzɪt/ *n.* 预付定金

instalment /ɪn'stɔːlmənt/ *n.* 分期付款
price /praɪs/ *n.* 价格
millionaire /ˌmɪljə'neə/ *n.* 百万富翁

Notes on the text 课文注释

1 大多数两个以上音节的形容词可与 more/less 连用构成其比较级形式, 与 most/least 连用构成其最高级形式, 如本课中的几个例子: This model's less expensive than that one; The other model's more expensive; It's the most expensive model in the shop.

2 it's not as good as the expensive one, 它不如那种价格高的好。not as ... as ... 可以用来进行比较, 意思是, 放在前面的人或物在程度上低于后面的人或物。

3 buy ... on instalments, 以分期付款的方式购买。

参考译文

弗里斯先生: 我非常喜欢这台电视机。请问它多少钱?
店　　员: 这是店里最贵的型号。它的售价是 500 英镑。

弗里斯夫人: 这对我们来说太贵了。我们花不起那么多钱。

店　　员: 这种型号的比那种要便宜些。它只要 300 英镑。但是, 它当然没有价钱高的那种好。

弗里斯先生: 我不喜欢这种型号。那一种型号价格是贵一些, 但它值这么多钱。

弗里斯先生: 我们可以用分期付款的方式购买吗?
店　　员: 当然可以。您可以先付 30 英镑定金, 然后每月 14 镑, 3 年付清。

弗里斯先生: 你喜欢吗, 亲爱的?
弗里斯夫人: 我当然喜欢, 但是我不喜欢这个价钱。你总是要买最好的, 可我们买不起。有时候你以为自己是个百万富翁!
弗里斯先生: 百万富翁是不会分期付款买东西的!

Lesson 112 How do they compare? 比一比

 Listen to the tape and answer the questions.
听录音并回答问题。

As . . . as 像……一样

a

sweet

b
tall

c

short

d
old

e

blunt

f

sharp

Not as . . . as 不像……一样

g

clean

h

fat

i

smart

j

light

k

new

l

expensive

m

This test is
difficult.

n

This test is
more difficult.

o

This is the most difficult
test I have ever done!

p

This book is
interesting.

q

This book is
less interesting.

r

This is the least interesting
book I have ever read!

Written exercises 书面练习

A Complete these sentences.
   模仿例句完成以下句子。

Examples:

This dress is long, but that one is _____ .
This dress is long, but that one is longer.
Tom is intelligent, but Bill is _____ .
Tom is intelligent, but Bill is more intelligent.

1 This book is cheap, but that one is _____ .
2 This book is expensive, but that one is _____ .
3 This question is easy, but that one is _____ .
4 This question is difficult, but that one is _____ .

B Write questions and answers.
   模仿例句提问并回答。

Example:

green apple/sweet/red apple
Is the green apple as sweet as the red apple?
No, it isn't. The green apple isn't as sweet as the red apple.

1 policeman/tall/policewoman   3 boy/old/girl   5 blue car/clean/red car
2 man/short/woman   4 red pencil/blunt/green pencil 6 woman/fat/man

C Write new sentences.
   模仿例句改写以下句子。

Examples:

This test is less difficult. (ever done)
No, it isn't. It is more difficult.
It's the most difficult test I've ever done.

My book is more interesting than yours. (ever read)
No, it isn't. It is less interesting.
It's the least interesting book I've ever read.

1 My radio is less expensive than yours. (ever seen)
2 Tom is less intelligent than Bill. (person/ever met)
3 My book is less interesting than yours. (ever read)
4 This test is more difficult. (ever done)

Lesson 113　Small change　零钱

 Listen to the tape then answer this question.
Who has got some small change?
听录音，然后回答问题。谁有零钱？

CONDUCTOR :	Fares, please!
MAN :	Trafalgar Square, please.
CONDUCTOR :	I'm sorry, sir.
	I can't change a ten-pound note.
	Haven't you got
	any small change?
MAN :	I've got no small change,
	I'm afraid.
CONDUCTOR :	I'll ask some of the passengers.

CONDUCTOR :	Have you any small change, sir?
1st PASSENGER :	I'm sorry.
	I've got none.
2nd PASSENGER :	I haven't got any either.

CONDUCTOR :	Can you change
	this ten-pound note, madam?
3rd PASSENGER :	I'm afraid I can't.
4th PASSENGER :	Neither can I.

CONDUCTOR :	I'm very sorry, sir.
	You must get off the bus.
	None of our passengers
	can change this note.
	They're all millionaires!

TWO TRAMPS :	Except us.
1st TRAMP :	I've got some small change.
2nd TRAMP :	So have I.

New words and expressions 生词和短语

conductor /kən'dʌktə/ *n.* 售票员

fare /feə/ *n.* 车费, 车票

change /tʃeɪndʒ/ *v.* 兑换（钱）

note /nəʊt/ *n.* 纸币

passenger /'pæsɪndʒə/ *n.* 乘客

none /nʌn/ *pron.* 没有任何东西

neither /'naɪðə/ *adv.* 也不

get off 下车

tramp /træmp/ *n.* 流浪汉

except /ɪk'sept/ *prep.* 除……外

Notes on the text 课文注释

1 Fares, please! 请买票! 这是公共车辆售票员用语。

2 Trafalgar Square, 特拉法加广场, 位于伦敦市区。

3 I've got no small change, 我没有一点儿零钱。no +名词表示所指的东西全然没有, 以上这句话比 "I haven't got any small change." 更强调没有任何一点儿零钱。

4 I've got none. 这里是指零钱（不可数名词）。none 也可与可数名词连用, 如 none of our passengers can change this note.

5 Neither can I.
当有人说了一句否定意义的话, 其否定的内容也适于你或另外的人或事物时, 可以采用这种简略的句式。注意这种简略句式中主语和动词（包括 be）的顺序。

6 get off the bus, 下车。

7 So have I.
当有人说了一句肯定意义的话, 其肯定的内容也适于你或另外的人或事物时, 可以采用这种简略的句式。注意这种简略句式中主语和动词（包括 be）的顺序。

参考译文

售票员: 请买票!

男　子: 请买一张到特拉法加广场的票。

售票员: 对不起, 我找不开 10 英镑的钞票。您没有零钱吗?

男　子: 恐怕我没有零钱。

售票员: 我来问问其他乘客。

售票员: 先生, 您有零钱吗?

乘客 1: 对不起, 我没有。

乘客 2: 我也没有。

售票员: 夫人, 您能把这 10 英镑的钞票换开吗?

乘客 3: 恐怕不能。

乘客 4: 我也不能。

售票员: 非常抱歉, 先生。您必须下车。我们的乘客中没人能换开这张钞票。他们都是百万富翁!

二流浪汉: 我们俩除外。

流浪汉 1: 我有零钱。

流浪汉 2: 我也有。

Lesson 114 I've got none. 我没有。

 Listen to the tape and answer the questions.
听录音并回答问题。

o

Have you got any
chocolate?

p

I haven't got any.
I've got no chocolate.
I've got none.

q

I haven't any either.
Neither have I.

r

Have you got any
envelopes?

s

I haven't got any.
I've got no envelopes.
I've got none.

t

I haven't any either.
Neither have I.

u

Have you got any
cake?

v

I've got some.

w

So have I.

x

Have you got any
biscuits?

y

I've got some.

z

So have I.

231

Written exercises 书面练习

A Rewrite these sentences.
   模仿例句改写以下句子, 用 no 来表示否定 。

Example:

There isn't any milk in that bottle. *There is no milk in that bottle.*

1 There aren't any books on that shelf.
2 I haven't got any money.

3 There isn't any coffee in this tin.
4 I didn't see any cars in the street.

B Answer these questions.
   模仿例句回答以下问题 。

Example:

Have you got any beer?
No, I haven't got any beer.
I've got no beer. I've got none.

1 Have you got any milk?
2 Have you got any envelopes?

3 Have you got any magazines?
4 Have you got any bread?

C Write new sentences.
   模仿例句完成以下句子 。

Example:

I'm not tired.
Neither am I. I'm not tired, either.

1 I'm not hungry.
2 I didn't meet him.

3 I wasn't at church yesterday.
4 I don't like ice cream.

5 I can't swim.
6 I'm not a doctor.

D Write new sentences.
   模仿例句完成以下句子 。

Example:

I'm tired.
So am I. I'm tired, too.

1 I'm hungry.
2 I met him.

3 I was at church yesterday.
4 I like ice cream.

5 I can swim.
6 I'm a doctor.

Lesson 115 Knock, knock! 敲敲门!

Listen to the tape then answer this question. What does Jim have to drink?
听录音,然后回答问题。吉姆只能喝什么饮料?

HELEN : Isn't there anyone at home?

JIM : I'll knock again, Helen.

Everything's very quiet.

I'm sure there's no one at home.

HELEN : But that's impossible.

Carol and Tom invited us to lunch.

Look through the window.

HELEN : Can you see anything?

JIM : Nothing at all.

HELEN : Let's try the back door.

JIM : Look! Everyone's in the garden.

CAROL : Hello, Helen. Hello, Jim.

TOM : Everybody wants to have lunch

in the garden.

It's nice and warm out here.

CAROL : Come and have something to drink.

JIM : Thanks, Carol.

May I have a glass of beer please?

CAROL : Beer?

There's none left.

You can have some lemonade.

JIM : Lemonade!

TOM : Don't believe her, Jim.

She's only joking.

Have some beer!

233

New words and expressions 生词和短语

anyone /'eniwʌn/ *pron.* （用于疑问句、否定式）
　　任何人
knock /nɒk/ *v.* 敲，打
everything /'evriθɪŋ/ *pron.* 一切事物
quiet /'kwaɪət/ *adj.* 宁静的，安静的
impossible /ɪm'pɒsɪbəl/ *adj.* 不可能的

invite /ɪn'vaɪt/ *v.* 邀请
anything /'eniθɪŋ/ *pron.* 任何东西
nothing /'nʌθɪŋ/ *pron.* 什么也没有
lemonade /ˌlemə'neɪd/ *n.* 柠檬水
joke /dʒəʊk/ *v.* 开玩笑

Notes on the text 课文注释

1　Isn't there anyone at home? 家里没人吗? 在英语中，由 some, any, no, every 与 -one, -thing 组成的复合词，起代词作用，常被称为不定代词，这是因为我们常常不清楚其所指的是谁或什么。

2　nice and . . .
用于形容词或副词前以加强语气。一般表示褒义，但有时也用于贬义。

3　There's none left. 一点儿都没剩下。
句中的 left 是个过去分词，用来修饰 none。

参考译文

海　伦： 家里没有人吗?

吉　姆： 海伦，我再敲一次。毫无动静，肯定家里没有人。

海　伦： 但这是不可能的。卡罗尔和汤姆请我们来吃午饭。从窗子往里看看。

海　伦： 你能看见什么吗?

吉　姆： 什么也看不见。

海　伦： 让我们到后门去试试。

吉　姆： 瞧! 大家都在花园里。

卡罗尔： 你好，海伦。你好，吉姆。

汤　姆： 大家都想在花园里吃午饭。这外面挺暖和。

卡罗尔： 来喝点什么。

吉　姆： 谢谢，卡罗尔。给我一杯啤酒好吗?

卡罗尔： 啤酒? 一点都不剩了。你可以喝点柠檬水。

吉　姆： 柠檬水!

汤　姆： 吉姆，别信她的。她只是在开玩笑。喝点啤酒吧!

Lesson 116 Every, no, any and some 每一、无、若干和一些

 Listen to the tape and answer the questions.
听录音并回答问题。

Every	None	Any	Some
Everyone	No one	Anyone	Someone
Everybody	Nobody	Anybody	Somebody
Everything	Nothing	Anything	Something
Everywhere	Nowhere	Anywhere	Somewhere

a

Everyone is asleep.
Everybody is asleep.

b

Everything is untidy.

c

I looked for my pen
everywhere.

d

Is there anyone
at home?
Is there anybody at home?

e

Is there anything
in that box?

f

I couldn't find my pen
anywhere.

g

There's no one
at home.
There's nobody
at home.

h

There's nothing
in this box.

i

Where did you go
yesterday?
Nowhere. I stayed
at home.

j

There's someone
in the garden.
There's somebody
in the garden.

k

There's something
under that chair!

l

My glasses must be
somewhere!
You're wearing them!

235

New words and expressions 生词和短语

asleep /əˈsliːp/ *adj.* 睡觉, 睡着（用作表语）

glasses /ˈglɑːsiz/ *n.* 眼镜

Written exercises 书面练习

A Rewrite these sentences.
　　模仿例句改写以下句子。

Example:

I didn't buy *anything*. *I bought nothing.*

1 I didn't do *anything*.　　2 I didn't see *anyone*.　　3 I didn't go *anywhere*.　　4 I didn't meet *anybody*.

B Answer these questions using *any/no* with -one, -body, -thing, -where.
　　模仿例句回答以下问题。

Example:

Did you see anyone?

No, I didn't see anyone. I saw no one.

1 Did you hear anything?　　3 Did you go anywhere?　　5 Did you write to anybody?
2 Did you speak to anyone?　　4 Did you buy anything?　　6 Did you meet anyone?

C Rewrite these sentences.
　　模仿例句改写以下句子。

Example:

They're all watching television.

Everyone's watching television.

1 They're all looking out of the window.　　3 They're all eating.
2 They're all hurrying to work.　　4 They're all drinking lemonade.

D Answer these questions.
　　模仿例句回答以下问题。

Example:

Have you got anything to wear? — *No, I haven't got anything to wear. I've got nothing to wear.*
What about Penny? — *She's got something to wear.*

1 Have you got anything to eat? What about Sam?
2 Have you got anything to do? What about the children?
3 Have you got anything to drink? What about Jane?
4 Have you got anything to read? What about Alan?

Lesson 117　Tommy's breakfast 汤米的早餐

 Listen to the tape then answer this question.
What does she mean by 'change' in the last sentence?
听录音，然后回答问题。最后一句话中的 "change" 是什么意思？

When my husband was going
into the dining room this morning,
he dropped some coins on the floor.

1

There were coins everywhere.
We looked for them,
but we could not find them all.

2

While we were having breakfast,
our little boy, Tommy,
found two small coins on the floor.

3

He put them both into his mouth.
We both tried to get the coins,
but it was too late.
Tommy had already swallowed them!

4

Later that morning,
when I was doing the housework,
my husband phoned me
from the office.

5

'How's Tommy?' he asked.
'I don't know,' I answered,
'Tommy's been to the toilet
three times this morning,
but I haven't had any change yet!'

6

New words and expressions 生词和短语

dining room 饭厅
coin /kɔɪn/ *n.* 硬币
mouth /maʊθ/ *n.* 嘴

swallow /'swɒləʊ/ *v.* 吞下
later /'leɪtə/ *adv.* 后来
toilet /'tɔɪlɪt/ *n.* 厕所, 盥洗室

Notes on the text 课文注释

1 在英文中表示过去某时正在进行的动作, 要用过去进行时。与现在进行时相比, 过去进行时的区别就在于要用 be 的过去式。过去进行时的例子有: When my husband was going into the dining room this morning . . . ; While we were having breakfast . . . 等。

2 them all, all 用来强调每一个硬币。从语法上来讲, all 是 them 的同位语。紧跟在一个名词或代词后, 进一步说明前面名词或代词是谁或什么东西的名词或代词, 叫同位语。

3 our little boy, Tommy,
   Tommy 是 boy 的同位语。

4 put them both . . .
   both 是 them 的同位语。

5 we both . . .
   both 是 we 的同位语。

6 Tommy had already swallowed them!
   句中用了过去完成时。过去完成时用来表示两个动作中, 发生在前的那个动作。显然, 句中 "咽下硬币" 的动作发生在夫妇俩能够把硬币从汤米手中抢过来之前。

7 later that morning, 那天上午的晚些时候。
   later 是副词 late 的比较级。

8 any change,
   change 是个多义词, 既有 "零钱" 的意思, 也有 "变化" 的意思。此处既可指 "硬币", 亦可指 "情况的变化"。这是 "双关" 修辞法。

参考译文

今天早晨我丈夫走进饭厅时, 把一些硬币掉在地上了。

到处都是硬币。我们虽然找了, 但没能把它们全部找到。

正当我们吃早饭时, 我们的儿子小汤米在地上找到了两枚小硬币。

他把这两枚硬币全都放进了嘴里。我们俩都试图把这两枚硬币弄出来, 但太迟了。汤米已经把硬币咽了下去!

那天上午的晚些时候, 当我正做家务时, 我丈夫从办公室打来电话。

"汤米怎么样?" 他问。"我不知道。" 我回答说。"今天上午汤米去了 3 次厕所了, 但我还没看到硬币!"

Lesson 118 What were you doing? 你那时正在做什么？

 Listen to the tape and answer the questions.
听录音并回答问题。

m

Someone knocked at the door
when I was having breakfast.

n

When I was leaving the house,
the postman arrived.

o

Just as I was opening the
front door, the telephone rang.

p

She slipped and hurt herself
while she was getting off the bus.

q

He cut himself
while he was shaving.

r

My wife was cooking the dinner
while I was working in the garden.

New words and expressions 生词和短语

ring /rɪŋ/ (rang /ræŋ/, rung /rʌŋ/) v. （钟、铃）鸣响

Written exercises 书面练习

A Rewrite these sentences using *when*.
模仿例句用 *when* 把两个句子合并成一句 。

Example:

He arrived. I had a bath. *He arrived when I was having a bath.*

1 He knocked at the door. I answered the phone.

2 He came downstairs. I had breakfast.

3 The phone rang. I washed the dishes.

4 The boss arrived. She typed a letter.

5 The train left. I bought the tickets.

6 It rained heavily. I drove to London.

B   Answer these questions.
模仿例句回答以下问题。

Example:

What were you doing when he arrived? (have a bath)
When he arrived I was having a bath.

1   What were you doing when he arrived? (cook a meal)
2   What were you doing when he arrived? (wash the dishes)
3   What were you doing when he arrived? (work in the garden)
4   What were you doing when he arrived? (type letters)
5   What were you doing when he arrived? (shave)
6   What were you doing when he arrived? (boil the milk)
7   What were you doing when he arrived? (phone my sister)
8   What were you doing when he arrived? (dust the bedroom)

C   Answer these questions.
模仿例句回答以下问题。

Example:

What was he doing while you were cooking the dinner?
(work in the garden)
While I was cooking the dinner, he was working in the garden.

1   What was he doing while you were cooking the dinner?
    (have a wash)
2   What was he doing while you were cooking the dinner?
    (watch television)
3   What was he doing while you were cooking the dinner?
    (clean his shoes)
4   What was he doing while you were cooking the dinner?
    (listen to the radio)
5   What was he doing while you were cooking the dinner?
    (change his suit)
6   What was he doing while you were cooking the dinner?
    (sit in the dining room)
7   What was he doing while you were cooking the dinner?
    (read the paper)
8   What was he doing while you were cooking the dinner?
    (drive home from work)

Lesson 119 A true story 一个真实的故事

 Listen to the tape then answer this question.
Who called out to the thieves in the dark?
听录音，然后回答问题。谁在暗处对窃贼喊了一声？

Do you like stories?
I want to tell you a true story.
It happened to a friend of mine a year ago.

While my friend, George, was reading in bed,
two thieves climbed into his kitchen.

After they had entered the house,
they went into the dining room.
It was very dark,
so they turned on a torch.

Suddenly, they heard a voice behind them.
'What's up? What's up?' someone called.
The thieves dropped the torch
and ran away as quickly as they could.

George heard the noise
and came downstairs quickly.

He turned on the light,
but he couldn't see anyone.
The thieves had already gone.

But George's parrot, Henry, was still there.
'What's up, George?' he called.
'Nothing, Henry,' George said and smiled.
'Go back to sleep.'

New words and expressions 生词和短语

story /'stɔːri/ n. 故事

happen /'hæpən/ v. 发生

thief /θiːf/ （复数 thieves /θiːvz/） n. 贼

enter /'entə/ v. 进入

dark /dɑːk/ adj. 黑暗的

torch /tɔːtʃ/ n. 手电筒

voice /vɔɪs/ n. （说话的）声音

parrot /'pærət/ n. 鹦鹉

Notes on the text 课文注释

1　as quickly as they could 是状语, 修饰 ran away 。第 1 个 as 是副词, 第 2 个 as 是连词, 引导比较状语从句 。could 后省略了 run, 是 "能跑多快就跑多快" 的意思 。

2　What's up? 干什么? 有什么事?

3　he called,

　　he 指 parrot 。英语中, 动物有时用 he 或 she 代替, 是 "拟人" 的写法 。

4　go back to sleep, 继续睡觉 。

参考译文

你喜欢听故事吗? 我要告诉你一个真实的故事 。这是一年前发生在我的一个朋友身上的故事 。

当我的朋友乔治在床上看书时, 两个小偷爬进了他的厨房 。

他们进到屋里后, 走进了饭厅 。饭厅里很暗, 于是他们打开了手电筒 。

突然他们听到身后有声音 。"什么事? 什么事?" 有人叫着 。小偷扔下了手电筒, 飞快地逃走了 。

乔治听到了响声, 迅速地下了楼 。

他打开灯, 但不见一个人 。小偷逃走了 。

但是乔治的鹦鹉亨利仍在那里 。"什么事, 乔治?" 它叫着 。"没事, 亨利 。" 乔治笑着说, "接着睡觉吧 。"

Lesson 120　It had already happened. 事情已经发生了。

 Listen to the tape and answer the questions.
听录音并回答问题。

s

I asked the price of the car,
but they had already sold it.

t

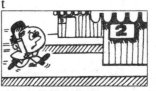

I ran to the platform quickly,
but the train had already left.

u

He gave us our exercise books
after he had corrected them.

v

She went on holiday
after she had taken the examination.

w

She had finished the housework
before she went out.

x

We had had dinner
before they arrived.

New words and expressions 生词和短语

exercise book /'eksəsaɪz-bʊk/ n. 练习本

Written exercises 书面练习

A　Rewrite these sentences using after.
用 after 把两个句子合并为一。

Example:

She went home. She typed the letter.
She went home after she had typed the letter.

1　He dropped the vase. He took it into the living room.

2　He bought another car. He sold his old one.

3　He swept the floor. He dusted everything.

4　She drank the milk. She boiled it.

5　He turned off the television. He saw the programme.

6　He went to bed. He did his homework.

B　Answer these questions.
　　模仿例句回答以下问题 。

Example:

Have you met him?

Yes, I have just met him. I had never met him before.

1　Have you seen it?

2　Have you read it?

3　Have you tried it?

4　Have you been there?

5　Have you written a letter in English?

6　Have you watched this programme?

C　Answer these questions.
　　模仿例句回答以下问题 。

Example:

Why didn't you sweep the floor? (She)

It was too late. She had already swept it.

1　Why didn't you paint the bookcase? (He)

2　Why didn't you dust the dressing table? (She)

3　Why didn't you telephone him? (You)

4　Why didn't you correct it? (You)

5　Why didn't you shut the door? (They)

6　Why didn't you make the bed? (She)

D　Write new sentences using *after*.
　　模仿例句, 使用 after 改写以下句子 。

Example:

Did you read the book? Yes, but I saw the film first.

I read the book after I had seen the film.

1　Did you go to the doctor? Yes, but I made an appointment first.

2　Did the boss leave the office? Yes, but he finished work first.

3　Did your wife go out? Yes, but she finished the housework first.

4　Did your teacher give you your exercise book? Yes, but he corrected it first.

5　Did your sister go on holiday? Yes, but she took the examination first.

6　Did you buy a new car? Yes, but I sold my old one first.

Lesson 121　The man in a hat　戴帽子的男士

Listen to the tape then answer this question.
Why didn't Caroline recognize the customer straight away?
听录音,然后回答问题。为什么卡罗琳没有马上认出那位顾客?

CUSTOMER : I bought
two expensive dictionaries here
half an hour ago,
but I forgot
to take them with me.

MANAGER : Who served you, sir?
CUSTOMER : The lady who is standing
behind the counter.

MANAGER : Which books did you buy?
CUSTOMER : The books
which are on the counter.

MANAGER : Did you serve this gentleman
half an hour ago, Caroline?
He says he's the man
who bought these books.
CAROLINE : I can't remember.
The man who I served
was wearing a hat.

MANAGER : Have you got a hat, sir?
CUSTOMER : Yes, I have.
MANAGER : Would you put it on, please?
CUSTOMER : All right.

MANAGER : Is this the man
that you served, Caroline?
CAROLINE : Yes.
I recognize him now.

New words and expressions 生词和短语

customer /ˈkʌstəmə/ n. 顾客

forget /fəˈget/ (forgot /fəˈgɒt/, forgotten /fəˈgɒtn/)
        v. 忘记

manager /ˈmænɪdʒə/ n. 经理

serve /sɜːv/ v. 照应, 服务, 接待

counter /ˈkaʊntə/ n. 柜台

recognize /ˈrekəgnaɪz/ v. 认出

Notes on the text 课文注释

1   to take them with me 把它们带上 。
    them 指 "两本词典"。

2   The lady who is standing behind the counter.
    这是一个省略句, 完整的句子是 "The lady who is standing behind the counter served me." 其中 who is standing behind the counter 是一个以关系代词 who 引导的定语从句, 用来修饰前面的名词 the lady 。本课带有定语从句的复合句还有: The books which are on the counter; He says he's the man who bought these books; The man who I served was wearing a hat; Is this the man that you served 等, 其中which, who, whom, that 均为关系代词 。

3   The man who I served was wearing a hat.
    这是另一个定语从句的例子 。由于被修饰的名词 the man 在定语从句中是动词 served 的宾语, 因此, 关系代词应该用宾格 whom, 但在口语中往往用主格who 。

参考译文

顾　客: 半小时以前我在这里买了两本很贵的辞典, 但是我忘了拿走 。

经　理: 是谁接待您的, 先生?
顾　客: 站在柜台后面的那位女士 。

经　理: 您买的是两本什么书?
顾　客: 就是柜台上的那两本 。

经　理: 卡罗琳, 半小时前你接待过这位先生吗? 他说他就是买这两本书的人 。
卡罗琳: 我记不起来了 。我接待的那个人戴着一顶帽子 。

经　理: 先生, 您有帽子吗?
顾　客: 有的, 我有帽子 。
经　理: 请您把帽子戴上好吗?
顾　客: 好吧 。

经　理: 卡罗琳, 这就是你接待过的那个人吗?
卡罗琳: 是他 。我现在认出他来了 。

Lesson 122 Who (whom), which and that 关系代词

 Listen to the tape and answer the questions.
听录音并回答问题。

1

Who served you?
The man who/that is
standing behind the
counter.

2

Who served you?
The woman who/that is
standing behind the
counter.

3

Who is making all
that noise?
The men who/that are
repairing the road.

4

I served him
yesterday.
He is the man who(m)/
that I served
yesterday.

5

I served her
yesterday.
She is the woman
who(m)/that I served
yesterday.

6

I saw them
yesterday.
They are the men
who(m)/that I saw
yesterday.

7

Which book did
you buy?
The book which/that
is on the counter.

8

Which books did
you buy?
The books which/that
are on the counter.

9

Which dog is yours?
The dog which/that
is carrying that
basket.

New words and expressions 生词和短语

road /rəʊd/ n. 路

Written exercises 书面练习

A Rewrite these sentences using *who, whom* or *which*.
用 *who, whom* 或 *which* 把以下每对句子改写成一句话 。

Examples:

She is the girl. *She* met me yesterday.
She is the girl who met me yesterday.

She is the girl. I met *her* yesterday.
She is the girl who (or whom) I met yesterday.

This is the book. I bought *it* yesterday.
This is the book which I bought yesterday.

1　This is the car. The mechanic repaired *it* yesterday.

2　He is the man. I invited *him* to the party.

3　These are the things. I bought *them* yesterday.

4　He is the man. *He* came here last week.

5　He is the policeman. *He* caught the thieves.

6　She is the nurse. *She* looked after me.

7　She is the woman. I met *her* at the party.

8　I am the person. *I* wrote to you.

B Write questions and answers.
模仿例句提问并回答 。

Example:

He served me.
Who served you? That man?
Yes, he's the man who served me.

1　She met him.　　3　She made it.　　5　He shut it.　　7　He told me.

2　He sat there.　　4　He read it.　　6　She took it.　　8　She saw me.

C Write questions and answers.
模仿例句提问并回答 。

Example:

I met him yesterday.
Whom did you meet yesterday? That man?
Yes, he's the man whom I met yesterday.

1　I saw him.　　　3　I invited him.　　5　I found him in the garden.　　7　I heard her.

2　I telephoned her.　4　I took him to the cinema.　6　I drove her to London.　　8　I remembered him.

248

Lesson 123 A trip to Australia 澳大利亚之行

Listen to the tape then answer this question.
Who is the man with the beard?
听录音，然后回答问题 。那个长着络腮胡子的人是谁?

MIKE : Look, Scott.
This is a photograph I took
during my trip to Australia.
SCOTT : Let me see it, Mike.

1

SCOTT : This is a good photograph.
Who are these people?
MIKE : They're people I met during the trip.

2

MIKE : That's the ship
we travelled on.
SCOTT : What a beautiful ship!

3

SCOTT : Who's this?
MIKE : That's the man I told you about.
Remember?
SCOTT : Ah yes.
The one who offered you
a job in Australia.
MIKE : That's right.

4

SCOTT : Who's this?
MIKE : Guess!
SCOTT : It's not you, is it?
MIKE : That's right.

5

MIKE : I grew a beard during the trip,
but I shaved it off
when I came home.
SCOTT : Why did you shave it off?
MIKE : My wife didn't like it!

6

New words and expressions 生词和短语

during /'djʊərɪŋ/ *prep.* 在……期间

trip /trɪp/ *n.* 旅行

travel /'trævəl/ *v.* 旅行

offer /'ɒfə/ *v.* 提供

job /dʒɒb/ *n.* 工作

guess /ges/ *v.* 猜

grow /grəʊ/ (grew /gruː/, grown /grəʊn/) *v.* 长,
让……生长

beard /bɪəd/ *n.* （下巴上的）胡子, 络腮胡子

Notes on the text 课文注释

1 This is a photograph I took . . .

这句话中的 I took during my trip to Australia 是一个定语从句, 用来修饰a photograph; 由于所修饰的名词在从句中作动词 took 的宾语, 因此, 引导从句的关系代词 that 往往省略。

2 They're people I met during the trip.

与注 1 的情况相同, 关系代词 whom 往往省略。

参考译文

迈　克：看, 这是我到澳大利亚旅行时拍的一张照片。

斯科特：让我看看, 迈克。

斯科特：这是一张很好的照片。这些人是谁?

迈　克：他们是我旅行时认识的人。

迈　克：这是我们所乘的那条船。

斯科特：多漂亮的船啊!

斯科特：这是谁?

迈　克：这就是我跟你说过的那个人。还记得吗?

斯科特：啊, 记得。就是在澳大利亚给你工作做的那个人。

迈　克：对。

斯科特：这是谁?

迈　克：你猜!

斯科特：这不是你, 对吗?

迈　克：不, 是我。

迈　克：我在旅行时留了胡子, 但我回到家时就把它刮了。

斯科特：你为什么把它刮了?

迈　克：我妻子不喜欢!

Lesson 124　(Who) / (whom), (which) and (that) 关系代词

 Listen to the tape and answer the questions.
听录音并回答问题。

1

Who served you?
The man standing
behind the counter.

2

Who served you?
The woman standing
behind the counter.

3

Who is making all
that noise?
The men repairing the
road.

4

I served him
yesterday.
He is the man
I served yesterday.

5

I served her
yesterday.
She is the woman
I served yesterday.

6

I saw them
yesterday.
They are the men
I saw yesterday.

7

What's this?
This is the book
I bought yesterday.

8

What are these?
These are the books
I bought yesterday.

9

What's this?
This is the kitten
I found in the garden.

New words and expressions 生词和短语

kitten /'kɪtn/ *n.* 小猫

Written exercises 书面练习

A Rewrite these sentences.
模仿例句把以下每对句子改写成一句话：

Examples:

She is the girl. I met *her* yesterday.
She is the girl I met yesterday.
This is the ship. I travelled on *it*.
This is the ship I travelled on.

This is the book. I bought *it* yesterday.
This is the book I bought yesterday.

1 She is the woman. I drove *her* to London.
2 That's the film. I saw *it*.
3 That's the man. I spoke to *him*.

4 They are the thieves. The police caught *them*.
5 These are the letters. I typed *them*.
6 These are the people. You asked me about *them*.

B Write questions and answers.
模仿例句提问并回答 。

Example:

I met that man yesterday.
Which man? That man?
Yes, that's the man I met yesterday.

1 I saw that man yesterday.
2 I repaired that car yesterday.
3 I drove that woman to London yesterday.

4 I bought that umbrella yesterday.
5 I took that medicine yesterday.
6 I invited that man to my house yesterday.

C Write new sentences.
模仿例句改写以下句子 。

Example:

This is the film. I told you about it.
That's right. This is the film you told me about.

1 This is the village. I wrote to you about it.
2 He is the person. I have heard about him.
3 This is the test. I spoke to you about it.

4 She is the woman. I read about her.
5 This is something new. I haven't thought about it.
6 This is something. I must decide about it.

Lesson 125 Tea for two 两个人一起喝茶

 Listen to the tape then answer this question.
Does Susan have tea by herself?
听录音，然后回答问题 。苏珊是一个人喝茶吗?

SUSAN : Can't you come in
and have tea now, Peter?

PETER : Not yet.
I must water the garden first.

1

SUSAN : Do you have to water it now?

PETER : I'm afraid I must.
Look at it!
It's terribly dry.

2

SUSAN : What a nuisance!

PETER : Last summer it was very dry, too.
Don't you remember?
I had to water it every day.

SUSAN : Well, I'll have tea by myself.

3

SUSAN : That was quick!
Have you finished already?

PETER : Yes.
Look out of the window.

4

SUSAN : It's raining!
That means
you don't need to water the garden.

PETER : That was a pleasant surprise.
It means I can have tea, instead.

5

New words and expressions 生词和短语

water /'wɔːtə/ v. 浇水

terribly /'terɪbli/ adv. 非常

dry /draɪ/ adj. 干燥的, 干的

nuisance /'njuːsəns/ n. 讨厌的东西或人

mean /miːn/ (meant /ment/, meant) v. 意味着, 意思是

surprise /sə'praɪz/ n. 惊奇, 意外的事

Notes on the text 课文注释

1 have to（过去式 had to）, 不得不, 必须 。
   have to 强调客观需要多一些 。must 则着重说明主观看法 。
2 What a nuisance! 真讨厌!
3 by myself, 我自己, 独自 。同样, 我们可以说 by yourself, by himself, by herself, by itself, by ourselves, by yourselves, by themselves, by oneself 。

参考译文

苏珊 ： 彼得, 你现在能进来喝茶吗?
彼得 ： 还不能 。我得先给花园浇水 。

苏珊 ： 你一定得现在浇吗?
彼得 ： 恐怕我得现在浇 。你看看, 干得厉害 。

苏珊 ： 真讨厌!
彼得 ： 去年夏天也是干得很 。你不记得了吗? 我不得不每天浇水 。
苏珊 ： 好吧, 我一个人喝茶了 。

苏珊 ： 好快啊! 你已经浇完了?
彼得 ： 是的 。你看看窗外 。

苏珊 ： 下雨了! 这就是说, 你不必给花园浇水了 。
彼得 ： 这是意想不到的好事 。这意味着我反倒可以喝茶了 。

Lesson 126 Have to and do not need to 不得不和不必要

 Listen to the tape and answer the questions.
听录音并回答问题 。

1

Do you have to go now?
Yes, I have to leave
immediately.

2

Do you have to get up early
tomorrow morning?
Yes, I'll have to get up
at six o'clock.

3

Did you have to take a taxi?
I'm afraid I had to.
I couldn't get a bus.

4

Hasn't your friend arrived yet?
How long have you had to wait?
I've had to wait for two hours!

5

Do you have to water the garden?
No, I don't need to water it now.
It's going to rain.

6

Do we have to walk to the station?
No, we don't need to.
We can catch a bus.

New words and expressions 生词和短语

immediately /ɪ'miːdiətli/ *adv.* 立即地

Written exercises 书面练习

A Write questions and answers.
抄写以下句子，然后提问并写出相应的否定句。

Examples:

You have to leave early.
Do you have to leave early?
You don't have to leave early.

She must leave early.
Must she leave early?
She needn't leave early.

1 She has to decide immediately.
2 She must decide immediately.

3 We have to take a taxi.
4 We must take a taxi.

B Answer these questions.
用 *have to* 或 *has to* 回答问题。

Example:

I must go now. What about you?
I have to go, too.

1 I must telephone him. What about you?
2 I must wait for him. What about Mary?

3 I must meet her. What about Jim?
4 I must travel by ship. What about Tom and Mary?

C Write questions.
模仿例句改写提问。

Example:

I must go now.
Do you really have to go now?

1 I must telephone him.
2 Mary must wait for him.

3 Jim must meet her.
4 Tom and Mary must travel by ship.

Lesson 127　A famous actress　著名的女演员

Listen to the tape then answer this question.
Who is only twenty-nine, and why is it so unclear?

听录音，然后回答问题。谁只有 29 岁？为什么这件事如此含糊不清？

KATE :　Can you recognize that woman, Liz?

LIZ :　　I think I can, Kate.

It must be Karen Marsh, the actress.

KATE :　I thought so.

Who's that beside her?

LIZ :　　That must be Conrad Reeves.

KATE :　Conrad Reeves, the actor?

It can't be.

Let me have another look.

I think you're right!

Isn't he her third husband?

LIZ :　　No. He must be her fourth or fifth.

KATE :　Doesn't Karen Marsh look old!

LIZ :　　She does, doesn't she!

I read she's twenty-nine,

but she must be at least forty.

KATE :　I'm sure she is.

LIZ :　　She was a famous actress

when I was still at school.

KATE :　That was a long time ago, wasn't it?

LIZ :　　Not *that* long ago!

I'm not more than twenty-nine myself.

New words and expressions 生词和短语

famous /'feɪməs/ *adj.* 著名的

actress /'æktrɪs/ *n.* 女演员

at least /ət-'liːst/ 至少

actor /'æktə/ *n.* 男演员

read /riːd/ (read /red/, read) *v.* 通过阅读得知

Notes on the text 课文注释

1　在 It must be Karen Marsh ... 这一句中, must be 是英文中用来表示根据事实所作的推论, 往往译为 "一定"。must be 的否定式是 can't be, 如 Kate 的话 "It can't be." 是对 Liz 的推论 ("That must be Conrad Reeves.") 的否定。同时, 请注意这里的 can't be (表示不可能) 和第 45 课中 I can't type this letter. (表示能力) 的区别。

2　Who's that beside her?

本句中 that 指人。

3　her fourth or fifth后面省略了 husband。

4　Not *that* long ago!

句中的that 是副词, 指像 Kate所说的 "那么" 遥远, 可译作 "那样"、"那么"。课文中用斜体印刷表示一种强调, 显然 Liz 对 Kate 的判断和对她本人年龄的估算很不满意。

参考译文

凯特：莉兹, 你能认出那个女人吗?

莉兹：我想我认得出来, 凯特。那一定是女演员卡伦·马什。

凯特：我也这样想。她旁边的那个人是谁?

莉兹：一定是康拉德·里弗斯。

凯特：康拉德·里弗斯, 那个男演员吗? 不可能是。让我再看一看。我想你是对的。他不是她的第 3 任丈夫吗?

莉兹：不, 他一定是她的第 4 任或第 5 任丈夫。

凯特：卡伦看上去可够老的!

莉兹：是的, 谁说不是呢! 我从报上看到她是 29 岁, 但她一定至少有 40 岁了。

凯特：我肯定她有 40 岁了。

莉兹：当我还是学生时, 她就是个著名的演员了。

凯特：那是好久以前的事了, 是吗?

莉兹：不, 没有那么久。我自己现在还没 29 岁呢。

Lesson 128 He can't be . . . 他不可能……
He must be . . . 他肯定是……

Listen to the tape and answer the questions.
听录音并回答问题。

1

He can't be ill.
He must be tired.

2

It can't be my new hat.
It must be my old one.

3

She can't be Danish.
She must be Swedish.

4

He can't be a dentist.
He must be a doctor.

5

She can't be forty.
She must be fifty.

6

It can't be the 20th.
It must be the 21st.

7

He can't be the youngest.
He must be the oldest.

8

He can't be reading.
He must be sleeping.

Written exercises 书面练习

A Rewrite these sentences, using either *has to* or *I think he is probably...*
    模仿例句，使用 has to 或 I think he is probably ...改写以下句子 。

Examples:

He must be home before six o'clock.

He has to be home before six o'clock.

He must be tired.

I think he is probably tired.

1 He must be here at six o'clock.
2 He must be busy.
3 He must be at the office early tomorrow.
4 He must be sleeping.
5 He must be French.
6 He must be in France next week.
7 He must be an engineer.

B Write new sentences.
    模仿例句改写下列句子 。

Example:

I think she's Danish. (Swedish)

I don't think so. She can't be Danish.
She must be Swedish.

1   I think she's Italian. (Greek)
2   I think he's English. (American)
3   I think they're Canadian. (Australian)
4   I think he's a mechanic. (engineer)
5   I think he's a bus conductor. (bus driver)
6   I think he's a sales rep. (the boss)
7   I think he's twenty-four. (thirty)
8   I think they're five. (seven)
9   I think he's seventy-six. (over eighty)
10 I think she's fifty-five. (under fifty)
11 I think it's the 21st today. (20th)
12 I think it's Tuesday today. (Wednesday)
13 I think it's the 2nd today. (3rd)
14 I think it's cheap. (expensive)
15 I think it's easy. (difficult)
16 I think she's old. (young)
17 I think they're early. (late)
18 I think he's reading. (sleeping)
19 I think they're listening to the radio. (watching television)
20 I think she's retiring. (looking for a new job)

Lesson 129 Seventy miles an hour 时速 70 英里

Listen to the tape then answer this question.
What does Ann advise her husband to do next time?
听录音，然后回答问题。安建议她的丈夫下次做什么？

ANN : Look, Gary!
That policeman's waving to you.
He wants you to stop.

POLICEMAN : Where do you think you are?
On a race track?
You must have been driving
at seventy miles an hour.
GARY : I can't have been.
POLICEMAN : I was doing eighty
when I overtook you.

POLICEMAN : Didn't you see the speed limit?
GARY : I'm afraid I didn't, officer.
I must have been dreaming.
ANN : He wasn't dreaming, officer.
I was telling him to drive slowly.
GARY : That's why I didn't see the sign.

POLICEMAN : Let me see your driving licence.

POLICEMAN : I won't charge you this time.
But you'd better not do it again!
GARY : Thank you.
I'll certainly be more careful.

ANN : I told you to drive slowly, Gary.
GARY : You always tell me
to drive slowly, darling.
ANN : Well, next time
you'd better take my advice!

New words and expressions 生词和短语

wave /weɪv/ v. 招手

track /træk/ n. 跑道

mile /maɪl/ n. 英里

overtake /ˌəʊvə'teɪk/ (overtook, overtaken) v.
    从后面超越, 超车

speed limit /'spiːd ˌlɪmɪt/ 限速

dream /driːm/ v. 做梦, 思想不集中

sign /saɪn/ n. 标记, 牌子

driving licence 驾驶执照

charge /tʃɑːdʒ/ v. 罚款

darling /'dɑːlɪŋ/ n. 亲爱的（用作表示称呼）

Notes on the text 课文注释

1 Where do you think you are?

   do you think 是用在特殊疑问句中的插入语, 用来征询见解或表达看法 。

2 must have been driving,

   这种结构用来表示对过去正进行的事情的推测 。可译为 "一定" 或 "准是" 。

3 at seventy miles an hour, 每小时70英里的速度 。

4 I was doing eighty when I overtook you.

   其中的动词 do 表示 "以……速度行进" 。

5 But you'd better not do it again!

   you'd better = you had better, 后面加动词原形 。

   had better 用于建议在将来某一具体场合采取动作, 而不用于一般情况, 比 should 语气更为强烈,
   常有威胁 、告诫或催促的意味 。

6 you'd better take my advice! 你最好还是听从我的劝告 。take one's advice 是 "听从劝告" 的意思 。

参考译文

  安： 瞧, 加里! 那个警察正朝你挥手呢 。他要你停下来 。

警察： 你认为你现在是在哪儿? 在赛车道上吗? 你刚才一定是以每小时 70 英里的速度开车 。

加里： 我不会开得那样快的 。

警察： 我是以每小时 80 英里的速度赶上你的 。

警察： 难道你没看见限速牌吗?

加里： 恐怕我没有看见, 警官 。我一定是思想开小差了 。

  安： 警官, 他思想没有开小差 。我刚才正告诉他开慢点 。

加里： 所以我才没看见那牌子 。

警察： 让我看一看你的驾驶执照 。

警察： 这次我就不罚你款了 。但你最好不要再开得这样快 。

加里： 谢谢您 。我以后一定会多加注意 。

  安： 加里, 我刚才叫你开慢点吧 。

加里： 你总是叫我开慢点, 亲爱的 。

  安： 好啦, 下次你最好还是听从我的劝告吧!

Lesson 130 He can't have been . . . 他那时不可能······
He must have been . . . 他那时肯定是······

Listen to the tape and answer the questions.
听录音并回答问题。

1

He can't have been ill.
He must have been tired.

2

It can't have been my new hat.
It must have been my old one.

3

She can't have been Danish.
She must have been Swedish.

4

He can't have been a dentist.
He must have been a doctor.

5

She can't have been forty.
She must have been fifty.

6

It can't have been the 20th.
It must have been the 21st.

7

He can't have been the youngest.
He must have been the oldest.

8

He can't have been reading.
He must have been sleeping.

Written exercises 书面练习

A Complete these sentences using *had to* or *must have been*.
　完成以下句子, 用 *had to* 或 *must have been* 填空 。

Example:

He is very tired because he *had to* get up early this morning.
He didn't get up early this morning. He must have been tired.

1　He didn't come to work yesterday. He _____ ill.
2　He didn't come to the office this morning. He _____ stay at home.
3　I don't think she was Austrian. She _____ German.
4　I lost my pen so I _____ buy a new one.
5　He forgot his case so he _____ return home.
6　She didn't hear the phone. She _____ sleeping.

B Write new sentences.
　模仿例句改写以下句子 。

Example:

I think she was Danish. (Swedish)
I don't think she was. She can't have been Danish.
She must have been Swedish.

1　I think they were Canadian. (Australian)
2　I think she was Finnish. (Russian)
3　I think they were Japanese. (Chinese)
4　I think they were butchers. (bakers)
5　I think she was a dentist. (doctor)
6　I think he was a sales rep. (the boss)
7　I think she was seventeen. (twenty-one)
8　I think they were five. (seven)
9　I think he was seventy-six. (over eighty)
10　I think she was fifty-five. (under fifty)
11　I think it was the 17th yesterday. (16th)
12　I think it was Tuesday yesterday. (Wednesday)
13　I think it was the 19th yesterday. (20th)
14　I think it was cheap. (expensive)
15　I think it was easy. (difficult)
16　I think she was old. (young)
17　I think he was ill. (tired)
18　I think they were listening to the radio. (watching television)
19　I think she was retiring. (looking for a new job)
20　I think they were sitting. (standing)

Lesson 131 Don't be so sure! 别那么肯定!

 Listen to the tape then answer this question.
What's the problem about deciding on a holiday?
听录音,然后回答问题。决定如何度假有什么为难的地方?

MARTIN : Where are you going to
spend your holidays this year, Gary?

GARY : We may go abroad.
I'm not sure.
My wife wants to go to Egypt.
I'd like to go there, too.
We can't make up our minds.

MARTIN : Will you travel by sea or by air?

GARY : We may travel by sea.

MARTIN : It's cheaper, isn't it?

GARY : It may be cheaper,
but it takes a long time.

MARTIN : I'm sure you'll enjoy yourselves.

GARY : Don't be so sure.
We might not go anywhere.
My wife always worries too much.
Who's going to look after the dog?
Who's going to look after the house?
Who's going to look after the garden?
We have this problem every year.
In the end, we stay at home
and look after everything!

New words and expressions 生词和短语

Egypt /ˈiːdʒɪpt/ *n.* 埃及

abroad /əˈbrɔːd/ *adv.* 国外

worry /ˈwʌri/ *v.* 担忧

Notes on the text 课文注释

1　We may go abroad. 我们可能去国外 。
　　在英文中用 may 来表示可能发生的事情, 在 may 后面加动词原形 。请注意 may 表示的是一种可能性, 这与第 127 课所讲的表示有根据的推论是有区别的 。

2　make up our minds, 打定主意 。

3　Don't be so sure. 别那么肯定 。
　　在祈使句中, be 动词的否定形式要用 don't be, 这种结构常常用于劝告 。

4　We might not go anywhere. 我们可能哪里也去不成 。
　　might 可以用来表示一种可能性, 但它表示的"肯定"程度还不如may 。和 may 一样, might 所表示的是现在或将来的一种可能性 。

5　look after, 照看 。

6　in the end, 最后 。

参考译文

马丁：加里, 今年你们打算去哪里度假?

加里：我们可能到国外去, 但我不敢肯定 。我妻子想到埃及去, 我也想去那儿 。我们还拿不定主意 。

马丁：你们乘船去, 还是乘飞机去?

加里：我们可能乘船去 。

马丁：这更便宜些, 是吗?

加里：可能是便宜些, 但花的时间长 。

马丁：我肯定你们一定会玩得很痛快 。

加里：别那么肯定 。我们可能哪里也去不成 。我妻子总是担心这担心那的 。谁来照看狗啦, 谁来看管房子啦, 谁来照料花园啦, 我们每年都碰到这类问题 。末了, 我们呆在家里来照看一切 。

Lesson 132 He may be . . . 他可能是……
He may have been . . . 他可能已经……
I'm not sure. 我不敢肯定。

 Listen to the tape and answer the questions.
听录音并回答问题。

1

Where's Harry?

He may be in his room.

I'm not sure.

2

Where will he go?

He may go to the cinema.

I'm not sure.

3

Why is he late?

He may be busy.

I'm not sure.

4

What is he doing?

He may be reading.

I'm not sure.

5

Why was he late?

He may have been busy.

I'm not sure.

6

What was he doing?

He may have been reading.

I'm not sure.

Written exercises 书面练习

A Read the conversation in Lesson 131 again. Then answer these questions.
重读第 131 课的对话, 然后回答以下问题 。

1 Is Martin talking to Gary?
2 Where may Gary and his wife go this year?
3 Who wants to go to Egypt?
4 How will they travel?
5 Isn't it cheaper to travel by sea?
6 Doesn't it take a long time?
7 Why might Gary and his wife not go anywhere?

B Answer these questions.
模仿例句回答以下问题 。

Examples:

Do you think she is Danish? (Swedish)
I'm not sure. She may be Swedish.

Do you think she was Danish? (Swedish)
I'm not sure. She may have been Swedish.

1 Do you think they are Canadian? (Australian)
2 Do you think she is Finnish? (Russian)
3 Do you think they are Japanese? (Chinese)
4 Do you think they were butchers? (bakers)
5 Do you think she was a dentist? (doctor)
6 Do you think he is a sales rep? (the boss)
7 Do you think she is seventeen? (twenty-one)
8 Do you think they were five? (seven)
9 Do you think he was seventy-six? (over eighty)
10 Do you think she was fifty-five? (under fifty)
11 Do you think it is the 17th today? (16th)
12 Do you think it was Tuesday yesterday? (Wednesday)
13 Do you think it is the 19th today? (20th)
14 Do you think it is cheap? (expensive)
15 Do you think it was easy? (difficult)
16 Do you think she was old? (young)
17 Do you think he was ill? (tired)
18 Do you think they are listening to the radio? (watching television)
19 Do you think she was retiring? (looking for a new job)
20 Do you think they are sitting? (standing)

Lesson 133 Sensational news! 爆炸性新闻!

 Listen to the tape then answer this question. What reasons did Karen Marsh give for wanting to retire?
听录音,然后回答问题。卡伦·马什说她为什么想要退休?

REPORTER : Have you just made
a new film, Miss Marsh?

MISS MARSH : Yes, I have.

REPORTER : Are you going to make another?

MISS MARSH : No, I'm not.
I'm going to retire.
I feel very tired.
I don't want to make another film
for a long time.

1

KATE : Let's buy a newspaper, Liz.
Listen to this!
'Karen Marsh: Sensational News!
By our reporter, Alan Jones.
Karen Marsh arrived
at London Airport today.
She was wearing a blue dress
and a mink coat.
She told me
she had just made a new film.
She said
she was not going to make another.
She said she was going to retire.
She told reporters she felt very tired
and didn't want to make
another film for a long time.'

LIZ : I wonder why!

2

New words and expressions 生词和短语

reporter /rɪˈpɔːtə/ *n.* 记者

sensational /senˈseɪʃənəl/ *adj.* 爆炸性的, 耸人听闻的

mink coat /ˈmɪŋk-kəʊt/ 貂皮大衣

Notes on the text 课文注释

1　Let's = Let us 常用于第一人称的祈使句中, 用来表示请求、建议、命令。

2　She told me she had just made a new film. 她告诉我她刚拍完一部新片子。
　　这是间接引语的又一个例子, 这句话中含有一个用过去时引述动词的结构。如果我们对比一下 Marsh 小姐对记者说的话 (直接引语) 和报上刊载的记者的复述 (间接引语), 就不难发现, 间接引语的动词时态往往要倒移。而这种倒移的普遍规则是: 现在时变成过去时, 现在完成时变成过去完成时。

3　I wonder why! 我很想知道为什么!

参考译文

记　　者：您刚拍完一部新电影吗, 马什小姐?

马什小姐：是的, 我刚拍完。

记　　者：您准备再拍一部吗?

马什小姐：不, 我不准备拍了。我准备退休了。我感觉累得很。我早就不想再拍片子了。

凯　　特：我们买份报纸吧, 莉兹。你听这段: "卡伦·马什: 爆炸性新闻! 由本报记者艾伦·琼斯报导。卡伦·马什今天到达伦敦机场。她穿着一身蓝色的裙子和一件貂皮大衣。她告诉我她刚拍完一部新片子。她说她不准备再拍电影了。她说她准备退休。她告诉记者她感到很疲劳, 早就不想再拍电影了。"

莉　　兹：我很想知道为什么!

Lesson 134 He said (that) he . . . 他曾说他……
He told me (that) he . . . 他曾告诉我说他……

 Listen to the tape and answer the questions.
听录音并回答问题。

1

I'm tired.

2

What did he say?
What did he tell you?

3

He said (that) he was tired.
He told me (that) he was tired.

4

I'm reading.

5

What did she say?
What did she tell you?

6

She said (that) she was reading.
She told me (that) she was reading.

7

We want our dinner.

8

What did they say?
What did they tell you?

9

They said (that) they wanted their dinner.
They told me (that) they wanted their dinner.

10

I've finished my homework.

11

What did he say?
What did he tell you?

12

He said (that) he had finished his homework.
He told me (that) he had finished his homework.

271

Written exercises 书面练习

A Read the conversation in Lesson 133 again. Then answer these questions.
   重读第 133 课的对话, 然后回答以下问题。

1 Has Miss Marsh just made a new film?
2 Who was asking her questions?
3 What is Miss Marsh going to do?
4 Why doesn't Miss Marsh want to make another film?

5 Who bought a newspaper?
6 Where did Miss Marsh arrive?
7 What was Miss Marsh wearing?

B Answer these questions.
   模仿例句回答以下问题。

Example:

I'm tired. — What did he say?
He said he was tired.

1 I'm busy. — What did he say?
2 She's cold. — What did he say?

3 The book's interesting. — What did she say?
4 They're hungry. — What did he say?

C Answer these questions.
   模仿例句回答以下问题。

Example:

I'm reading. — What did he tell you?
He told me he was reading.

1 I'm working. — What did he tell you?
2 She's leaving. — What did they tell you?

3 They're joking. — What did she tell you?
4 Tom's waiting. — What did he tell you?

D Answer these questions.
   模仿例句回答以下问题。

Example:

I've finished. — What did he tell you?
He told me he had finished.

1 I've met him. — What did he tell you?
2 I've lost it. — What did he tell you?

3 It has stopped. — What did she tell you?
4 She has arrived. — What did they tell you?

Lesson 135　The latest report　最新消息

 Listen to the tape then answer this question.
Is Karen Marsh going to retire, do you think?
听录音，然后回答问题。你认为卡伦·马什会退休吗？

REPORTER :　Are you really
　　　　　　going to retire, Miss Marsh?

MISS MARSH :　I may.
　　　　　　I can't make up my mind.
　　　　　　I will have to ask
　　　　　　my future husband.
　　　　　　He won't let me make another film.

REPORTER :　Your future husband, Miss Marsh?

MISS MARSH :　Yes. Let me introduce him to you.
　　　　　　His name is Carlos.
　　　　　　We're going to get married next week.

KATE :　Look, Liz!
　　　　Here's another report about
　　　　Karen Marsh.
　　　　Listen: 'Karen Marsh: The latest.
　　　　At her London Hotel today
　　　　Miss Marsh told reporters
　　　　she might retire.
　　　　She said she couldn't
　　　　make up her mind.
　　　　She said she would have to
　　　　ask her future husband.
　　　　She said her future husband
　　　　would not let her
　　　　make another film.
　　　　Then she introduced us to Carlos
　　　　and told us
　　　　they would get married next week.'

LIZ :　That's sensational news, isn't it,
　　　Kate?

KATE :　It certainly is.
　　　　He'll be her sixth husband!

New words and expressions 生词和短语

future /ˈfjuːtʃə/ *adj.* 未来的

get married 结婚

hotel /həʊˈtel/ *n.* 饭店

latest /ˈleɪtɪst/ *adj.* 最新的

introduce /ˌɪntrəˈdjuːs/ *v.* 介绍

Notes on the text 课文注释

1 请注意在直接引语变成间接引语的动词时态倒移过程中, 情态助动词的变化: may — might, can -- could, will — would 等, won't — wouldn't, going to — would, can't — couldn't 等 。

2 get married, 结婚 。

3 the latest, 这里是指最新消息 。

参考译文

记　　者: 马什小姐, 您真的准备退休吗?

马什小姐: 有可能退 。我还拿不定主意 。我得问一下我的未婚夫 。他不会再让我拍电影了 。

记　　者: 您的未婚夫, 马什小姐?

马什小姐: 是的, 让我把他给你们介绍一下 。他叫卡洛斯 。下星期我们就要结婚了 。

凯　　特: 看啊, 莉兹! 这又有一篇关于卡伦·马什的报道 。你听: "卡伦·马什: 最新消息 。今天在伦敦旅馆, 马什小姐告诉记者她可能要退休 。她说她还拿不定主意 。她说她得问问她的未婚夫 。她说她的未婚夫不会再让她拍电影 。然后她把我们介绍给卡洛斯, 并告诉我们说他们下星期结婚 。"

莉　　兹: 凯特, 这真是条轰动的消息, 是不是?

凯　　特: 当然啦 。他将是她的第 6 任丈夫!

Lesson 136　He said (that) he ... 他（曾）说他……
　　　　　　　He told me (that) he ... 他（曾）告诉我说他……

 Listen to the tape and answer the questions.
听录音并回答问题。

1

I'll leave
tomorrow.

2

What did he say?
What did he tell you?

3

He said (that) he would
leave tomorrow.
He told me (that) he
would leave tomorrow.

4

I can't do this
Maths problem.

5

What did he say?
What did he tell you?

6

He said (that) he couldn't
do this Maths problem.
He told me (that) he
couldn't do this Maths
problem.

7

I may return at
six o'clock.

8

What did she say?
What did she tell you?

9

She said (that) she might
return at six o'clock.
She told me (that) she
might return at six
o'clock.

Written exercises 书面练习

A Read the conversation in Lesson 135 again. Then answer these questions.
重读第 135 课的对话, 然后回答以下问题 。

1 Is Karen Marsh really going to retire, or is she still not sure?

2 She can't make up her mind, can she?

3 What is the name of her future husband?

4 When will they get married?

5 Where is Karen Marsh staying?

6 Does Karen Marsh introduce Carlos to the reporters?

7 How does Liz describe the news?

B Answer these questions.
模仿例句回答以下问题 。

Example:

I will leave tomorrow. — What did he say?
He said he would leave tomorrow.

1 Penny will open the window. — What did he say?

2 I will change some money. — What did she say?

3 It will rain tomorrow. — What did he say?

4 They will arrive later. — What did he say?

5 He will repair it. — What did she say?

6 I will write to him. — What did he say?

C Answer these questions.
模仿例句回答以下问题 。

Example:

I can do this Maths problem. — What did he tell you?
He told me he could do this Maths problem.

1 I can understand English. — What did he tell you?

2 I can recognize him. — What did she tell you?

3 They can afford it. — What did they tell you?

4 I can remember him. — What did she tell you?

5 I can change it. — What did he tell you?

6 I can finish it. — What did he tell you?

D Answer these questions.
模仿例句回答以下问题 。

Example:

I may go to the cinema. — What did he say?
He said he might go to the cinema.

1 They may arrive tomorrow. — What did they say?

2 I may retire. — What did he tell you?

3 I may telephone him. — What did she say?

4 I may sell it. — What did he tell you?

5 She may recognize you. — What did he say?

6 I may finish it. — What did she tell you?

Lesson 137 A pleasant dream 美好的梦

Listen to the tape then answer this question.
What would Julie like to do, if she had the money?
听录音, 然后回答问题 。如果朱莉有那笔钱, 她想做什么呢?

JULIE :   Are you doing the football pools, Brian?

BRIAN : Yes, I've nearly finished, Julie.

I'm sure we'll win something this week.

JULIE :   You always say that,

but we never win anything!

What will you do

if you win a lot of money?

BRIAN : If I win a lot of money

I'll buy you a mink coat.

JULIE :   I don't want a mink coat!

I want to see the world.

BRIAN : All right.

If we win a lot of money

we'll travel round the world

and we'll stay at the best hotels.

Then we'll return home

and buy a big house in the country.

We'll have a beautiful garden and . . .

JULIE :   But if we spend all that money

we'll be poor again.

What'll we do then?

BRIAN : If we spend all the money

we'll try and win the football pools again.

JULIE :   It's a pleasant dream

but everything depends on 'if'!

New words and expressions 生词和短语

football /'fʊtbɔːl/ n. 足球

pool /puːl/ n. 赌注

win /wɪn/ (won /wʌn/, won) v. 赢

world /wɜːld/ n. 世界

poor /pʊə/ adj. 贫穷的

depend /dɪ'pend/ v. 依靠(on)

Notes on the text 课文注释

1 football pools, 英国流行的一种赌博方式, 靠在足球比赛结果上的赌注来决定输赢。

2 if you win a lot of money, 如果你赢了许多钱。

   这是一个表示条件的状语从句。在英文中, 条件是指某一事情实现之后(状语从句中的动作)其他事情(主句中的动作)才能发生, 通常译作"假如"。如果条件状语从句用于询问或谈论十分可能发生的事情, 那么条件状语从句中常用一般现在时, 而主句中则用一般将来时。a lot of 既可与可数名词也可与不可数名词相连。

3 depend on, 取决于, 依靠。

参考译文

朱　莉：布赖恩, 你正在下足球赛的赌注吗?

布赖恩：是的。我这就做完了, 朱莉。我敢肯定这星期我们会赢一点什么的。

朱　莉：你老是那样说, 但是我们从来没赢过! 要是你赢了许多钱, 你打算做什么呢?

布赖恩：要是我赢了许多钱, 我给你买件貂皮大衣。

朱　莉：我不要貂皮大衣。我要去见见世面。

布赖恩：好吧。要是我们赢了很多钱, 我们就去周游世界, 并且住最好的旅馆。然后我们返回家园, 在乡下买幢大房子。我们将有一个漂亮的花园和……

朱　莉：但是如果我们把所有钱都花光了, 我们又会变穷的。那时我们怎么办呢?

布赖恩：如果我们花光了所有钱, 我们设法在足球赛赌注上再赢一次。

朱　莉：这是个美好的梦, 但一切都取决于"如果"!

Lesson 138 If ... 如果……

Listen to the tape and answer the questions.
听录音并回答问题。

1

If you break this window,
you'll have to pay for it!

2

If you don't hurry,
we'll miss the train.

3

If he falls,
he'll hurt himself.

4

If it rains tomorrow,
we won't go to the seaside.

5

If you feel better,
you can get up.

6

If he sells that car,
he can buy a new one.

Written exercises 书面练习

A Read the conversation in Lesson 137 again. Then answer these questions.
重读第 137 课的对话, 然后回答以下问题。

1 What is Brian doing?
2 Has Brian ever won anything on the football pools?
3 What will Brian buy his wife if he wins a lot of money?
4 She doesn't want a mink coat, does she?
5 What does Julie want instead of a mink coat?
6 What will Brian do if he spends all the money?
7 It's only a dream, isn't it?
8 What does it all depend on?

B   Answer these questions.
模仿例句回答以下问题。

Example:

What will you do if you win a lot of money?
Stay at the best hotels.
If I win a lot of money, I'll stay at the best hotels.

1   What will he do if he misses the bus?
    Take a taxi.
2   What will he do if he doesn't sell his old car?
    He won't buy a new one.
3   What will you do if they offer you more money?
    Work less.
4   What will he do if she doesn't type the letter?
    Type it himself.
5   What will the children do if they come home early?
    Play in the garden.
6   What will you do if you are ill tomorrow?
    I won't go to work.
7   What will you do if you go to the party?
    Enjoy myself.
8   What will you do if he asks you?
    Tell him the truth.
9   What will they do if it rains tomorrow?
    Stay at home.

C   Write sentences using these words.
模仿例句改写以下句子。

Example:

Stay at the best hotels. (He)
He can stay at the best hotels if he is rich.

1   Live abroad. (She)
2   Travel round the world. (He)
3   Buy a new house. (He)
4   Have a long holiday. (They)
5   Enjoy myself. (I)
6   Offer your boss a job. (You)
7   Fly to Tokyo. (He)
8   Work less. (She)

Lesson 139 Is that you, John? 是你吗, 约翰?

Listen to the tape then answer this question.
Which John Smith does Graham Turner think he is talking to?
听录音, 然后回答问题。格雷厄姆·特纳以为他在和哪一个约翰·史密斯
通话?

GRAHAM TURNER : Is that you, John?

JOHN SMITH : Yes, speaking.

GRAHAM TURNER : Tell Mary we'll be late
for dinner this evening.

JOHN SMITH : I'm afraid I don't understand.

GRAHAM TURNER : Hasn't Mary told you?
She invited Charlotte and me
to dinner this evening.
I said I would be
at your house at six o'clock,
but the boss wants me
to do some extra work.
I'll have to stay at the office.
I don't know when I'll finish.
Oh, and by the way,
my wife wants to know
if Mary needs any help.

JOHN SMITH : I don't know what you're talking about.

GRAHAM TURNER : That is John Smith, isn't it?

JOHN SMITH : Yes, I'm John Smith.

GRAHAM TURNER : You are John Smith, the engineer, aren't you?

JOHN SMITH : That's right.

GRAHAM TURNER : You work
for the Overseas Engineering Company, don't you?

JOHN SMITH : No, I don't.
I'm John Smith the telephone engineer
and I'm repairing your telephone line.

New words and expressions 生词和短语

extra /ˈekstrə/ *adj.* 额外的

overseas /ˌəʊvəˈsiːz/ *adj.* 海外的, 国外的

engineering /ˌendʒɪˈnɪərɪŋ/ *n.* 工程

company /ˈkʌmpəni/ *n.* 公司

line /laɪn/ *n.* 线路

Notes on the text 课文注释

1   Is that you, John?

Yes, speaking.

这两句话是朋友间打电话时的常用语。speaking 可译作"请讲"。

2   Tell Mary we'll be late . . .

句中 we will be late . . . 是一个宾语从句, 作动词 tell 的宾语。这个宾语从句省略了引导词 that。

3   She invited Charlotte and me to dinner this evening. 她邀请我和夏洛特今晚去吃饭。在英语中, 为了表示客气常常把其他人的姓名放在"我"之前, 请注意中英文不同的语序。

4   I don't know when I'll finish.

本句中也有一个宾语从句, 从句中的引导词 when 不能省略。类似的例子还有: My wife wants to know if Mary needs any help; I don't know what you're talking about 等。

5   by the way, 顺便（问, 说）。

参考译文

格雷厄姆·特纳: 是你吗, 约翰?

约 翰·史 密 斯: 是我, 请讲。

格雷厄姆·特纳: 你告诉玛丽, 今晚吃饭我们将晚到一会儿。

约 翰·史 密 斯: 恐怕我还不明白您的意思。

格雷厄姆·特纳: 玛丽没有告诉你吗? 她邀请我和夏洛特今晚去吃饭。我说过我 6 点到你家, 但老板要我加班。我不得不留在办公室, 不知道什么时候才能结束。喔, 顺便问一句, 我妻子想知道玛丽是否需要帮忙。

约 翰·史 密 斯: 我不知道您在说些什么。

格雷厄姆·特纳: 你是约翰·史密斯, 对吗?

约 翰·史 密 斯: 是的, 我是约翰·史密斯。

格雷厄姆·特纳: 你是工程师约翰·史密斯, 对吗?

约 翰·史 密 斯: 对。

格雷厄姆·特纳: 你在海外工程公司上班, 是吗?

约 翰·史 密 斯: 不, 不是。我是电话工程师约翰·史密斯, 我正在修理您的电话线。

Lesson 140 He wants to know if/why/what/when
他想知道是否／为什么／什么／什么时候

 Listen to the tape and answer the questions.
听录音并回答问题。

1

Are you tired?

Why are you tired?

2

What does he want
to know?
What does he want
to know?

3

He wants to know
if you are tired.
He wants to know
why you are tired.

4

Are you reading?

What are you
reading?

5

What does he want
to know?
What does he want
to know?

6

He wants to know
if you are reading.
He wants to know
what you are reading.

7

Does Tom always do
his homework?

When does Tom do his
homework?

8

What does he want
to know?

What does he want
to know?

9

He wants to know if
Tom always does his
homework.
He wants to know when
Tom does his homework.

Written exercises 书面练习

A   Read the conversation in Lesson 139 again. Then answer these questions.
重读第 139 课的对话, 然后回答以下问题。

1   Isn't Graham Turner speaking to John Smith?
2   Who invited Mr. and Mrs. Turner to dinner?
3   What time did Graham Turner say he would be there?
4   Why can't he be there at six o'clock?
5   Graham Turner doesn't know when he will finish work, does he?
6   What does Mr. Turner's wife want to know?

B   Write new sentences.
模仿例句改写以下句子。

Example:

Are you tired? Why?

I want to know if you are tired. Tell me if you are tired.
I want to know why you are tired. Tell me why you are tired.

1   Are you late? Why?   2   Are you dirty? Why?   3   Are you lazy? Why?   4   Are you busy? Why?

C   Write new sentences.
模仿例句改写以下句子。

Example:

Are you reading? What?

I want to know if you are reading. Tell me if you are reading.
I want to know what you are reading. Tell me what you are reading.

1   Are you writing? What?   3   Are you painting? What?
2   Are you cooking? What?   4   Are you playing? What?

D   Write new sentences.
模仿例句改写以下句子。

Example:

Did Tom go to bed early? When?

I want to know if Tom went to bed early. Tell me if Tom went to bed early.
I want to know when Tom went to bed. Tell me when Tom went to bed.

1   Did Tom get up early? When?   3   Did Tom do his homework yesterday? When?
2   Did Tom arrive late? When?   4   Did Tom have a bath yesterday? When?

Lesson 141 Sally's first train ride 萨莉第一次乘火车旅行

Listen to the tape then answer this question.
Why was the mother embarrassed?
听录音, 然后回答问题 。为什么母亲感到很尴尬?

Last week, my four-year-old daughter, Sally,

was invited to a children's party.

I decided to take her by train.

Sally was very excited

because she had never travelled

on a train before.

She sat near the window

and asked questions

about everything she saw.

Suddenly, a middle-aged lady

got on the train

and sat opposite Sally.

'Hello, little girl,' she said.

Sally did not answer,

but looked at her curiously.

The lady was dressed in a blue coat

and a large, funny hat.

After the train had left the station,

the lady opened her handbag and took out her powder compact.

She then began to make up her face.

'Why are you doing that?' Sally asked.

'To make myself beautiful,' the lady answered.

She put away her compact and smiled kindly.

'But you are still ugly,' Sally said.

Sally was amused,

but I was very embarrassed!

New words and expressions 生词和短语

excited /ɪk'saɪtɪd/ *adj.* 兴奋的

get on 登上

middle-aged /ˌmɪdl-'eɪdʒd/ *adj.* 中年的

opposite /'ɒpəzɪt/ *prep.* 在……对面

curiously /'kjʊəriəsli/ *adv.* 好奇地

funny /'fʌni/ *adj.* 可笑的, 滑稽的

powder /'paʊdə/ *n.* 香粉

compact /'kɒmpækt/ *n.* 带镜的化妆盒

kindly /'kaɪndli/ *adv.* 和蔼地

ugly /'ʌgli/ *adj.* 丑陋的

amused /ə'mjuːzd/ *adj.* 有趣的

smile /smaɪl/ *v.* 微笑

embarrassed /ɪm'bærəst/ *adj.* 尴尬的, 窘迫的

Notes on the text 课文注释

1　my four-year-old daughter, 我那 4 岁的女儿。

　　four-year-old 是名词daughter的定语, 常常用连字符连在一起, 组成一个复合形容词。注意在这个复合词中仅用 year, 而不用复数。

2　Sally was invited to a children's party.

　　这是一个被动语态的例子。在英文中, 如果想避免用含混不清的词（如 someone 等）作主语, 常常可使用被动语态。被动语态由相应的 be 动词加上过去分词组成。

3　she had never travelled on a train before,

　　副词 before 通常用于完成时（现在完成时或过去完成时）的句子里, ago 用在过去时的句子里。

4　be dressed in . . ., 穿戴……。

5　make up her face, 往她的脸上施脂粉。

6　make myself beautiful, 把自己打扮漂亮。

参考译文

　　上周, 我 4 岁的女儿萨莉被邀请去参加一个儿童聚会。我决定带她乘火车去。萨莉非常激动, 因为她从未乘过火车。她靠车窗坐着, 对她所看到的一切都要问个明白。突然, 一个中年妇女上了火车, 坐在萨莉的对面。"你好, 小姑娘。"她说。萨莉没回答, 却好奇地看着她。那位妇女穿着一件蓝色的大衣, 戴着一顶大而滑稽的帽子。火车开出车站后, 那位妇女打开了手提包, 拿出了粉盒。然后她开始打扮起来。"你为什么要那样做呢?"萨莉问。"为了把自己打扮漂亮啊。"那位妇女答道。她放好了粉盒, 慈祥地微笑着。"可是你仍然难看呀。"萨莉说。萨莉感到很有趣, 而我却很尴尬！

Lesson 142 Someone invited Sally to a party.

有人邀请萨莉出席一个聚会。

Sally was invited to a party. 萨莉应邀出席一个聚会。

 Listen to the tape and answer the questions.
听录音并回答问题。

1

She is embarrassed.

2

They are worried.

3

Does anyone ever repair
this car?

4

Someone repairs it regularly.
It is repaired regularly.

5

Does anyone ever correct
these exercise books?

6

Someone corrects them regularly.
They are corrected regularly.

7

Did anyone meet him at the
station this morning?

8

Someone met him at the station
this morning.
He was met at the station this
morning.

New words and expressions 生词和短语

worried /ˈwʌrid/ *adj.* 担心的, 担忧的

regularly /ˈreɡjʊləli/ *adv.* 经常地, 定期地

Written exercises 书面练习

A Read the story in Lesson 141 again. Then answer these questions.
重读第 141 课的故事, 然后回答以下问题 。

1 How old is Sally?
2 Why did Sally's mother decide to take her by train?
3 Where did Sally sit?
4 Who got on the train?

5 How was the lady dressed?
6 What did the lady do?
7 Why did the lady make up her face?
8 Did Sally think the lady was beautiful?

B Answer these questions.
用主动语态和被动语态两种形式来回答以下问题 。

Examples:

Does anyone ever open this window? *Someone opens it regularly. It is opened regularly.*
Does anyone ever open these windows? *Someone opens them regularly. They are opened regularly.*

1 Does anyone ever air this room?
2 Does anyone ever clean these rooms?
3 Does anyone ever empty this basket?
4 Does anyone ever sharpen this knife?
5 Does anyone ever turn on these taps?

6 Does anyone ever water these flowers?
7 Does anyone ever repair this car?
8 Does anyone ever dust this cupboard?
9 Does anyone ever correct these exercise books?
10 Does anyone ever shut this window?

C Answer these questions.
模仿例句回答以下问题 。

Examples:

Did anyone open this window?
Someone opened it. It was opened this morning.

Did anyone open these windows?
Someone opened them. They were opened this morning.

1 Did anyone water these flowers?
2 Did anyone repair this car?
3 Did anyone dust this cupboard?
4 Did anyone correct these exercise books?
5 Did anyone shut this window?

6 Did anyone buy these models?
7 Did anyone sweep this floor?
8 Did anyone take them to school?
9 Did anyone meet them at the station?
10 Did anyone tell them?

Lesson 143 A walk through the woods 林中散步

Listen to the tape then answer this question.
What was so funny about the words on the sign?
听录音，然后回答问题。牌子上的字有什么可笑的地方？

I live in a very old town

which is surrounded by beautiful woods.

It is a famous beauty spot.

On Sundays, hundreds of people

come from the city

to see our town

and to walk through the woods.

Visitors have been asked

to keep the woods clean and tidy.

Litter baskets have been placed under the trees,

but people still throw their rubbish everywhere.

Last Wednesday, I went for a walk in the woods.

What I saw

made me very sad.

I counted seven old cars

and three old refrigerators.

The litter baskets were empty

and the ground was covered with

pieces of paper, cigarette ends, old tyres,

empty bottles and rusty tins.

Among the rubbish,

I found a sign which said,

'Anyone who leaves litter in these woods

will be prosecuted !'

New words and expressions 生词和短语

surround /sə'raʊnd/ v. 包围

wood /wʊd/ n. 树林

beauty spot /'bjuːti-spɒt/ 风景点

hundred /'hʌndrɪd/ n. 百

city /'sɪti/ n. 城市

through /θruː/ prep. 穿过

visitor /'vɪzɪtə/ n. 参观者, 游客, 来访者

tidy /'taɪdi/ adj. 整齐的

litter /'lɪtə/ n. 杂乱的东西

litter basket 废物筐

place /pleɪs/ v. 放

throw /θrəʊ/ (threw /θruː/, thrown /θrəʊn/) v. 扔, 抛

rubbish /'rʌbɪʃ/ n. 垃圾

count /kaʊnt/ v. 数, 点

cover /'kʌvə/ v. 覆盖

piece /piːs/ n. 碎片

tyre /taɪə/ n. 轮胎

rusty /'rʌsti/ adj. 生锈的

among /ə'mʌŋ/ prep. 在……之间

prosecute /'prɒsɪkjuːt/ v. 依法处置

Notes on the text 课文注释

1   was covered with . . . , 覆盖 …… 。

2   What I saw made me very sad.

句中的主语 what I saw 是一个以 what 引导的名词性从句。

3   I found a sign which said . . .

这里的 said 不当 "说" 讲, 而是 "写着……"。

参考译文

　　我住在一个由美丽的树林环绕的古老小镇上。这是一个著名的风景胜地。每逢星期天, 有许许多多的人从城里来参观我们的小镇, 并在树林中散步。游客已被告知要保持树林的整洁。树下都已设置了废物筐, 但是人们仍到处扔垃圾。上星期三我到树林里去散步。我所见到的一切使我非常难过。我数了一下, 有 7 辆旧汽车和 3 个旧冰箱。废物筐是空的, 而满地都是纸片、烟头、旧轮胎、空瓶子和生锈的空罐头盒。在垃圾堆中我发现了一块牌子, 上面写着: "凡在此树林里丢弃垃圾者, 将依法处置。"

Lesson 144 He hasn't been served yet. 还没有人来招待他。
He will be served soon. 很快会有人来招待他的。

 Listen to the tape and answer the questions.
听录音并回答问题。

1

Hasn't anyone repaired this car yet?

2

It has already been repaired!

3

Hasn't anyone corrected
these exercise books yet?

4

They have already been corrected!

5

Hasn't anyone caught the
thief yet?

6

He hasn't been caught yet.
He will be caught soon!

7

Hasn't anyone caught the
thieves yet?

8

They haven't been caught yet.
They will be caught soon!

Written exercises 书面练习

A Read the piece in Lesson 143 again. Then answer these questions.
   重读第 143 课课文，然后回答以下问题：

1 Where does the writer live?
2 Why do visitors often come from the city?
3 What have visitors been asked to do?
4 Where have litter baskets been placed?

5 Where did the writer go last Wednesday?
6 He saw a lot of rubbish, didn't he?
7 What did he see among the rubbish?
8 What did the sign say?

B Answer these questions.
   模仿例句回答以下问题。

Examples:

Hasn't anyone opened the window yet?
Someone has opened it. It has already been opened.

Hasn't anyone opened the windows yet?
Someone has opened them. They have already been opened.

1 Hasn't anyone aired this room yet?
2 Hasn't anyone cleaned these rooms yet?
3 Hasn't anyone emptied this basket yet?
4 Hasn't anyone sharpened this knife yet?
5 Hasn't anyone turned on the taps yet?

6 Hasn't anyone bought these models yet?
7 Hasn't anyone swept the floor yet?
8 Hasn't anyone taken them to school yet?
9 Hasn't anyone invited them yet?
10 Hasn't anyone told them yet?

C Answer these questions.
   模仿例句回答以下问题。

Examples:

Hasn't anyone opened the window yet?
It hasn't been opened yet. It will be opened tomorrow.

Hasn't anyone opened the windows yet?
They haven't been opened yet. They will be opened tomorrow.

1 Hasn't anyone aired this room yet?
2 Hasn't anyone cleaned these rooms yet?
3 Hasn't anyone emptied this basket yet?
4 Hasn't anyone sharpened this knife yet?
5 Hasn't anyone turned on the taps yet?

6 Hasn't anyone watered these flowers yet?
7 Hasn't anyone repaired this car yet?
8 Hasn't anyone dusted the cupboard yet?
9 Hasn't anyone corrected these exercise books yet?
10 Hasn't anyone shut the window yet?

Appendix 1: Personal names 附录 1：人名中英文对照表

英文（课）	译文
Amy (29)	艾米
Andy (99)	安迪
Ann (47)	安
Anna (13)	安娜
Billy Steward (69)	比利·斯图尔特
Bird (49)	伯德（姓）
Blake (5)	布莱克（姓）
Bob (45)	鲍勃
Brian (137)	布赖恩
Carlos (135)	卡洛斯
Carol (79)	卡罗尔
Carter (99)	卡特（姓）
Catherine (91)	凯瑟琳
Chang-woo (5)	昌宇
Charlotte (109)	夏洛特
Christine (47)	克里斯廷
Claire Taylor (17)	克莱尔·泰勒
Conrad Reeves (127)	康拉德·里弗斯
Croft (77)	克罗夫特（姓）
Dan (37)	丹
Dave (11)	戴夫
David Hall (97)	大卫·霍尔
Dimitri (51)	迪米特里
Emma (9)	埃玛
Frith (111)	弗里斯（姓）
Gary (103)	加里
George (37)	乔治
Graham Turner (139)	格雷厄姆·特纳
Hans (5)	汉斯
Helen (9)	海伦
Henry (119)	亨利
Ian (89)	伊恩
Jack (31)	杰克
Jackson (17)	杰克逊（姓）
Jane (71)	简
Jean (31)	琼
Jenny (91)	詹尼
Jeremy Short (17)	杰里米·肖特
Jill (65)	吉尔
Jim (115), Jimmy (61)	吉姆, 吉米
John (139)	约翰
Johnson (67)	约翰逊（姓）
Jones (29)	琼斯（姓）
Julie (137)	朱莉
Karen Marsh (127)	卡伦·马什
Kate (127)	凯特
Ken (85)	肯
Liz (127)	莉兹
Louis (13)	路易丝
Lucy (99)	露西
Martin (131)	马丁
Mary (139)	玛丽
Michael Baker (17)	迈克尔·贝克
Mike (123)	迈克
Mills (73)	米尔斯（姓）
Naoko (5)	直子
Nicola Grey (17)	尼古拉·格雷
Nigel (89)	奈杰尔
Pamela (45)	帕梅拉
Pauline (71)	波琳
Penny (39)	彭妮
Peter (125)	彼得
Richard (103)	理查德
Richards (17)	理查兹（姓）
Robert (7)	罗伯特
Ron Marston (71)	朗·马斯顿
Sally (31)	萨莉
Sam (39)	萨姆
Sandra (105)	桑德拉
Sawyer (55)	索耶（姓）
Scott (123)	斯科特
Smith (25)	史密斯（姓）
Sophie Dupont (5)	索菲娅·杜邦
Steven (9)	史帝文
Susan (37)	苏珊
Tim (11)	蒂姆
Tom (79), Tommy (117)	汤姆, 汤米
Tony (9)	托尼
Turner (139)	特纳（姓）
Williams (61)	威廉斯（姓）
Wood (87)	伍德（姓）

Appendix 2: Geographical names 附录 2： 地名中英文对照表

英文（课）	译文	英文（课）	译文	英文（课）	译文
Athens (94)	雅典	Geneva (94)	日内瓦	Poland (54)	波兰
Australia (54)	澳大利亚	Germany (52)	德国	Rome (94)	罗马
Austria (54)	奥地利	Greece (51)	希腊	Russia (52)	俄罗斯
Berlin (94)	柏林	Holland (52)	荷兰	Scotland (101)	苏格兰
Bombay (94)	孟买	India (54)	印度	Seoul (94)	首尔
Brazil (52)	巴西	Italy (52)	意大利	Spain (52)	西班牙
Canada (54)	加拿大	Japan (54)	日本	Stockholm (94)	斯德哥尔摩
China (54)	中国	Madrid (93)	马德里	Sweden (52)	瑞典
Denmark (70)	丹麦	Moscow (94)	莫斯科	Sydney (94)	悉尼
Egypt (131)	埃及	New York (93)	纽约	Thailand (54)	泰国
England (52)	英国	Nigeria (54)	尼日利亚	Tokyo (93)	东京
Finland (54)	芬兰	Norway (52)	挪威	Turkey (54)	土耳其
France (52)	法国	Paris (85)	巴黎	U. S., the (52)	美国

Appendix 3: Phonetic symbols 附录 3： 英语音标

单元音和双元音

音标	例词	音标	例词	音标	例词
iː	beat	u	actuality	eɪ	make
ɪ	bit	ɑː	car	aɪ	buy
e	let	ɔː	born	ɔɪ	boy
æ	cat	uː	moon	əʊ	go
ɒ	hot	ɜː	bird	aʊ	now
ʌ	but	ʊ	put	ɪə	real
ə	about			eə	pair
i	happy			ʊə	sure
				iə	peculiar

辅音

音标	例词	音标	例词	音标	例词
p	pen	f	five	h	how
b	bed	v	view	m	man
t	tea	θ	thin	n	no
d	day	ð	then	ŋ	sung
k	key	s	so	l	let
g	get	z	zoo	r	red
tʃ	chair	ʃ	ship	j	yet
dʒ	jump	ʒ	measure	w	wet

新概念英语系列·全套产品目录

教材及教学辅导用书	书号 *
新概念英语 1（另配录音带 2 盒）	1346-6 (01)
新概念英语 2（另配录音带 3 盒）	1347-3 (01)
新概念英语 3（另配录音带 3 盒）	1348-0 (01)
新概念英语 4（另配录音带 3 盒）	1349-7 (01)
新概念英语 教师用书 1（另配录音带 4 盒）	1350-3
新概念英语 教师用书 2（另配录音带 4 盒）	1351-0
新概念英语 教师用书 3（另配录音带 4 盒）	1771-6
新概念英语 教师用书 4（另配录音带 4 盒）	1841-6
新概念英语 练习册 1	1840-9
新概念英语 练习册 2	1723-5
新概念英语 练习册 3	2482-0
新概念英语 练习册 4	2775-3
新概念英语 自学导读 1	1799-0
新概念英语 自学导读 2	1733-4
新概念英语 自学导读 3	1940-6
新概念英语 自学导读 4	2512-4
新概念英语 练习详解 1	2225-3
新概念英语 练习详解 2	1812-6
新概念英语 练习详解 3	1873-7
新概念英语 练习详解 4	2329-8
新概念英语 词汇随身听速记手册 1（另配录音带 4 盒）	3063-0
新概念英语 词汇随身听速记手册 2（另配录音带 4 盒）	3150-7
新概念英语 词汇随身听速记手册 3（另配录音带 7 盒）	3151-4
新概念英语 词汇练习 1	4208-4
新概念英语 词汇练习 2	5632-6
新概念英语 词汇练习 3	4390-6
新概念英语 词汇练习 4	5633-3
新概念英语 语法练习 1	3304-4
新概念英语 语法练习 2	4591-7
新概念英语 语法练习 3	4308-1
新概念英语 口语练习 1	4391-3
新概念英语 口语练习 2	4573-3
新概念英语 口语练习 3	4752-2
新概念英语 口语练习 4	4792-8

教材及教学辅导用书	书号 *
新概念英语 词汇大全	1727-3
新概念英语 语法手册	4230-5
新概念英语（1）课本同步讲解辅导 VCD	
新概念英语（2）课本同步讲解辅导 VCD	
新概念英语（3）课本同步讲解辅导 VCD	
新概念英语（4）课本同步讲解辅导 VCD	
新概念英语（盒装版）	
新概念英语 1（含 CD 3 张）	6729-2
新概念英语 2（含 CD 3 张）	6730-8
新概念英语 3（含 CD 3 张）	6731-5
新概念英语 4（含 CD 3 张）	6732-2
新概念英语 1（含录音带 2 盒）	6725-4
新概念英语 2（含录音带 3 盒）	6726-1
新概念英语 3（含录音带 3 盒）	6727-8
新概念英语 4（含录音带 3 盒）	6728-5
新概念英语青少版	
新概念英语青少版 学生用书 1A（含 mp3 和动画 DVD）	7354-5
新概念英语青少版 学生用书 1B（含 mp3 和动画 DVD）	7356-9
新概念英语青少版 学生用书 2A（含 mp3 和动画 DVD）	7371-2
新概念英语青少版 学生用书 2B（含 mp3 和动画 DVD）	7372-9
新概念英语青少版 学生用书 3A（含 mp3 和动画 DVD）	7373-6
新概念英语青少版 学生用书 3B（含 mp3 和动画 DVD）	7374-3
新概念英语青少版 练习册 1A	7355-2
新概念英语青少版 练习册 1B	7357-6
新概念英语青少版 练习册 2A	7375-0
新概念英语青少版 练习册 2B	7376-7
新概念英语青少版 练习册 3A	7377-4
新概念英语青少版 练习册 3B	7378-1
新概念英语青少版 教师用书 1（含 mp3）（另配录音带）	7368-2
新概念英语青少版 教师用书 2（含 mp3）（另配录音带）	7369-9
新概念英语青少版 教师用书 3（含 mp3）（另配录音带）	7370-5

* 本产品目录中书号为完整书号的后 5 位；如订书，请在前面加 978-7-5600-。

　　上述图书和音像产品全国各大书店均有销售。欢迎登录新概念英语官方教学网站 **www.ncehome.com** 查询具体信息。